Bridging Tourism Theory and Practice
Volume 1

Tourism Branding:
Communities in Action

Series Editors:
Jafar Jafari
Department of Hospitality and Tourism, University of Wisconsin-Stout, Menomonie, Wisconsin 54751, USA.
Tel (715) 232 2339; Fax (715) 232 3200; Email <jafari@uwstout.edu>

Liping A. Cai
Purdue Tourism and Hospitality Research Center, Purdue University, West Lafayette, Indiana 47907, USA.
Tel (765) 494 8384; Fax (765) 496 1168; Email <liping@purdue.edu>

Recognizing the increasing gap between what is researched in the academic community and what is practiced in the tourism industry, this book series aims to bring together perspectives from both banks in order to discuss, exchange, and debate issues critical to the advancement of tourism. The series intends to create a platform for the academics and practitioners to share theories and practices with each other and, more significantly, to serve as a collaborative venue for meaningful synthesis.

Each volume will feature a distinct theme by focusing on a current or upcoming niche or "hot" topic. It will show how theories and practices inform each other; how both have evolved, advanced, and been applied; and/ or how industry best practices have benefited from, and contributed to, theoretical developments. Volume editors or authors have both strong academic credentials and informed consulting or other practical experiences. In general, the book series seeks a synergy of how concepts can inform actions, and vice versa. It will inspire the new generation of researchers who can translate academic discoveries to deliverable results valuable to practitioners.

Forthcoming volumes in this book series

Tourism in the Muslim World
Noel Scott and Jafar Jafari, eds.

Tourism as an Instrument of Development: A Case Study
Eduarod Fayos-Sola, ed.

Bridging Tourism Theory and Practice
Volume 1

Tourism Branding: Communities in Action

LIPING A. CAI
Purdue University, USA

WILLIAM C. GARTNER
University of Minnesota, USA

ANA MARÍA MUNAR
Copenhagen Business School, Denmark

United Kingdom • North America • Japan
India • Malaysia • China

Emerald Group Publishing Limited
Howard House, Wagon Lane, Bingley BD16 1WA, UK

First edition 2009

Copyright © 2009 Emerald Group Publishing Limited

Reprints and permission service
Contact: booksandseries@emeraldinsight.com

British Library Cataloguing in Publication Data
A catalogue record for this book is available from the British Library

ISBN: 978-1-84950-720-2
ISSN: 2042-1443 (Series)

Awarded in recognition of
Emerald's production
department's adherence to
quality systems and processes
when preparing scholarly
journals for print

INVESTOR IN PEOPLE

Contents

PART II: FROM THEORIES TO PRACTICES

Chapter 1

TOURISM BRANDING
A Community Affair

Liping A. Cai
Purdue University, USA

William C. Gartner
University of Minnesota, USA

Ana María Munar
Copenhagen Business School, Denmark

Abridgement: Academic inquiries have predominantly treated destination branding as a marketing phenomenon that happens to involve tourists as customers in a marketplace. The practice of it has been entrenched in deploying tactical marketing tools such as attention-grabbing slogans. This opening chapter provides a critical review of destination and place branding literature, as well as a synopsis of each of the 15 chapters assembled in this state-of-the-art collection. Considering tourism branding as a community affair, this volume is distinguished from previous publications by adopting a global and more multidisciplinary approach and by placing the subject of tourism branding outside of the conventional domains of marketing and destination. By having the host community at the central stage, many chapters explicitly consider

Tourism Branding: Communities in Action
Bridging Tourism Theory and Practice, Volume 1, 1–14
Copyright © 2009 by Emerald Group Publishing Limited
All rights of reproduction in any form reserved
ISSN: 2042-1443/doi:10.1108/S2042-1443(2009)0000001003

different stakeholders in the process of branding. Built on theoretical foundations with both empirical findings and practical cases, this book brings together different perspectives and offers an intellectual and open dialogue among academics and practitioners of the field. **Keywords:** community affair; stakeholders; tourist experience.

INTRODUCTION

Tourism Australia could not have been happier when in March 2006 a British regulatory authority tried to ban its new brand slogan "So Where the Bloody Hell Are You?" and keep the national television audience from being exposed to the A$180-million campaign. Although it is unknown if Tourism Australia's advertising agency had planned for and fully expected the regulatory reaction, the ban was "a marketer's dream," claimed its then managing director Morrison (Ioltravel 2006). There is no evidence yet that the controversy proves the cliché that there is no such thing as bad publicity, it nevertheless elevated awareness for a campaign that could not have accomplished the same without it. As more and more destinations—from big countries to small towns—jump on the bandwagon of branding, Tourism Australia's marketing coup underscores the focus on catchy slogans and other creative advertising gimmicks to grab tourists' attention.

As brand elements, slogans and taglines play an indispensable role in brand positioning and identity building. The role is particularly critical for destinations and locations whose names already exist and are not replaceable. However, the extent to which a slogan or tagline contributes to the success of destination branding depends not only on the uniqueness of it but more importantly on its substance and the destination's ability to deliver and sustain what the slogan promises. Canadian bloggers complained about Americans ripping off their destination slogans and blasted US ad agencies for recycling the same or similar taglines for different destinations (Wright 2007). A Canadian territory launched "Larger than Life" in 2006. Months later, "We live larger than life" prominently appeared in the branding literature of a city in Alaska, USA. The slogan of "Pure and Simple" was created for two different cities by two marketing firms that are related, and as it turns out, the phrase had already been trademarked by a third community (Koonce and Ferguson 2007). Although no instances of duplicated destination slogans are reported for country brands, a *Wall Street Journal* reporter observed that "international ad campaigns sound surprisingly, and blandly, similar" (Stanley 2006:B1). Tourism Australia's controversial new slogan perhaps was a deliberate attempt to break away from or stand out in the crowd. The questions remains, though, does the pursuit of uniqueness of slogans get translated into additional new arrivals, repeat visitation, and other favorable market responses? Furthermore and more importantly, beyond creative and sensational rhetoric, what does destination branding truly embody?

TOURISM BRANDING BEYOND MARKETING

The practice of destination branding is not new, although the interest in it has reached new levels. Focused academic interest in the subject started about a decade ago when Gnoth organized a special track on "Branding Tourism Destination" at the 1998 American Marketing Science Conference. The proceedings of the contributions to this track were not published. In 1999, the *Journal of Vacation Marketing* devoted a special issue (volume 5, issue 3) to the theme of destination branding, although the thematic papers were more about image than branding. The authors of its lead paper defined branding as "what images people have of [a destination] and what kind of relationship they have with it" (Nickerson and Moisey 1999:217). Another contributor defined a brand in general marketing terms and pointed out its core objective as "producing a consistent, focused communication strategy" (Hall 1999: 230). Other contributions made reference to some branding terms. Overall, the two concepts of destination image and branding were used interchangeably and not delineated in this journal's special issue.

The Status Quo

A special issue of the *Journal of Brand Management* in 2002 featured both theoretical and practical articles on marketing countries and nations as brands. In its foreword, the editor maintained that branding in general is neither a broad nor an infinitely complex discipline; "it is really rather narrow—and is heavily overpopulated" (Anholt 2002:229). The majority of articles in the special issue, however, deal with country or nation marketing and branding in general. They are not about branding countries and nations exclusively as tourism destinations. In addition, in 2002, Morgan, Pritchard, and Pride edited a collection of contributions in a book, *Destination Branding: Creating the Unique Destination Proposition*. The authors hailed the topic as a significant development in the marketing of destinations and places. They released the second edition of the book in 2006 to capture the rapid progress of destination branding in the short intervening period. With additional international case studies, the authors intended the new edition to enable "the reader to place destination branding in a wider context, to recognize more clearly the complex challenges facing marketers and to explore how a variety of places has met those challenges" (Morgan, Pritchard and Pride 2006a, 2006b:4).

This second edition includes two articles initially collected in the aforementioned 2002 special issue of *Journal of Brand Management*. They are "Branding the nation: the historical context" by Olins and "Country as brand, product and beyond: a place marketing and brand management perspective" by Kotler and Gertner. Setting the tone for the new collection, Olin's work illustrates how a nation did and can reinvent itself and draws many analogies between the management of nation and corporate brands. The piece by Kotler and Gertner examines the effects of country-of-origin on consumers' attitude toward its products and services and discusses ways countries can be marketed and their brands can be managed through strategic place marketing. The authors conclude their article by outlining a five-step strategic management approach to country branding, which begins with an analysis of strengths, weaknesses, opportunities, and threats as the first step.

More recently, *Tourism Analysis* presented a double-issue special on "Building Destination Brands." The editors pointed out that branding has become a popular marketing tool in the last decade, and there has been an increasing academic interest in examining how branding works for places and destinations. Yet, "The destination branding literature is still a far cry from the level and quality of research we find in the generic product and services marketing literature, mostly because of the complexity of the connotations that comes with the term 'destination'" (Gnoth, Baloglu, Ekinci and Sirakaya-Turk 2007:340). With the purpose of broadening the understanding of theory and practice of destination branding, the editors compiled a diverse collection of 12 empirical papers or case studies, in addition to their introduction and a theoretical discussion. The brands examined in the empirical collection range from country to region, county, city, and resort hotel. The issues cover development and management of destination brands; image, identity, positioning, and personality; and market segmentation.

In the *Tourism Analysis* collection, Gnoth provides a theoretical discussion on the structure of destination brands and how they are different from product brands. He regards branding a destination as offering values for touristic consumption and defines a concept of a destination's capital as consisting of the cultural, natural, and economic dimensions of its people.

He proposed a model that relates the capital to destination brand architecture and tourism experience. Two contributions stand out from the rest of the empirical collection. Instead of the widely held approach to studying destination image from a tourist perspective, they investigated, respectively, the residents' perceptions of, and their attitudes toward, a city brand. Despite Gnoth's holistic conceptual contribution and the two studies on residents, the overall context in which this special issue is presented remains entrenched in destination or place marketing. Like other publications on this topic, branding is regarded as a tool of marketing in practice, and destination branding is seen an "emerging field of destination marketing" (Gnoth et al 2007:340) in academic discourse. Although there is evidence that destinations establish branding as a long-term strategy, the implementation of it inescapably focuses on applications of promotional techniques developed in product and service marketing, as is the case of the new destination slogan for Australia. Academic investigations predominantly treat it as a marketing phenomenon that happens to involve tourists as customers in a marketplace, albeit with the recognition that such marketplace bears unique characteristics.

The Broader New Frontiers

This book treats a traditional marketing subject from multidisciplinary perspectives. It attempts to free branding research and practice in tourism from the shackles of marketing that are dominated by the conventional approach of product, price, place, and promotion (4Ps). An opinion piece in *Business Week* (Kiley and Helm 2007) attributes the high turnover of chief marketing officers to the bewildering New Media. In closer analysis, their failure to live up to the challenge of New Media is only the symptom. The root cause is their inability to get out of the rational 4Ps box. There have been numerous contemporary marketing innovations in practice and theory such as experience (experiential) marketing, relationship marketing, personal marketing, one-on-one marketing, and permission marketing. These innovations all aim at attracting and retaining customers through building relationships and creating positive experiences. Individually, however, these concepts remain piece meals. They are constrained by conventional economic theories of rationality that are underpinning the 4Ps. In a society where purchasing and consumption decisions are increasingly emotional, conventional theories of rationality in economic terms alone cannot answer all questions.

The practices of and academic inquiries into branding to date are also framed by the conventional understanding of destinations in economic terms. Although debates about its definition generate more confusion than clarity, Framke (2002) has categorized various definitions into two useful schools of thoughts. One is conventional and business-oriented; and the other is sociocultural. The conventional definition regards destinations as geographical units in a hierarchy from self-contained centers to cities, provinces, regions, and countries. These units are convenient for economic planning and statistical gathering. Such definition is supply-driven and considers tourists as rational economic consumers. The sociocultural understanding of destinations, on the contrary, regards them as structures and images unconstrained by geographical boundaries and developed by continuous process of social interactions. Tourists are seen as consumers and social actors at once seeking experiences in a tourism space where they interact with each other and with experience providers. The quality of the interaction determines the quality of the experience given and received, which in turn affects the attachment of tourists to the tourism space.

To advance the practice and study of destination branding, the traditional marketing approach and the conventional understanding are no longer adequate and may be a hindrance. M&C Saatchi may have created a catchy and unique slogan for Tourism Australia. It generated enormous amount of attention, as well as controversy. The slogan might very well resonate with how tourists perceive Australia and what they expect. But the critical question is how the Australians feel about it. At the time of its launch, strong opposing opinions were already abundant in Australia and New Zealand. Critics there call it "a profane turnoff" (Stanley 2006). Advertising messages set expectations. What expectations does the "bloody" slogan set for tourists? What experience does the slogan promise? The ad agency does not take the role of host in the tourism space to meet the expectation and to deliver the promise. The people in Australian cities and towns do. For tourists to have a positive interactive experience and to nurture their loyalty to a destination, the community must participate in developing its brand.

This book is distinguished from previous publications in three major aspects. First, it adopts a global and more multidisciplinary approach and brings the subject of branding outside of the conventional domains of marketing and destination. Second, the multidisciplinary thinking enables the explicit consideration of different stakeholders in the process of branding. The host community occupies the central stage throughout the three parts of the book. Third, built on theoretical foundations with both empirical findings and practical cases, this book brings together different perspectives and offers an intellectual and open dialogue among academics and practitioners of the field. The book adopts "tourism branding" instead of "destination branding" as the key term for the title. However, the term is more suggestive than definitive at this stage. Although some authors may explicitly define it in their appropriate contexts, others contributors may choose other definitions that best fit their theses.

Global Concepts. The first part of the book is conceptual in nature and collects five chapters immediately following this introduction. In Chapter 2, Munar presents a stimulating essay on the relationship between branding and globalization. She identifies the expansion of the world market and the use of information and telecommunication technologies as the two globalization processes that exert the most impact on branding. Founded on various theories of globalization as it relates to tourism, the author argues that, due to the intensity and speed in which the two processes are evolving, the conventional research and practice of tourism branding are severely challenged. This chapter illustrates that although the global market expansion in tourism enhances the significant needs for strong brands, the digitization of experience made by tourists, and the expansion of virtual communities are now confronting academe and practitioners for more innovative approaches to branding destinations and businesses. One such approach may be the empowerment of the tourists. The author cautions, though, that this and other strategies must recognize the roles of residents, employees, and managers throughout the branding.

Chapter 3 continues the theme of the dual globalization processes, but focuses on a series of conceptual propositions that examine how virtual destination branding can be achieved through building virtualized image. By adopting the concepts of telepresence and integrated informational response, Hyun and Cai propose a model and explain how communication stimuli including both online and offline media can affect various components of virtualized destination image, which in turn influence the behavioral responses of tourists. The authors reiterate and expand the conventional constructs of destination image in the context of digitalized experience and tourist virtual communities. The chapter offers 14 prepositions that illustrate the relationships among virtualized destination image, its antecedents and consequences in the virtual destination branding model.

Gartner puts forward a theory of brand equity for destinations in Chapter 4 that examines five dimensions. These dimensions are awareness, image, loyalty, quality, and value. The author offers suggestions and cases that explain and illustrate how brand equity can be built by using market characteristics and their relationship to the different dimensions. This contribution further examines the differences and similarities between destination and product brands. The author observes that these two brands share the characteristic of novelty, but differ in the characteristics of stability and tangibility. They are also distinct in their respective internal and external perspectives. An internal perspective occurs when managers emphasize the use of resources to achieve a customer response. An external perspective occurs in the way customers interpret brand meaning and use it to enhance their personal purchase decision.

The internal and external perspectives are further probed in Chapter 5 as supply- and demand-side approaches in a conceptual discussion by Ruzzier and Ruzzier. They argue that the incorporation of both perspectives allows different stakeholders of a destination to be included in the branding process. Recognizing the lack of academic attention to the concept of brand identity, the authors propose a supply-side process by which the identity of a destination brand is developed and built. The role of the host community is highlighted as an important part of the supply-side, and a case is cited for a brief illustration of the process. Empirical works are also presented in the discussion on the demand-side approach to building brand equity. By integrating the two approaches, the chapter considers the supply-side brand identity as a management function, the demand-side brand equity as a marketing function, and destination branding as encompassing both.

The stakeholders' participation in the destination branding process is further elaborated in Chapter 6 by Park, Cai, and Lehto. Adapting the theoretical constructs of an interorganizational collaborative process to destination setting, the authors propose a community-based approach to destination branding. Their analysis of existing destination branding research and practice reveal that there are considerable limitations and constraints for a destination marketing organization (DMO) to establish a sustainable brand identity and gain support from a diverse array of community stakeholders. Their synthesis of extant literature supports the proposition that branding can benefit from collaborative approaches, which have been examined conceptually and empirically in the contexts of community-based tourism planning and development. Furthermore, the authors demonstrate that a community-based collaborative process must be integrated with the building of destination brand equity from the perspective of tourists. In this regard, the chapter examines and reconciles two existing brand equity models and offers a destination branding model that is both community- and consumer-based.

From Theories to Practices. The second part of the book consists of five contributions that link theories to practices through empirical investigations or synthesis of empirical findings. Cai begins this part (Chapter 7) with a look at a small community in the rural Midwest, USA. By invoking the social exchange theory as the foundation and its complex exchange system as the conceptual framework, Cai elaborates the uniqueness of rural destination as a social structure rather than as product or single organization. He proposes a tourism branding model and illustrates it through the case study of the rural community. The model advocates a community-based approach to image research as a platform on which the tourism branding process takes place. The chapter reports the comparative findings on the destination's image as projected by a DMO, perceived by current and potential tourists, and desired by the host community. By highlighting the role of the host community's participation in branding a rural destination, Cai informs the definition of tourism branding as a continuing process to create affective experiences through building and sustaining a consistent destination identity and image that emotionally bonds with the host community and resonates with tourists. This chapter also demonstrates how a branding process can adopt a straightforward approach to what often seems to be a confusing and complex problem.

Chapter 8 looks at a practical component of a destination's offering, local cuisine, as a basis for brand building. It uses an internal perspective, a resident survey, to determine how residents react to the international tourists with respect to their local food offerings. Lin segments local residents into three groups, based on survey responses: "indifferent," "ambivalent," and "supportive." The latter group had the most interest in being involved in culinary tourism activities. The "ambivalent" residents were conservative in making recommendations to international tourists about local food. The "indifferent" group had a low level of support for tourism activities. The work by Lin shows that the internal branding perspective rarely ever yields unanimous agreement on each and every destination attribute as a basis for destination branding. However, the knowledge of where different group of stakeholders stand is a necessary step in this overall process. The chapter also suggests the value of adding "local flavor" into a destination brand that eventually results.

Chapter 9, by Valls, Sierra, Bañuelos, and Ochoa, describes a branding strategy that first tries to narrow the potential items included in a branding strategy to a manageable set. Using expert opinions the authors looked at a range of factors that would influence potential tourists. They then tested this set with tourists who were asked to rate ten different Spanish destinations with respect to the factors identified. This is a winnowing process that first identifies what is important and then attempts to determine the strength of each one of them with respect to different destinations. The study used a relatively older technique (first used in tourism in the 80s by Goodrich and then Gartner and Hunt), multidimensional scaling, which is relatively easy to implement and interpret. It is a rather simple but powerful technique that should be used by more destinations before brand building begins. This chapter shows how methodological techniques, derived from theory, can be usefully applied in a destination branding context. It also serves as a precursor to Chapter 11 where Tasci and Gartner explore the brand building process from both the internal and the external perspectives.

Chapter 10 provides some firsthand singular accounts of what Spain was trying to achieve from both practitioner and academic viewpoints. Aramberri makes the case that the sun and sea which Spain had in abundance formed the basis for attracting not the elite, the traditional travelers in Europe, but the masses that were being economically democratized by the systems put in place after World War II. However, much of what Spain tried to achieve in the way of a touristic image was misguided. The country, in its promotional material, most often depicted scenes of culture and history. When nature was featured, it was primarily mountains or inland natural features. Only a small percentage actually featured what was to become Spain's most recognizable image, that of its beaches and seaside communities. The chapter suggests, although not explicitly, that the internal and external perspectives of destination images and brands do not often match. Failure on the part of the internal brand developers to recognize this fact often results in expensively misguided brand building efforts. In this case, the external perspective on its brand was so strong that eventually the Spanish national tourism authority figured it out and embraced sun, sand, and sea as the elements of its brand building.

Chapter 11 by Tasci and Gartner is devoted to providing a practical framework for destination authorities to follow when developing their brand. It emphasizes many of the points brought out in previous chapters and brings them together as a guide for "do it yourself branding—sans consultants." The authors also argue that both qualitative and quantitative methods of data collection should be used to determine present brand positioning and future direction. Most of the data collection methods used in previous chapters have been around for a long time. However, until they are used in concert and brought to bear on the issue of brand development, the full picture will not be understood. Brand development may be time consuming, but following the path outlined by Tasci and Gartner, it would be complete and provide a fuller picture of the direction that should be taken. The authors refer to the supply and demand sides of the brand development puzzle. Simply put, the supply side consists of an internal perspective and the demand side the external perspective. At some point, they must come together for destination branding to be successful from a marketing and sociocultural perspective, a theme explored in more detail in Chapter 5 and seen throughout this book. This chapter provides the framework needed for the objectives of market growth tied to tourism development with increased quality of life for local residents to both be achievable in the process of destination branding.

Practical Cases. The third part of the book consists of five cases. They are contributed by the practitioners of tourism branding, with some in collaboration with academic investigators. Chapter 12 by Kouris provides an example of how branding is used as a tool to reposition a mature mass destination, Greece. This contribution highlights the relevance of image building in branding and its relation to brand equity. The author outlines the research initiatives that were undertaken to develop a model for the repositioning of the brand and presents ten different implementation strategies. The chapter details an analysis of the complexity of building a national brand as the endorsement of a formal architecture system with a myriad of region, city, and cluster brands.

This complexity is examined from a different standpoint by Jørgensen and Munar in the case study of Copenhagen, Denmark. Chapter 13 explores how Copenhagen has been addressing its branding strategy in relation to three main issues: the relationship between destination branding and the national capacity to insource valuable resources, the need to reframe the concept of branding involving the tourists and the host community, and the importance of networking as a winning business model for cities. The case enlightens the interconnection between destination branding and national political strategy, while presenting a thorough analysis of the organization Wonderful Copenhagen, the official convention and visitor bureau for the greater Copenhagen area, and its branding strategies.

Chapters 14 and 15 continue the theme of branding for cities. In Chapter 14, Baker proposes a consultative model for destination brand planning. The model emphasizes the engagement of community stakeholders to generate their buy-in and support. The chapter provides some practical tools for tourism organizations and demonstrates through lively examples how industry leaders in several US cities tackle the branding process for their respective communities. A successful consultant himself, Baker shares in this chapter how a consultancy firm may deal with the task of facilitating a branding process by having in mind that people are ultimately the most influential and credible communicators of the experiences. The different strategies that destinations can use when planning branding strategies are further probed in Chapter 15. By presenting two cases in South Korea, Lee examines different ways of developing brand identity as a critical component in the process of branding a city. One of the two cases illustrates a process of redefining traditional cultural assets to develop a brand identity in the contemporary context. Lee suggests that such strategy is suited to cities that have an abundant cultural heritage but are less developed. The second case shows how cities that do not have a distinctive heritage can create new cultural assets to amass a new city identity and image. Through contrasting two different strategies in the cases, Lee explores how they can be implemented effectively. The chapter highlights the importance of coordinated marketing programs in developing a city identity and interconnectedness between city branding and tourism industry.

The last practical case, Chapter 16 extends the discussion of tourism branding from the perspective of hospitality organizations. del Olmo and Munar examine the strategic branding for hospitality through the case of Sol Meliá, the 12th largest hotel chain in the world. The authors illustrates how branding has been moving upwards from first being a niche of the marketing and sales department toward being a strategic asset and then becoming the core of the company's organizational structure and corporate strategy. The chapter explains the process conducted by the hotel chain to streamline its brand portfolio, and highlights the relationship between brand strategy and financial management, as well as the importance to involve customers and employees in the branding process. del Olmo and Munar illustrate how the company's brand equity relates to its long-term strategy and how Sol Meliá's branding strategy reflects a change toward an open-networking innovation culture in hospitality organizations. The case presents a series of management tools that can be applied by hospitality practitioners.

CONCLUSION

Tourism Australia's slogan "So Where the Bloody Hell Are You?" has turned out to be short lived. On October 8, 2008, the Australian DMO started a new global advertising blitz when it abandoned the two-year old controversial marketing gimmick that failed in key markets (Sinclair 2008). In a media release, according to Australia Tourism Minister Martin Ferguson (2008) "Australia's tourism industry is currently facing a difficult period and this significant change in direction from Tourism Australia comes at a very important time." It is worth noting that the new campaign broke again in the United Kingdom. This time, it was launched without a provocative slogan. Instead, the advertising theme is based on a storyline that was inspired by the upcoming epic movie, *Australia*. The theme is accompanied with a soft tagline of "Come Walkabout." In so doing, the campaign moved towards illustrating "how people would feel after a holiday in Australia" instead of showing Australian attractions, and it received strong support from tourism industry stakeholders (Sinclair 2008).

It remains to be seen if the new theme and tagline will undo any damage of the previous slogan and increase the equity of the Australian brand. However, the emphasis on experience and consequent feelings and the support of industry stakeholders seem to resonate with fundamentals of branding that many chapters in this book theorize or promote. The greater challenge facing Tourism Australia and other destination communities, big or small, is the deliverability of promise imbedded in their brand element, be it a loud slogan or soft tagline. Furthermore, the experience promised and delivered to tourists must be sustained to achieve their loyalty to the destination brand.

Starbucks has been a shining star when it comes to building a strong consumer brand. The brand has been in trouble lately. In early February 2007, Starbucks Chairman Howard Schultz acknowledged in a memo that the brand's rapid growth in the past 10 years had led to the watering down of the Starbucks experience. Schultz was concerned with the sustainability of the brand and its adverse impact on its core value of customer experience. In other words, Starbucks was undoing what had made it a strong brand. Schultz's warning apparently came too late; and his concern has in fact materialized. Within a year, the company's stock value plummeted by 42% "on signs that consumers were falling out of love with Starbucks" (Huffington 2008). In response, Starbucks scheduled to close more than 600 stores in the United States in 2008. Even more dramatic is the company's initiative that for three hours on Tuesday every single one of its remaining stores is shut down, so that its employees can receive a refresher course on how best to improve the coffee customer experience (Huffington 2008).

Destinations that strive to build a strong brand have much to learn from the self-discipline, as well as the lessons of Starbucks. The company has not degraded any of its product offerings. What has been lost is the authentic experience that its employees used to be depended on to deliver, and do so consistently. To achieve sustainability, tourism branding—be it for a destination or tourism organizations and businesses within the destination—must be a dynamic process in which employees and communities actively participate. Happy Branding!

Acknowledgement

Several contributors to this book developed the chapters from their earlier talks given at Tourism Branding-IV Innovation and Tourism International Seminar organized by the Directorate General for Research, Technological Development and Innovation of the Government of the Balearic Islands, Spain (26–28 September 2007), and at the Second International Conference on Destination Branding and Marketing organized by the Institute for Tourism Studies, Macao (17–19 December 2007).

PART I

GLOBAL CONCEPTS

Chapter 2

CHALLENGING THE BRAND

Ana María Munar
Copenhagen Business School, Denmark

Abridgement: The study explores the issue of branding in tourism from the perspective of two processes related to globalization: the expansion of the world market and the use of information and communication technologies. The question addressed is how these processes affect tourism branding. This chapter shows that while the global market expansion in tourism enhances the relevance of brands, the digitalization of the experience made by the tourists and the expansion of virtual communities both represent an unprecedented challenge to the research and practice of tourism branding. The analysis reveals an empowerment of the tourists which may affect the residents, employees, and managers' roles in branding. The chapter ends with new organizational strategies of brand enhancement which take into consideration the digitalization era. **Keywords:** branding; globalization processes; tourist digital natives; information technologies.

INTRODUCTION

The idea of branding finds its origin in the 19th century (Room 1992) and is related to the market economy. It has existed for centuries as a way of distinguishing the goods of different producers. The capacity of the brand to

Tourism Branding: Communities in Action
Bridging Tourism Theory and Practice, Volume 1, 17–35
Copyright © 2009 by Emerald Group Publishing Limited
All rights of reproduction in any form reserved
ISSN: 2042-1443/doi:10.1108/S2042-1443(2009)0000001004

differentiate a product and the benefits of having a well-known name, rather than bulk commodities or generic goods, have long been appreciated by the business world (Anholt 2003). A brand can be understood as the projection of feelings that a given name or symbol has for a given individual. The name can belong to a company, a person, a thing, or a place. However, brand conceptualization is far more complex, and most academics agree that it is much more than a logo or an advertising theme. As explained by Konecnik and Gartner, a brand may be understood as a "legal instrument, logo, company, identity system, image, personality, relationship, and/or as adding value" (2007:400). Furthermore, according to Urry (2003), products can be considered to be the effect of the brand than vice versa. Brands have the power to produce lifestyles, which is essentially cultural, not residing in the workplaces, workforces, or the objects produced and sold.

Brands in tourism can be found in many categories of goods and services influencing many diverse facets of tourist activities (Cai 2002). A brand enables tourism producers to charge more money for their products and services, while it also gives them the responsibility of maintaining and enhancing the brand reputation. However, the changing values of a specific tourist will affect the perception and the feelings that he/she may have toward the brand. For example, a tourist with a stronger conviction toward the problems of climate change may turn out to have positive feelings toward tourism companies with environmentally friendly policies regarding the control of CO_2 emissions. A brand is not a tangible value (Anholt 2003) and a tourism one belongs to the mind of the tourist. The perception of a tourism brand is the dynamic reality of the brand. It is a historically and sociocultural-rooted phenomenon.

Today's tourists live in a world of increased interconnectivity (Mulgan 1998) and transnational information flows (Castells 1996) which may necessarily affect the way in which they relate to the brands. The rise of a global information platform has further enhanced globalization processes. This platform is the product of a convergence of the personal computer, the capability of the fiber optic cable to increase access to digital information, and the emergence of workflow software, which enables people to collaborate on a specific digital content (Friedman 2005). Although many studies have been focusing on the issue of tourism products branding (Cai 2002) and an increasing number of them have been concentrating on destination branding (Cai 2002; Konecnik and Gartner 2007; Murphy, Moscardo and Benckendorff 2007; Ooi 2006), little has been said of the relationship between globalization forces and the phenomenon of branding in tourism. To which extent the increasing importance of branding in tourism relates to the globalization processes remains a rather unexplored issue. Although research of branding in tourism from a globalization perspective is seldom, a general opinion exists among scholars that tourism is increasingly globalized (Reid 2003; Reiser 2001; Wang 2000; Wood 2000).

This chapter is concerned with branding in tourism from the perspective of two processes related to globalization: the expansion of the world market and the use of information and communication technologies. Due to the intensity and speed in which these two processes are evolving, the understanding of branding is severely challenged. Therefore, the question addressed in the analysis is how the phenomenon of tourism branding is affected by these globalization processes.

GLOBALIZATION AND TOURISM BRANDING

The conceptual framework for this study is based on the theoretical contributions to the understanding of globalization of Held, McGrew, Goldblatt and Perraton (1999) and others such as Robertson (1995), Castells (1996), Giddens (1990), Bauman (1998), Beck (2000), Stiglitz (2003), Bhagwati (2004), and Friedman (2005). There are also many studies that have focused on the relationship of tourism and globalization such as the works of Urry (2001), Wang (2000), Wood (2000), Wahab and Cooper (2001), Reiser (2001), Reid (2003), Teo and Li (2003), Burns (2004), Salazar (2005, 2006), Hjalager (2007), and Munar (2007). The theories that provide the grounding for this study are related to a transformationalist account (Held et al 1999) toward globalization processes. From this perspective, globalization is responsible for the deep transformation of all the spheres of human activity at the beginning of the new century. However, the transformationalist thesis is not responding to a linear logic, as it does not claim to know an ideal model of globalization nor the last stage of globalization. Compared to other theoretical contributions (De la Dehesa 2000; Ohmae 1990), it does not understand globalization as a perfect global market or a global civilization. Globalization, according to the transformationalist approach, is understood as a process deep rooted in history and also as the face of late modernity, which subsequently has a connection to tourism as a social phenomenon that is in itself an expression of modernity. Globalization in this study is conceptualized in the following way:

> The concept of globalization implies first and foremost, a
> stretching of social, political, and economic activities across

frontiers such that events, decisions, and activities in one
region of the world can come to have significance for
individuals and communities in distant regions of the world.
In this sense, it embodies trans-regional interconnectedness,
the widening reach of networks of social activity and power,
and the possibility of action at distance. (Held et al 1999:15)

Related perspectives on global processes and tourism can be found in the
works of Urry (1990) and Wang (2000). There are also others who present
the understanding of non-linear methods as something fundamental in the
study of complex systems (Farrell and Twining-Ward 2004; Milne and
Ateljevic 2001). Reiser (2001) in his study of the Otago Peninsula makes a
claim for the plural understanding of globalization as well as for a historical
approach to the phenomenon. Besides, several studies have claimed the
need of surpassing the everlasting dichotomy of local–global, particular–
universal, and we–others (Brown 1998; Burns 2004; Chang, Milne, Fallon
and Pohlmann 1996; Teo and Li 2003; Teo and Yeoh 1997). Salazar (2005,
2006) employs the theoretical concept of glocalization (Robertson 1995),
while Wood (2000) uses the feature of deterritorialization in his study
on cruise tourism, and Göymen (2000) analyzes globalization challenges
to the dynamics of nation-state policies in Turkey. These authors share
with the transformationalists the use of new ways of understanding social
change through glocalization (Robertson 1995), inclusive distinctions
(Beck 2000), self-interpretation (Held 1997), and connexity (Mulgan 1998).
The main features of the transformationalist approach on globalization are
related to the study of the spatio-temporal and the organizational attributes
(Held et al 1999). The analysis of the spatio-temporal dimensions
(time, space, and velocity of change) focuses on the increase in intensity of
interactivity and interdependency among world regions. The examination
of the organizational dimensions deals with the infrastructure that allows
globalization processes, the institutionalization of global networks and
power, the pattern of global stratification, and the dominants mode of global
interaction.

The literature shows that, although during recent years many researchers
have included the study of globalization in their analyses, a complete
systemic theoretical understanding of the term has not emerged. Most
contributions are a collection of views of different positions on globalization, a sum of theories and statements focusing on specific issues, and a
common understanding of the phenomenon still lacking among tourism
researchers. Hjalager (2007:439) argues that it is "remarkable how little the

literature has discussed the broader manifestations of globalization in tourism, and how limited interest has been in applying theory to the field."

This analysis is also based on the theories of branding as explained by Anholt (2003) and branding in tourism as presented in the studies of Cai (2002), Konecnik and Gartner (2007), Lee, Cai and O'Leary (2006), Ooi (2004, 2006), Baker (2007), and Murphy et al (2006). The theoretical approach is related to both the findings of an exploratory analysis of the use of information and communication technologies in tourism and a content examination of websites, Internet platforms, and the media. An increase in the stretching of the interrelations of the people of the world through frontiers entails the enhancement of globalization processes. This stretching of the social, political, and economic activities and the high increase of interconnectedness of the information age (Castells 1996) mean that today millions of people have access to an enormous amount of information as well as increased diversity among the typology of goods and commodities in their local marketplace. Both the expansion of the tourism marketplace and the evolution of the use of information technologies have a relevant impact on tourism branding. Therefore, the analysis examines in the first place the globalization of the marketplace.

Expanded Tourism Marketplace

The globalized economy has led to a 16-fold increase in world trade since World War II, worth over US$4 trillion per year (Henderson 1999). This spectacular growth is parallel to the increased participation in the World Trade Organization. "In 1947, only 23 nations participated in the first round of trade negotiations" (Hills 2005:26). Today, 151 countries are participating in the ninth round: the Doha Round (WTO 2007). More than two-thirds of these countries are developing countries (WTO 2007). Not many decades ago, most people in developed countries had access to their national goods. It was a case of limited access to information and restricted market width. Nowadays, any huge local supermarket or department store of the Organisation for Economic Co-operation and Development countries can provide an enormous display of variety of a huge amount of products: from sauces or beverages to children's toys. When compared to the choices that people had just 50 years ago, the increase is spectacular.

The change has been even more impressive in the post-communist regimes that, following the decline of the Soviet Empire, embraced a market economy. In just a few years, the post-communist consumers went from a homogenized, state-controlled, limited range of goods and commodities to a large variety of products. At the beginning of the 1990s, for the Eastern countries of Europe, the symbol of their newly won Bill of Rights became not the diversity of political parties or some recovered national traditions but the global marketing campaigns of the trans-national companies. Tourism was to be included in the new range of goods and services destined to become available to the population of the world.

The Berlin Wall fell and citizens obtained, among other things, the right to be tourists. The dream of escaping from the ordinary to the land of nonordinary (Jafari 1987) was no longer stopped by the sign of a military frontier. As the New World Order started, the people of the world won the right to search for Spring throughout the whole year, and this could be offered by tourism destinations worldwide (Beck 2000). At the same time, as the New World Order made its entrance on the global scene, tourism became more readily available to millions who entered the consumer society for the first time. According to the study conducted by Bentley—quoted in *The State of the World 2004*—there are more than 1.7 billion people in the consumer society. Nearly half of them are living in the developing world, with 240 million in China alone (Worldwatch Institute 2004). It is not just citizens of the former Soviet bloc who now enjoy the new pleasures of a market society but also the Far East where the market is gaining ground. The Pacific zone and Eastern Asia have become new commercial centers, showing a high growth in tourism with a 20% share of the international tourism arrivals and 22% of receipts in the year 2007 (UNWTO 2008). Furthermore, China reached the fifth position in the ranking by international tourism spenders, and the Middle East was the fastest growing region in 2007 (UNWTO 2008). Globalization is being driven not only by individuals but also by a much more diverse non-Western group of individuals (Friedman 2005). Nevertheless, not all people can consume tourism products, pay for a hotel room, or buy a whole travel package arrangement. Although the number of consumers is large, there are still one billion people living in extreme poverty (World Bank 2007). The World Development Report explains that "opportunities for the consumption of private goods differ vastly between rich and poor countries. Mean annual consumption expenditures range from Purchasing Power Parity $279 in Nigeria to $17,232 in Luxemburg. This means that the citizen in Luxembourg enjoys monetary resources 62 times higher than the average Nigerian" (World Bank 2006:6).

Globalization of markets means that when looking spatially at the local level, the local consumer is confronted with an increasing amount of information that demands a lot of time and effort before making the final choice of buying one product. Globalization has the effect of multiplying the names of brands that are known as well as the spatial dimension in which these names can come to be known. The global tourism market has also expanded geographically with new destinations all around the world and an increased diversification of the classification of tourism activities such as wellness tourism, city tourism, business and conference tourism, rural tourism, risk tourism, dark tourism, and medical tourism. This process of diversification has received the label of new tourism (Poon 1996).

In the situation of increased variety and complexity, the trust and the confidence placed in a known brand save the consumer a lot of time and worry. Branding can be considered as a powerful strategy which allows the product to stand out from its competition in the minds of customers in terms of benefits and promises (Lee, Lee and Lee 2005). Branding allows a product to be heard in a noisy, overloaded environment. This capability of branding becomes even more relevant with the global market expansion. Tourists do not need to know a lot about how the new planes of Air Berlin operate compared to those of another company, or how the Intercontinental hotel meets sanitary regulations in the spa facilities. It is much easier to rely on the sincerity and good reputation of the brand. If the last experience in a hotel was pleasant, then it will help the stressed family to plan their next holiday more easily and to book rooms at a hotel of the same brand. If the tourist is looking for a great culinary experience, he/she may well search for the restaurants of the destination which have been awarded one or more Michelin stars. According to Anholt (2003), brands provide businesses with the possibility of achieving sustainable wealth, thanks to the loyalty of the customer base, the ready recognition of new products, and the relative cheapness of retaining loyal customers compared to the cost of continually finding new ones.

The increased diversification of goods at the local level of consumption due to the process of economic globalization, while expanding the possibilities of choice among the tourists, increases the importance of the brands. In tourism, it is possible to identify different types of brands. One classification may be established by the public–private category: tourism organizations being public or private—that is, the World Tourism Organization or the Pacific Asia Travel Association and private companies such as Marriot or Sol Meliá. Another classification may focus on the destination vs. product category. Destinations that relate to the branding of a place, this being a nation, a region, or a town, are always an emotive subject (Anholt 2003), and they have some major distinctive elements (Cai 2002; Murphy et al 2006; Ooi 2004). The stakeholders will be different, depending on the category—these being the residents in the case of a brand related to a specific place and the employees or members in the case of a brand not related to a destination. All these different typologies will be indistinctively called tourism brands throughout the study. The mention of a brand related to a destination will be specified when relevant.

Virtual Tourism Communities

The increase of diversity at local level puts brand reputation at the forefront of the strategy for either a tourism company or a destination that strives to be competitive. Companies and destinations compete to be the most attractive to the tourist mind. However, this task of creating a strong and coherent brand is challenged by the revolution of information and communication technology. This revolution increases the sources of information received by the possible tourists. Castells (1996) explains this phenomenon in his trilogy on the information age. The enhancement of the World Wide Web provides a ground where groupings of individuals and organizations are able to interact meaningfully providing individualized, interactive communication across frontiers. The new information platform is shaped by the constant interactivity with its millions of users around the globe. Some of these users are the "digital natives," the first generation to grow up with information technology, surrounded by computer games, Internet, instant messaging, and emails (Prensky 2001). According to Friedman (2005), at the beginning of the 21st century, the information society is entering a new phase characterized by a huge increase in the digitalization, virtualization, and automatization of processes and products. Knowledge has been digitalized, and digital natives use technology to package and transport their knowledge and images throughout the world telecommunication systems. It is possible to assume that the enormous collage of information sources will increase as the new "digital natives" become the new professionals and climb to higher social, economic, and cultural positions. Furthermore, the personal computer and the development of more customer-friendly software products are enabling ordinary people to upload and download information from the Internet without being programmers (Buhalis 2003).

The upload and download phenomenon brings the use of Internet facilities into a new stage of development, a development that can also be called the "C2C market"—from customer to customer (Jensen 2007). The development of Internet community as a new way of providing services and information is in its first stage. A good example of a sharing knowledge community is Wikipedia, an online encyclopedia with over 1.5 million articles produced by users. In tourism, the same concept is developed with Wikitravel (2007a), "a project to create a free, complete, up to date and reliable worldwide travel guide." Wikitravel allows people to share their knowledge on destinations and is available in 19 languages. The English Wikitravel announces that it can provide more than 16,000 destination guides and other articles from around the globe.

The main shift of the upload–download phenomenon is that the user becomes the producer and the consumer at the same time, without the need for including traditional business in the process. Furthermore, the product is offered free of charge (Jensen 2007). It is difficult not to imagine the challenge that this type of knowledge-sharing communities can become for well-established tourism guide brands such as *Lonely Planet*. Still the website of *Lonely Planet* shows that efforts are already being made to allow their customers to blog (texts written by tourists, digitalized and posted on some Internet platform) as well as to podcast (the audio/visual version of blogging) videos of their travels and share them with the rest of the world (Lonely Planet 2007). However, the question for tourism organizations is how to find a strategic balance in more hybrid forms of public/private or professional/amateur services with increased decentralized information tools and still profit from it while maintaining a coherent brand. The widening of the Internet as an information source is fast developing.

> Podcasts involve individuals producing their own audio and video files—music, commentary, books, poetry readings, singing recitals, anything you can imagine that can be done by voice or video—which can then be uploaded onto Internet platforms, like Apple iTunes. These podcasts are then downloaded by users or subscribers, who listen to them or watch them on their computer, iPod, MP3 player, cell phone, or other portable device. (Friedman 2005:120)

A good example of the possibilities of the uploading–downloading phenomenon is the massive use of the image bank of YouTube. Tourists no longer need to go to an official website to take a look at a destination. By typing in the name of Ibiza in YouTube search, it is possible to see videos of the activities of other tourists who were there in the past week. Many of these images have a "real life" approach, without any or only a minimum of manipulation (YouTube 2007). Besides the image of the new generation of tourist digital natives, the emergence of the "Pro-Am" is to be considered.

The term "Pro-Am" appeared at the pamphlet entitled "The Pro-Am revolution: How enthusiasts are changing our economy and society," written by Leadbeater and Miller (2004). According to their analysis, the past two decades have seen the appearance of the Pro-Ams: a new class of amateur who works to professional standards. Thanks to the new information platforms, these Pro-Ams are creating new, distributed organizational models that will be innovative, adaptative, and low cost. Some of these are world renowned for their contribution to community-developed software such as Linux, the open-source software, or the Mozilla Foundation, which released the free Web browser Firefox (Friedman 2005); others were the protagonists of the Jubilee 2000 debt campaign that started in the mid-1990s and had a petition with 24 million signatures by the year 2000. There are many Pro-Ams who are enthusiastic about tourism experiences and are willing to share them in the form of travel guides, diaries, reviews, or films. The previously mentioned Wikitravel is a good illustration of how amateurs in tourism guides provide a community-made product that try to match professional standards. Furthermore, an example as Couchsurfing, a website that allows tourists to choose the coach at resident homes as means of accommodation and presents itself as "a worldwide network for making connections between travelers and the local communities they visit," shows how the new platform allows for both knowledge sharing and the introduction of innovative customer-based products.

By taking a look at the thousands of guides, videos, and images portraying destinations and products, it seems that the times in which it was possible to pursue control over the brand image are long gone. Urry (2001) mentions how the Internet enables a type of horizontal communication that cannot be effectively surveilled, controlled, or censored by national societies. The new communication platform cannot be controlled by either single-destination management offices or companies. The knowledge of these professional amateurs combined with the interactive participation of all kinds of persons, which make use of micro-cameras in mobile phones and instant connection to the Internet, makes it possible to post images of places in real time. All those billions of bytes of accessible information provide the nurturing of a huge unprecedented platform of communication and interconnection.

The websites of many destinations and companies have to face the challenge of a change of perspective: from being informational windows with a top–down presentation to one of enhanced customer participation. This change toward down–down communication challenges traditional marketing orientations as well as company cultures. In their study of US state tourism websites, Lee, Cai and O'Leary (2006:824) concludes his analysis by indicating that state marketing managers have to confront the heterogeneity of their products as well as avoid decentralization tendencies to project a "uniquely concentrated brand personality." Ooi (2006:6) mentions that "branding inadvertently frames and packages the destination into a relatively well-defined and coherent product, which focuses on attractions and activities that are considered significant and relevant to the brand values." Nevertheless, globalization of digitalized information maximizes decentralization tendencies in tourism by breaking the framework and challenging the possibilities of packaging a coherent image. The expansion of the amount of information and the lack of control of what is written, read, and seen on the Internet create a huge challenge for the companies or institutions that want to control the image of their brand.

Tourism is specially affected by the new possibilities of the global information age because historically tourists enjoy to film or take photos of their holidays. The local residents do not usually go around with a camera immortalizing the local bar or bus station. Nevertheless, tourists do take photos of their hotel rooms, the food they are served, the monument they visit, and so on. The evolvement of cell phones to include a photo and recording camera, plus an Internet connection, has provided the tourist with a mobile technological platform, which is a powerful tool to send information of their experience around the globe. Many examples of the increasing digitalization of experiences through podcasts can be found on the Internet. Tourists become virtual tourists at the Virtual Tourist website. This site invites their members to become part of the "virtual-tourist travel community in action" and receives more than 2,000 new postings on travel and holidays every 24 hours (Virtual Tourist 2007). Furthermore, the blogging reality is entering tourism as a tool widely used to read and write reviews on accommodation and travel services. Today's new digital tourists can post their diaries on the Internet. Tourists can also share the site with their community of friends, colleagues, and family so that they can take a look at the blog or send it as an email. Webs incorporate dialog features through blog and podcast possibilities for the tourists, and these last years have seen a tremendous increase on tourism social interactivity through computers.

Thanks to the new platform, the act of communication becomes a public scene where everybody can see what is written. Trip Advisor is one of the sites where it is possible to read reviews of tourism products and services. The site has proven to be a great financial success with a profit of $129 million on $260 million in revenue for the 12 months to June 30, 2008, attracting 20.3 million tourists in July 2008 alone (Weisman 2008).

Hotel owners and other companies may regard these sites as reliable sources of information on their business and products. However, they may also perceive them as a threat. The following is one example of the type of very critical personal comment that can easily be found in customer-generated content websites:

> After a long and grueling trip from Australia my wife and I were looking forward to a lovely stay in the heart of London. Unfortunately our initial impressions of London were significantly marred by the underwhelming reception we received from the reception staff at The Strand Palace. As we arrived early (7am) I asked if the hotel had any shower facilities so my wife and I could freshen up whilst awaiting check in. The response was not only discourteous it was outright rude. The reception staff seemed disinterested. To add insult to injury the hotel tried to charge my wife and I for baggage storage as we decided to stroll the streets whilst we waited until we could check-in (2 pounds per bag ... we had 4 bags!!!). The room was small with a large 70's styled bathroom. The only thing going for this hotel was location, which was fairly central however they have a lot to learn about customer service. I would not recommend nor would I stay here again. (Trip Advisor 2007a)

Any tourist can be a global image-maker or story teller by uploading information onto the Internet. TravelBlog is another popular website that enables wanna-be-tourists to read a collection of travel journals, diaries, and photos from around the world and allows tourists to update friends and family on their experiences. When this research was conducted, its website showed "325 updated blogs, 91 new bloggers, 3,126 new photos, and 67 forum post" and all that in only 24 hours (TravelBlog 2007). The same concept is found in IgoUgo (2007a), another online travel community website. As one PhD student on computer games explained: he never reads journals or newspapers because they are too slow to catch the changes. He gets the latest news on computer games from the blogs on the Internet. This tendency is also reaching the management of tourism businesses. As Fluxà, the manager of the Hotel Casa Camper in Barcelona, explained during a research interview on September 2007: "I always look at websites. I prefer to look in Trip Advisor and see how the reviews that we get are. I hate to get questioners in the hotels, it is annoying for the customers" (Fluxá cited in

Munar 2008). According to Fluxà, with over 100 customer reviews posted on websites such as Trip Advisor, it is enough to check them to know what is right and what is wrong with the hotel service. Besides, those reviews have a high degree of reliability. No wonder that the trademark slogan of Trip Advisor (2007b) is "Get the truth, then go." Other major companies such as Sol Meliá (2007a, 2007b), a hospitality brand with 406 hotels in 35 countries, pay consultancy firms to surf the web and analyze the content generated by their customers. When compared to Wikitravel, which exists due to the collaboration of thousands of "Pro-Ams" who share their knowledge worldwide, these other sites such as IgoUgo, Trip Advisor, or TravelBlog represent another type of community based on experience sharing.

Most blogs and podcasts in these sites are portraits of the tourism experience from a personal and subjective perspective. Some quotes to exemplify the type of subjective messages posted are as follows: a tourist talking about a hotel in California: "Why, oh why? Why didn't I check this site first? This place—so bad, there was a spontaneous support group for guests in the parking lot the day we left. None of this is hearsay ... Look at the pictures" (Trip Advisor 2007c); another tourist regarding a visit to Galleries Lafayette in Paris: "When my sister said that we were going to go to a department store, I thought to myself 'Oh great; another mall!' You have no idea how wrong I was ..." (IgoUgo 2007b); and finally, a tourist commenting on a meal at a restaurant in Kuwait: "This week we decided to try a Lebanese restaurant we had seen close to a place called Fresh where my friends have eaten before. The food, service and surroundings were so good, I rushed back here to tell you all about it. Anyone who is already in Kuwait must go and try this place out." The thousands of tourists' postings on the different sites provide many examples of this type of experience sharing. These are texts that do not say as much about knowledge delivery as they do about the human need for social communication.

The phenomenon of podcasting can be turned into a marketing tool, but a direct advertising approach to it can come to foster negative effects on the image of the brand. Two very different cases on corporate podcast appeared in the Danish economic newspaper *Børsen* (Larsen 2007). The first one was the case of Starbucks, the multinational coffee bar chain, which used podcast to produce commercial advertising. The firm received a negative feedback from its customers that developed popular hate-sides against the campaign on the Internet. The second one was the British Airway's production of a series of podcast episodes with "Dr. Sleep" (British Airways 2007), which aimed to assist sleep on flights and which achieved very good results, although it was not meant as an advertising campaign for the company. Now it is possible to search the web for sleep and British Airways appears as a reliable source of knowledge on the issue (Larsen 2007). The possibilities of blogging and also of podcasting are just beginning to be explored in tourism. An example of the possibilities of the use of podcast in the official branding of a destination is the website of the official tourism office in Dublin, which announces "the podcasts section of our site, here you can download our free podcast audio guides to Dublin," which they call the "iWalks" and also the "Malahide Castle Audio Guides" (Official Online Tourism Office for Dublin 2007). Baker (2007) mentions how Travel Oregon's GoSeeOregon.com has incorporated some of the features that allow tourists to share information.

Blogging is a massive phenomenon and there are more than 50 million bloggers; people who wish to share their knowledge with others and who do it through the Internet and throughout the world (Jensen 2007). The phenomenon stretches from the tourism examples that have just been examined to other areas such as journalism or the film industry (Friedman 2005; Jensen 2007). According to Baker (2007), despite all the marketing opportunities today, it is still the word of mouth that is the most powerful form of communication, and technology is amplifying its impact. The trend is only a few years old and there is still a lot more research to be done to establish the impacts of the new uses of the information and communication technologies in tourism. However, the exploratory research conducted and analyzed in the previous sections points toward a massive use of blogs and podcasts by tourists. As new generations of digital tourists gain economic, social, and cultural power, the use of these tools can be expected to become routine within the tourism experience, creating major challenges for the brand in the industry to follow (Table 1).

Tourism Brands Challenged

Even if the information age is a reality and examples of how tourists use digitalization to record and share experiences are everywhere, there are still examples of how branding tourism destination policies have not yet assimilated the changes. In a study made by Davies, principal of Orient Pacific Century Market Research, it is possible to read the following analysis based on controlling projection of brand identity:

> Every tourist destination in the world has a "brand image."
> If developed carefully the brand serves to differentiate a
> destination from competing destinations. However some

Table 1. Challenges to the Tourism Brand

Globalization Processes	Dimensions	Impacts on Tourism Branding
Tourism marketplace	Spatio-temporal, increase in intensity and volume and diversification of products	Enhancement of the importance of the brand
Information technologies	Expansion of ICTs (Information and Communication Technologies) as global mode of interaction	Empowerment of the tourist and fragmentation of brand coherence
	Increased intensity in customer social computing and expansion of Web 2.0	New information channels for tourism organizations

destinations do not have a brand strategy, and are supported by inconsistent advertising campaigns, creating a confused image to prospective customers. Image must be controlled by a clear projection of brand identity. (Davies 2003)

This type of argumentation for coherence and avoidance of fragmentation is common in the literature. A study on the branding of Denmark conducted by a Danish consultancy firm for the Danish Ministry of Economy and Enterprise explained that "greater positive attention demands that one communicates a coherent and truthful image of Denmark" (Red Associates 2006:5).

The existence of incoherent and fragmented marketing campaigns cannot project a clear brand. However, the new global challenge comes not as much from regional and national promotional campaigns lack of coordination as from the expanding possibilities of the digital era. The information-age risks, which may challenge the brand reputation, are most likely to be more diffused, dispersed, multidimensional, and ambiguous than risks of previous ages (Urry 2001). The hundreds of images and texts that circled the globe of several terror attacks such as the ones in Bali, natural disasters such as the fires in Greece, the tragic disappearance of Madeleine McCann (a little British girl) in the Portuguese tourist resort of Praia da Luz, or even a political crisis such as the one provoked by the publication in a Danish newspaper of the Muhammad caricatures could all have a deep and long-lasting impact on the image which a destination may have in the minds of future tourists. In this sense, the relevance of today's globalization interconnectivity is related to Beck's (2000) concept of Risk Society. In a World Risk Society, those issues that were usually handled behind closed doors and shared among a small group of people are made public and exposed worldwide from one day to the next—for example, economic investment decisions, the chemical composition of products and medicines, scientific research programs, the development of new technologies, or the unsatisfying tourism experience. The fragility of the brand can be seen in various cases such as the brand of Monsanto, a global agricultural company that nearly disappeared because of the news relating the company to genetically modified food (Urry 2001), or the accusations of child labor exploitation made against Nike (Azam 1999).

The new technologies in the hands of millions of consumers increase the risk tendency even more. An "internet-enabled camera phone is not just a camera; it is also a copy machine, with worldwide distribution potential" (Friedman 2005:198). One of the examples of how brands can face risks is the issue of climate change and air travel's CO_2 emissions. Rather than waiting for tourists to expose the climate risk of air travel to the whole world, Air France, through its website, has provided a service that allows the calculation of CO_2 emission. According to the company, "The calculator meets the strong demand for transparency from Air France customers, key accounts, corporate, and individual passengers, who would like to calculate the CO_2 emissions generated by their trip" (Airfrance 2007). How the empowerment of customers and employees can be achieved by the new upload and download phenomenon can be seen in the case of IBM. Truskowski, the company's Corporate Innovation Officer, developed a strategy that he named a "blog on steroids," where employees and customers are encouraged to blog their ideas on the company's future. Using intranet-based collaboration technology, IBM got 50,000 responses from their employees and—assisted by IT—distilled those into just three corporate values (Anthes 2006). IBM's new values, which include putting client needs first and fostering innovation, may seem obvious, but Truskowski explained that the participatory means by which they were developed gives them credibility with employees—something they would have lacked if they had been developed by "a senior executive sitting in Armonk" (cited in Anthes 2006). In October 2004, the company developed a so-called jam, a worldwide brainstorming session. It drew ideas from 33,000 employees, and IBM later implemented the top 35 suggestions as determined by an employee vote (Anthes 2006).

By exchanging employees for residents, the same procedures could be used to empower and involve local people in designing the image as well as the strategy of a destination brand. But the idea of strategic blogging and network collaboration can also be used by tourism organizations in positioning their goods and services. In the IBM example, the management facilitated a process of digital collaboration to enhance innovation in the corporation. However, many of the websites reviewed, such as Trip Advisor or YouTube, do not allow this possibility of strategic management, because their goals are much more diffused and unstructured and they are mainly focused on C2C sharing of information. The lack of residents' participation in the new social computing networks calls for the involvement of tourism stakeholders and policymakers who need to face the new challenges that the growing expansion and complexity of the market and the evolving of the new information technologies present for their destinations.

CONCLUSION

The globalization processes studied have major impacts on tourism branding. Brands that provide recognition, visibility, and loyalty are more relevant today than ever before due to the expansion of the global market and the diversification of tourism products. However, in the era of digital information global flows, the top–down approach to branding in organizations is deeply challenged. Tourist digital natives have begun to make more and more use of digitalization in the forms of blogs and podcasts sent by mobile phones, emails systems, or postings on tourism internet platforms. They use the new communication tools to both evaluate brands and create new ways of understanding the brand. Tourism brands are highly exposed when compared to those of other industries, because tourists traditionally record their experiences and share their stories. The future will bring new unexpected forms in which technical means of communication are combined with humans (Urry 2001). This may give tourists new unexpected possibilities of interacting with each other. In Friedman's words:

> This newfound power of individuals and communities to send up, out and around their own products and ideas, often for free, rather than just passively downloading them from commercial enterprises or traditional hierarchies, is fundamentally reshaping the flow of creativity, innovation, political mobilization and information gathering and dissemination. (Friedman 2005:94)

The best assurance for maintaining the good reputation of a brand is to live up to the quality and promises made to the tourist who is the consumer.

> People can't be deceived for long; ... the higher you raise their expectations, the more completely they reject your offering when they are disappointed; and you can't make people buy a bad product more than once. So every good marketer knows that his or her primary responsibility is to ensure that the product matches up to the promise, because misleading marketing is ineffective marketing. (Anholt 2003:12)

With globalization's information tools, the risks have become much bigger. The unhappy tourist may not only refuse to buy the product a second time but may well shout throughout the cyber world how bad and disappointing the experience happened to be.

A message that in the past may have remained within the realm of friends and relatives can now be dispatched to thousands of readers through the Internet. Brand coherence and control by companies and organizations is at stake because why should the opinion of a professional reviewer, writer, or journalist be more trustworthy than that of dozens of customers? Why should the planned and coherent image projected by the destination management office be more real and appropriate than hundreds of images of experiences shared by tourists? Why should professionals be better than the "Pro-Ams"? To assure a good brand reputation in tourism products and services, destination organizations will have to closely monitor social changes and trends that may end up having an effect on the values and feelings of tourists. Better research on what tourists say (their knowledge) and on what they really do (their praxis) may be demanded. To this purpose, many companies have started to utilize research methods of anthropology, ethnography, and other social sciences (Merit and Nielsen 2006).

The study shows how global technologies allow the empowerment of tourists vs. the organization's monopoly of the brand. Tourists are already actively playing a role in defining the image of destinations and their businesses, and this tendency can be expected to increase in the future. However, it is questionable to what extent the empowerment of the tourist toward destinations will be followed by an empowerment of the local population. As mentioned before, tourists are the ones who mostly use the possibilities of the upload and download phenomenon, share experiences, and write comments on tourism products, services, and destinations.

From all the different sites and examples reviewed in this chapter, the local population views on their local destinations seem missing as they are not going around taking photos of their ordinary life and posting them on tourism relevant sites. Even Wikitravel states that the site follows the principle "The traveler comes first" when making decisions about Wikitravel (2007b): "The idea is that all our work should be guided towards serving the travelers that are our readers." Residents of destinations do not appear to be part of any principle appearing on the Wikitravel project page.

This general tendency toward the empowerment of tourists could result in a huge gap of influence between the tourists and the residents. The latter may still have a lot to say through political mechanisms by electing local representatives and participating in debates to enhance the advertising campaigns for the destination. They may also agree upon which image they would like to be promoted throughout the world. However, these procedures relating to citizenship normally follow the strategy planned by the official destinations offices or local/national authorities. Local participation is mainly placed in the older paradigm of the top–down creation of the images of brands and far away from the increasing influence of the expansion of communication tools throughout the web.

If new strategies do not appear in tourism policy at the destination level, then in the future, many residents may find themselves with little influence on how they are increasingly perceived by the rest of the world. A policy that really wants to empower the local residents' image of the place needs to focus on these other participation tools such as podcasting, open debates, and cultural activities, which together may not be either top–down structured nor follow political procedures of decision-making, but which are much more participatory and flat in their structure. There are promising opportunities for further research on tourism experiences by studying the digitalization and sharing of information provided by the tourists. All such websites and internet platforms can be regarded as free access to large databases of customer practices, opinions, wishes, and needs; vital research that will be needed if organizations desire to improve their knowledge on the future of tourism branding.

Chapter 3

A MODEL OF VIRTUAL DESTINATION BRANDING

Martin Yongho Hyun
Catholic University of Daegu, South Korea

Liping A. Cai
Purdue University, USA

Abridgement: As more destinations jump on the bandwagon of branding, their marketing organizations increasingly employ the Internet as a convenient medium for promotion. This chapter argues that instead of extending their brand communications to the Web by simply digitizing the logos, taglines, and other elements, destinations can build brands virtually in an internet-mediated environment where virtual experience takes place. The study examines how branding can be achieved through building virtualized destination image. It adopts the concepts of telepresence, virtual experience, and integrated informational response and explains how online and offline communication stimuli can affect various components of virtualized image. This expands and modifies the conventional image constructs by specifying information sources as antecedents through telepresence and integrated behavioral responses as consequences. The relationships between the image, its antecedents, and consequences, and among the image constructs are illustrated

Tourism Branding: Communities in Action
Bridging Tourism Theory and Practice, Volume 1, 37–50
ISSN: 2042-1443/doi:10.1108/S2042-1443(2009)0000001005

through 14 propositions. The chapter concludes with a discussion of the net community in which residents and other stakeholders of communities actively participate in virtually building a strong destination brand. **Keywords:** telepresence; virtual experience; destination image; branding; integrated behavioral responses.

INTRODUCTION

The tourism industry in general has been among the major beneficiaries of e-commerce. Fast-evolving trends in technology, Internet infrastructure and culture, and online marketing are changing the ways people find information about destinations and purchase travel services and products. By 2005, there were already more than 79 million online consumers who used the Internet for travel plans in the United States, which was over half of the US tourists or 37% of the total adult population (Travel Industry Association of America 2005). However, the fruits of e-commerce in tourism are largely shared among mega travel e-mediaries that are established as internet brands such as Expedia and Travelocity, and transportation and lodging suppliers extending their brands to the Internet through integrated marketing communications. In contrast, destination communities, primarily represented by their destination marketing organizations (DMOs), have yet to take full advantage of the e-commerce opportunities presented by an increasingly globalized and digitized tourism industry.

The status quo of a DMO's participation in e-commerce can be best described as using the Internet as a new information medium typified by a website bearing the destination's name. Its functional features and capabilities vary, ranging from an online copy of a traditional flyer to a highly interactive portal with continuous updates. In the latter case, a DMO's website may be equipped with functionality for tourists to make reservations for hotel rooms and attraction admissions. Yet, it remains a complement to existing media, be it a travel guide, newspaper, magazine, radio, and television. Consumer-driven net communities have emerged as a primary information source for tourists and increasingly affect their decisionmaking processes. There is little evidence that DMOs are building virtual brands for these communities other than digitizing logos, taglines, and other brand elements created by their advertising agencies. As the academic inquiry into destination branding is still in its infancy, the research community has yet to explore it virtually as a new paradigm. This chapter examines how branding can be achieved through building virtualized image. The chapter adopts the concepts of telepresence, virtual experience, and integrated informational response. It explains how communication stimuli, including both online and offline information sources, can affect various components of virtualized image; and how such image influences the behavioral responses of tourists.

INTERNET-MEDIATED IMAGE AND BRANDING

A destination's image exerts a critical influence on tourists' choice due to the intangible nature of its offerings (Baloglu and Brinberg 1997; Cai 2002; Chen and Kerstetter 1999; Fakeye and Crompton 1991; Gartner 1993a, 1993b; McLellan and Foushee 1983; Um and Crompton 1990; Woodside and Lysonski 1989). As such, the image acts as a criterion to position and differentiate one place from its competitors (Ahmed 1991). A strong, positive, distinct, and recognizable image leads to a higher probability of it being chosen by tourists (Hunt 1975; Pearce 1982). Studies of destination image have progressed through three streams. They are information-stimuli focused (Fakeye and Crompton 1991; Gartner 1993a, 1993b; Gunn 1972; Phelps 1986), dynamic-stimuli approach (Baloglu and McCleary 1999a, 1999b; Beerli and Martín 2004; Stern and Krakover 1993), and technology-based (Cho, Wang and Fesenmaier 2002). The third stream is in response to the advent of the Internet and DMOs' use of it as a promotion tool due to the economical global accessibility to millions of users (Cai, Feng and Breiter 2004). In particular, by employing the concept of virtual experience, Cho (2002) examined how a Web-based virtual tour impacts destination image formation.

Defined as "psychological and emotional states that consumers undergo while interacting with products in 3D environment" (Li, Daughert and Biocca 2002:43), the term virtual experience has emerged as superior to both direct and indirect experience. The contention is that virtual experience has a greater impact on the three states of consumers' decisionmaking process than direct and indirect experience: mental imagery (cognitive), emotional responses (affective), and derived intentions. Cho's (2002) study suggested some effects of a virtual tour on destination image but stopped short of examining its structural relationships with virtual behavioral response, virtual experience or telepresence, and virtual antecedents such as offline and online information sources. The objective of this chapter is to conceptualize a virtual destination branding model by defining the components of virtualized image and by identifying its structural relationships with its antecedents and consequences in a branding context.

Telepresence and Destination Image

The terms of virtual experience and telepresence are often used interchangeably because both refer to a mediated environment. However, the latter seems to be a broader concept than the former. Telepresence can be applied to both offline and online media. However, virtual experience limits discussion to two-dimensional (2D) and three-dimensional (3D) environments on the Web. Cho and Fesenmaier (2001) noted that virtual experience derives from telepresence. Accordingly, Cho et al (2002:3) defined virtual experience as "an experience in a virtual environment using a computer-mediated environment and is based upon the concept of telepresence." As Shih (1998) mentioned, telepresence can result from any form of media such as TV, magazines, word-of-mouth, and the Web. Taking possible exposure to any media into consideration, consumers transport to offline and online mediated environments through telepresence, thereby leading to image formation and attitude toward an object.

Telepresence is a well-known mediating variable between information and consumers' attitudes (Fiore, Kim and Lee 2005; Suh and Chang 2006). It has been described as "the experience of presence in an environment by means of a communication medium" (Steuerm 1992:75), "an illusion of 'being there' in a mediated environment" (Li et al 2002:44), "a sense of presence in a mediated environment" (Klein 2003:42), or "a sense of being in a mediated space other than where the physical body is located" (Biocca 1997:3). It is the "extent to which consumers feel their existence in the virtual space" (Shih 1998:658). In sum, telepresence is a feeling of direct experience in a virtual environment created via an array of media.

The degree one feels telepresence is determined by two functional configurations of medium technology: interactivity and vividness. The former refers to the degree to which the use of a medium can influence the form or content of the mediated environment. The latter refers to the ability of a technology to produce a sensorially rich mediated environment (Klein 2003; Li et al 2002; Steuer 1992). Vividness can be measured by breadth and depth. Breadth refers to the number of sensory dimensions simultaneously presented by a communication medium, such as auditory, touch, taste, smell, and the visual senses (Klein 2003). Steuer (1992) argued that the redundant information from multi-sensory systems at the same time intensifies the perception of a particular environment. The result of this experiencing improves vividness. For example, television projects both the audio and visual systems; whereas radio addresses only the audio system. Thus, TV has greater sensory breadth (Li et al 2002). Traditional media such as television, telephone, print, and film are relatively low in breadth because they are mainly dependent on visual and auditory channels; whereas computer-based, newer media can enhance the breadth of mediated experience (Biocca 1997) by adding interactive functions such as changing, rotating, and zooming an attraction as tourists experience it at a real destination (Schlosser, Mick and Deighton 2003). Sensory depth refers to resolution within each of these perceptual channels (Klein 2003). For example, a 3D-based image has greater depth than a 2D-based image. Therefore, in most cases a telepresence from interactive media, such as 3D virtual environments, should be richer than indirect experience provided by print advertisements, television commercials (Klein 2003), or even 2D images on the Web (Li et al 2002).

In telepresence, interactivity has three components: speed, range, and mapping (Steuer 1992). Speed refers to the assimilation rate of input into the mediated environment. Real-time interaction is its most valuable representation of speed. Online chatting is typically real-time interaction. Films are not interactive at all. Range relates to the amount of change that can be effected on the mediated environment. For example, TV has a limited range of choices: on or off, which leads consumers to perceive their experience as more mediated. In contrast, the Web enables them to engage many controls such as changing color, rotating, and zooming, which allow the consumers to perceive the environment as less mediated by providing similarity to direct experience (Klein 2003). Successful mapping relies on how the mediated action can imitate, as closely as possible, humans' experience. For example, turning a steering wheel on a video game makes a virtual car move accordingly.

As Shih (1998) proposed, the more users are able to interact with the visual and auditory-based medium, the more they will feel immersed in the virtual environment, resulting in a more positive affect. Therefore, offline information produces lower telepresence than Web-mediated information since the former are less interactive than the latter. Furthermore, Web information classifies into 2D-based and 3D-based virtual information. The latter's features may result in a higher degree of telepresence (Coyle and Thorson 2001). This is in contrast to less vivid and interactive 2D photos and text-based Web features (Fiore and Jin 2003) since 2D-based-Web features are "non-interactive, static photograph and text-based message" (Li et al 2002:46).

According to Smith and Swinyard (1982, 1988), if the information on a product is closer to direct experience, consumers believe that it is more reliable, thereby, leading to a favorable attitude toward the product. In a hierarchical manner, mass media advertising has less effect on cognition, affect, and conation than a product trial depending on information acceptance level. In the tourism context, Gartner (1993a, 1993b) argued that, among traditional forms of information sources producing indirect experience, advertising classified as touristic information has low credibility, whereas word-of-mouth classified as non-touristic information has high credibility. Beerli and Martín (2004) found that with a greater impact of personal communication on image formation process than DMO promotions, word-of-mouth or past experience is closer to direct experience. Because a telepresence can provide real-life experience, which may lead to successful creation and communication of destination image (Cho and Fesenmaier 2001), it can have a greater impact than indirect experience on the three states of consumers' decisionmaking: cognition, affection, and conation (Li, Daugherty and Biocca 2001). In this regard, telepresence affects how a destination is perceived virtually in such an environment. In other words, this image can be virtualized with telepresence.

Virtualized Image, Antecedents, and Consequences

Virtualized image can be defined as an overall impression formed as a result of the interaction among virtual cognitive, affective, and global perceptions that online-individuals hold of a destination by experiencing its telepresence through exposures to offline and virtual information sources. Smith and Swinyard's (1982) traditional Integrated Information Response model, Cho's (2002) extended this model, and Gartner's (1993a, 1993b) image formation process are informative in identifying a structure where relationships among the virtualized image and its antecedents and consequences can be examined (Figure 1). The first assumption in the structure is that the virtualized image has four types of information sources as antecedents: DMO promotions, non-touristic information, 2D/text-based, and 3D-based virtual information. The first two form indirect experience. 2D/text-based virtual information forms virtual indirect experience (Li et al 2002), whereas 3D-based virtual information forms virtual direct experience (Griffith and Chen 2004). As Fasolo, Misuraca, McClelland and Cardaci (2006) noted, the animation of products with interactivity on the Web improves consumers' choice intention, because interactivity increases their tangibility (Koernig 2003).

Telepresence is the adapted determinant for information acceptance level. When an information source becomes increasingly more similar to direct experience, the degree of credibility for it increases (Smith and Swinyard

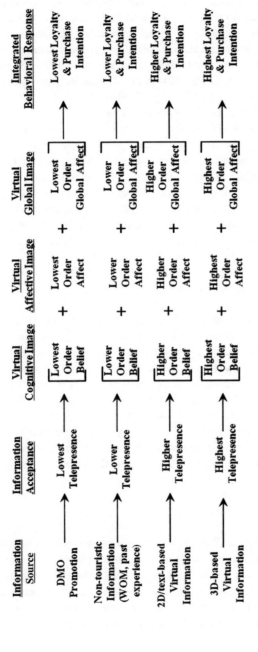

Figure 1 Virtualized Destination Image, Antecedents, and Consequences. Adapted from Smith and Swinyard (1982) and Cho (2002).

1988). Since a Web-mediated experience is much richer and more interactive than other mediated experience provided by prints ads or TV commercials, it is more similar to unmediated direct experience (Hopkins, Raymond and Mitra 2002). Virtual information can become more credible by improving the level of telepresence that makes consumers feel like having the actual experience. In Figure 1, the 3D-based virtual information results in the highest telepresence, followed by 2D-based virtual information, non-touristic information, and DMO promotions.

Virtualized destination image consists of three components: virtual cognitive, virtual affective and virtual global. Differentiated from existing image typologies where conation is considered as part of the image proper, it is treated in this study as the consequence of the image-integrated behavioral responses. The global component takes its place in the image proper. However, the relationships among the three image components remain intact in the absence of conation. Cognitive component refers to the perceptions of a destination's attributes; affective component consists of feelings and emotions derived from the perception; and global component is the product of the two, resulting from both cognitive and affective evaluations of the destination.

Conation as the consequence of virtualized image consists of the integrated behavioral responses of the resulting loyalty and purchase intention. Stern, Zinkhan and Holbrook (2002) argued that various responses to online image should be used for behavioral evaluation. In particular, they suggested loyalty as a critical behavioral response, in addition to purchase intention. Virtual loyalty is crucial for several reasons. First, it can significantly reduce the maintenance cost for website traffic (Hanson 1999). Second, it results in market efficiency by reducing consumers' search and decisionmaking costs (Laudon and Traver 2001). Third, it reduces new customer acquisition costs and increases the retention rate of current customers. Fourth, acquiring a new online customer requires a much higher cost than retaining an existing loyal customer (Hanson 1999; Laudon and Traver 2001).

The Model and Propositions

The seemingly hierarchical structure in Figure 1 illustrates how different types of information sources (ranging from DMO promotions and non-touristic information to 2D/text-based and 3D-based virtual information) lead to different levels of telepresence, which in turn influence the order and the strength of virtualized destination image. The integrated behavioral responses will vary accordingly. In reality, consumers can be exposed to any

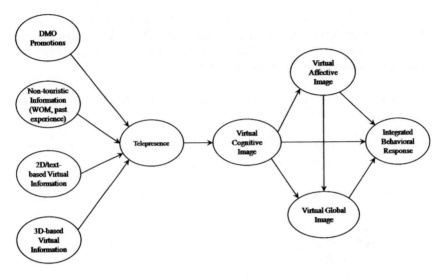

Figure 2 A Model of Virtual Destination Branding.

media before accessing DMO websites; and those online are known to be insatiable information seekers (Hyun, Wells and Huh 2003), as they attempt to obtain as much information as possible to reduce their perceived risk. Their telepresence is therefore a dynamic one and an aggregate result of being exposed to and seeking a multitude of information. The virtual branding model in Figure 2 reflects the dynamic nature of telepresence in relation to the four different types of information sources, the three virtualized image components, and the integrated behavioral responses. The remaining text of the chapter explores these relationships.

Extant literature is adequate to attest that information sources impact the formation of destination image (Fakeye and Crompton 1991; Gartner 1993a, 1993b; Gunn 1972; Jenkins 1999). However, few studies included virtual information sources, and the concept of telepresence is missing. Outside the research domain, telepresence is known as a mediating construct in the relationship between media channels and attitudes (Suh and Chang 2006). The impact of virtual information on telepresence was examined by Fiore et al (2005:39) who described the relation of interactivity technology to telepresence. They argued that interacting with a website determines the level of telepresence. Shih (1998) posited that telepresence relies on how closely computer-mediated experience simulates consumers' real-world interaction with a product. Choi, Miracle and Biocca's (2001) study showed that 3D-based nonverbal messages on a website have greater effect on the degree of telepresence than textual format cues. Cho (2002) proposed that TV-, Web-, and virtual reality-based (such as virtual tour) environments could produce different levels of virtual experience.

Proposition 1: *A causal relationship exists between DMO promotions and telepresence.*

Proposition 2: *A causal relationship exists between non-touristic information and telepresence.*

Proposition 3: *A causal relationship exists between 2D/text-based virtual information and telepresence.*

Proposition 4: *A causal relationship exists between 3D-based virtual information and telepresence.*

Computer-mediated environments induce a sense of telepresence (Klein 2003), which is enhanced by the use of 3D object visualizations. Virtual experience is much closer to direct experience than is indirect experience (Hoch and Deighton 1989). However, for telepresence to affect the order and strength of virtualized image, it should incorporate the advantages of direct, virtual, and indirect experience for consumer learning (Li et al 2001). When delineated as perceived information from indirect experience (Wright and Lynch 1995), close-up images enrich search attributes such as texture and color (Fiore et al 2005). Virtual model technology enables virtual tours to persuasively imitate experiential attributes (Li et al 2001), thus simulating direct experience during actual purchase (Wright and Lynch 1995). Virtual experience on the Web can have a greater impact than direct and indirect experience on the three states of consumers' decisionmaking: mental imagery or cognitive, emotional responses or affective, and derived intentions or conation (Li et al 2001). Yet, the influence will be even more profound with telepresence that incorporates direct, virtual, and indirect experience.

The interactive nature of a website enhances consumer attitudes toward the site and online purchasing (Fiore and Jin 2003). The interaction effect between vividness and interactivity can influence the level of telepresence that determines whether online consumers' attitudes form positively (Coyle and Thorson 2001; Eroglu, Machleit and Davis 2001). Furthermore, Fiore et al (2005) verified the mediating role of telepresence between virtual information, attitudes, intention to purchase, and willingness to patronize the online retailer. Choi et al (2001) argued that, stimulated by multi-modal presentations of messages, telepresence influences cognitive responses, Web visit intention, and brand purchase intention.

Proposition 5: *A causal relationship exists between telepresence and virtual cognitive image.*

Proposition 6: *A causal relationship exists between telepresence and virtual affective image.*

Proposition 7: *A causal relationship exists between telepresence and virtual global image.*

Proposition 8: *A causal relationship exists between telepresence and integrating behavioral responses.*

Destination image consists of cognitive, affective, and overall/global/ conative components (Baloglu and McCleary 1999a, 1999b; Castro, Armario and Ruiz 2007); and these components are hierarchical (Cai 2002; Gartner 1993a, 1993b). This understanding is in agreement with Fishbein and Ajzen's (1975) traditional attitude theory which hypothesizes sequentially causal relationships between cognition, affect, and conation. In extending the theory, Bagozzi (1982) adds one more proposition: the direct effect of cognition to conation. Hyun and Han's (2005) study supported the extended theory by empirically verifying the direct effect of cognitive image on overall image.

Furthermore, Baloglu (1997) and Lee, O'Leary and Hong (2002) indicated that the combination effect of cognitive and affective image results in overall image. Stern and Krakover's (1993) study concluded that appraisal perception (affect) played an intervening role between designative perception (cognition) and the composite image (global affect). Baloglu and McCleary (1999a, 1999b), Beerli and Martín (2004), Hyun, Han and Huh (2005), and Kim, Hyun and Han (2006) investigated image formation across different cultures. Their common finding is that cognitive image significantly influences affective and overall image, and that cognitive image indirectly affects overall image, which affective image mediates.

Proposition 9: *A causal relationship exists between virtual cognitive image and affective image.*

Proposition 10: *A causal relationship exists between virtual cognitive image and global image.*

Proposition 11: *A causal relationship exists between virtual affective image and global image.*

Stern et al (2002) argued that online behavioral responses should be measured by multi-attributes through adopting the concept of loyalty rather than one measure traditionally interpreted as intention to purchase. The more favorable the perception of a given destination, the more preferred it tends to be (Lee et al 2002). Current attitude and loyalty studies have investigated the association of destination image with behavioral responses such as intention to visit and loyalty across cultures (Dick and Basu 1994; Kim et al 2006). Web-based communication and retailing studies have limited observations of such a relationship by examining the causal effect of overall attitude or brand attitude to online buying intention (Fiore et al 2005; Li et al 2001, 2002; Suh and Chang 2006). Therefore, this discussion relies on the evidence provided by extant destination image studies to propose the relationship between image and integrated behavioral responses.

Cognition and affect can be influential factors for loyalty (Dick and Basu 1994; Lee et al 2002). In addition, Fishbein and Ajzen's attitude model and Bagozzi's extended attitude model indicate that cognition and affect directly and indirectly influence overt behavior. Empirical findings by Baloglu (1997), Hyun et al (2005), and Castro et al (2007) indicate that overall image directly influenced visit intention and loyalty. However, Kim et al (2006) revealed no impact of affect on loyalty. Since perceptions toward an object between unmediated and mediated environments are different, verification of whether or not traditionally proposed relationships between image components and behavioral responses can apply to the Web-mediated environment is necessary. As a result, the virtual destination branding model can have a theoretical formulation.

Proposition 12: *A causal relationship exists between virtual cognitive image and integrated behavioral responses.*

Proposition 13: *A causal relationship exists between virtual affective image and integrated behavioral responses.*

Proposition 14: *A causal relationship exists between virtual overall image and integrated behavioral responses.*

CONCLUSION

Consumers' experience is formed through their interaction with an environment (Gibson 1966). The degree of the interaction determines their position on the direct and indirect continuum of the experience. Direct experience solely derives from actual product contact, whereas the indirect type is generated from various sources such as word-of-mouth, brochures, and advertising (Li et al 2002). Several advantages exist for direct over indirect experience. First, the direct one is self-generated and the most trustworthy for consumers. Second, consumers may manage experience with product by controlling the focus and pace of inspection to maximize informational input. Third, such an interaction may result in more affective responses than from indirect experience (Millar and Millar 1996). This chapter posits that the Internet provides a mediated environment where the Web-based virtual experience takes place. Because of its many interactive capabilities, the virtual experience is closer to an unmediated environment— the direct polar of the experience continuum.

Defined as a feeling of direct experience in a virtual environment created through an array of media, telepresence is examined in this chapter as a mediating variable among four types of information sources and destination image. Virtual experience is represented by two types of information sources: 2D/text-based and 3D-based Web. The DMO promotion and non-touristic are the other two sources. Through literature review and synthesis, this chapter investigates the relationships among the four information sources, telepresence, the three-component virtualized destination image, and integrated behavioral responses. Fourteen propositions are developed as the result.

The construct of virtualized destination image in this chapter is conceptualized primarily by extending and modifying Gartner's theory of the image formation process (1993a, 1993b). A significant contribution to the theory is the specification of information sources as antecedents through the mediating variable of telepresence and the integrated behavioral responses as consequences. A critical departure from the theory is to treat the conation as a consequence instead of part of the image construct. These extension and modification, as well as the proposed relationships, should be empirically examined in future research to establish virtualized image as a viable construct in the virtual destination branding model. The empirical validity of the model will allow a DMO to take a more aggressive approach to branding by building a virtual or net community for tourists and residents alike. A net community is a fast-growing phenomenon in the online era. It provides a virtual space for tourists to dynamically exchange and share information. Consumers are increasingly becoming members of such communities to seek and offer opinions in selecting and evaluating products and services. Businesses of consumer goods and services are increasingly investing in and integrating net communities as part of their communication strategies to build or defend their brands.

A destination net community, however, calls for the active participation of residents and other stakeholders if a DMO employs it to virtually brand the destination. After all, it is the members of this community who will ultimately deliver the direct experience when tourists finally make it to the destination. As a limitation of this study, the proposed model does not explicitly consider this important aspect of branding. For tourism to be developed and practiced sustainably, branding depends on not only the support but more importantly the participation of residents in the host community. Factors that cultivate this support and motivate their participation include attachment to the community, level of knowledge about tourism and the local economy, level of contact with tourists, and perceived ability to influence the planning decisions. A destination net community affords a DMO the tools to positively influence these factors, for example, by initiating and facilitating a virtual dialogue between residents and tourists before they arrive in and after their departure from the destination. Such pre- and after-trip interactions in essence enrich tourists' virtual experience, enhance their destination image through strong telepresence, and cultivate their loyalty toward the destination. These issues warrant future conceptual inquiries and empirical investigations.

Chapter 4

DECONSTRUCTING BRAND EQUITY

William C. Gartner
University of Minnesota, USA

Abridgement: Destination brand equity is a recent line of enquiry within the academic community. The topic is still not well understood from a theoretical standpoint. This chapter attempts to frame the conceptual question of how to develop brand equity by providing some theoretical constructs for the nature of destination. Brand characteristics with respect to tangible and experiential products are examined, followed by the identification of its dimensions. Awareness, image, loyalty, quality, and value are identified as different dimensions existing within destination brands. Research that has dealt with these dimensions is discussed, with suggestions on how to build brand equity using market characteristics and their relationship to the different dimensions. Case studies are used to illustrate some of the main points from the theoretical discourse, including the issue of who controls brand identity under different development scenarios. **Keywords:** brand equity; destination brands; brand dimensions; image.

Tourism Branding: Communities in Action
Bridging Tourism Theory and Practice, Volume 1, 51–63
Copyright © 2009 by Emerald Group Publishing Limited
All rights of reproduction in any form reserved
ISSN: 2042-1443/doi:10.1108/S2042-1443(2009)0000001006

INTRODUCTION

Brand equity is an elusive concept when it comes to destinations. Its literature deals with a single product or a collection of like products marketed under the same name. What is clear is that branding is all about ownership. For example, marking livestock was a way to designate assets for producers. In its current marketing form, it is about creating a sense of ownership for customers, and it is through this process that brand equity is created.

According to Room (1992), the modern form of branding appeared in the 19th century and now includes legal instruments, logos, companies, identity systems, image, personality, and relationships. Using brands for marketing is probably one of the earliest forms of product differentiation. Under the Coliseum in Pula, Croatia, a structure dating back to the 1st century, a display of ancient amphora brands can be found. Amphorae, the vessels used to transport wine, were made of clay and were not meant to be returned to the producer. Yet, many amphorae are imprinted with the name of the producer. These names appear in a variety of script. One can assume the producer names, personally attributed, on non-returnable containers for an important beverage that could vastly differ in taste and quality must be some form of marketing to create brand equity. Adding value is the basis for all branding strategies (de Chernatony and McDonald 2001) and that is what these early wine producers were apparently attempting to do. Brands can add value, which gives equity. But can branding, as a part of a marketing strategy, be used to create brand equity for a destination is not yet known. The more inclusive definition of brands (Room 1992) suggests it can. The work in this area is still in its infancy (Cai 2002).

DESTINATION BRAND EQUITY

Brand equity is the process of not only creating ownership for a particular brand but the value of that ownership. It emerged originally from the literature on financial valuation in the 1990s (Barwise 1993). Yet, actually being able to measure it remains elusive (Yoo and Donthu 2001). For a consumer, product brand equity measurement should be pretty straightforward. It is simply the additional monetary return associated with the name of the brand. The difference between a generic equivalent and its branded counterpart is the additional amount of money that can be acquired in the marketplace from selling the brand name. However, if a generic equivalent does not exist, then its equity measurement becomes problematic. This is especially true for destinations as there is no generic equivalent to a geographic place. The valuation of a product brand therefore cannot be the same as occurs for destinations, which are not branded commodities, freely bought and sold, in an open marketplace. They are instead set places with a collection of assets both natural and sociocultural, making up unique properties of destinations and giving rise to its touristic value. In this sense, destination brand equity is related more to the number of tourists who choose the destination and their expenditure levels and length of stay. Poorly performing places, as will be discussed later in this chapter, would expect to receive fewer tourists, with shorter lengths of stay and lower levels of spending.

Brand Characteristics

Understanding the nature of destination brand equity requires an examination of the differences and similarities between product and destination brands. One of the major differences is brand stability. The former is enhanced when the customers know what they are buying. Its predictability arrives through product stability, meaning that it will deliver the expected performance no matter where it is purchased. Fast food companies have historically used product predictability to grow their market through franchise operations. However, many such brands slightly modify their products for different consumer tastes in international markets. For the most part, what makes them work is that customers, with a high degree of assurance, know what they are getting when they purchase the product. This is not the case for destination brands. They are dynamic places and change depending on the season and over time as the resident population fluctuates due to in- and out-migration. Destination known for winter skiing cannot sell the same experience during the summer. They also change in terms of development, service quality, and markets, as they move through the lifecycle (Butler 1980).

One major difference between destination and product brands is the experiential factor. The former are functional goods. They have substance that can be seen and felt. They have tangible features that can be identified and quantitatively measured, with relatively low risk associated with a purchase. Even products with a high price tag, and therefore higher risk associated with making the wrong purchase decision, generally have test periods where they can be returned for a full refund. Some purchases, such as over-the-counter medicine, fast food, and household cleaning products, may not always be returned if they do not perform as advertised, but consumers bear little financial risk from these inexpensive items. However, the cost of travel is not low, and tourists assume risk when they decide to take a trip. Since the tourism product is experiential and essentially different for each consumer, there is little predictability, stability, or recourse if expectations are not met. Delivering what is promised becomes a major concern for those trying to develop and support destination brands.

Novelty is an area of agreement between product and destination brands. Novelty, as it is used here, means providing a product or experience different from competitors. If a particular one is seen as providing a higher level of benefit than its competitor, its brand equity will be higher. Destinations also thrive on novelty. Since travel is a relatively expensive undertaking, those which can set themselves apart from their competitors on an experiential level are better able to enhance their brand equity. Travel is about difference both between home and destination and among different choices of locations. Without novelty they cannot be differentiated. The focus on novelty has led many to use their slogan or tagline to declare difference (Pride 2007). The slogan does not usually result in increased brand equity. One reason for this is that a destination must be seen as different, on a number of levels, to be considered as a worthy (time and money) place to visit. Difference is given when a potential tourist is in a destination selection mode. Its attributes cannot simply be declared as different but must be functionally so. Consumers must be aware of the difference vs. other destinations and what currently exists in the home environment. Novelty cannot simply be declared, it must be earned.

Brands have both internal and external perspectives. The first one relates to those providing the good or service. de Chernatony and McDonald (2001) argue that this occurs when managers emphasize the use of resources to achieve a customer response. Alternatively, an external perspective occurs in the way customers interpret brand meaning and use it to enhance their personal purchase decision. An example of internal branding occurs when new employees are assigned to training courses that serve to instill the corporate culture. In the process, the meaning and the benefits of a company brand are emphasized, and all employees should be able to communicate them to distributors and consumers. Destinations, on the contrary, are an agglomeration of businesses often competing for the same customers. They may be very effective at selling the benefits of their own brand but not as good at promoting a destination brand, especially if the destination marketing organization has not been active in developing a community-wide internal perspective. The external perspective, how the customer views the brand, may also be problematic. For example, destinations that rely on tour operators for tourists may not even be in control of their own brand building. A number of external perspectives may be working against each other leaving potential tourists with unclear expectations of the destination brand, a situation that will become more apparent later when discussing specific places.

Brands have dimensions (Aaker 1991; Yoo and Donthu 2001), for both product and destination brands. What these dimensions are has led to a relatively new set of research studies to uncover how they affect destination brand equity. Konecnik and Gartner (2007) uncovered four brand equity dimensions that apply to destinations. They are awareness, loyalty, image, and quality. These are the same dimensions identified by Aaker (1991) and Yoo and Donthu (2001). Tasci, Gartner and So (2007b) used these dimensions and added another: value. They found that different tourist segments evaluated each of these dimensions in different and significant ways.

Brand Equity Dimensions

Awareness is an essential dimension. It is the first step in building equity. A place must be known, in some context, before it can even be considered as a potential destination. Goodall (1993), Woodside and Lysonski (1989), and Howard and Sheth (1969) have uncovered four levels of awareness. From high to low, they are dominant, top of mind, familiarity, and knowledge. Dominant awareness does not always translate into enhanced brand equity. A case in point is the world's "hot spots" such as Iraq, Darfur, and Chad. These places have received extensive media coverage, but the human conflict that is portrayed does not translate into increased travel flow. The dominant or top of mind awareness is of negative value, in these cases, to building brand equity. That may not always be the case as awareness can lead to higher levels of future travel, such as for Vietnam, when the conflicts that created the awareness have receded into history. Awareness is the first step in creating brand equity, but it must be of a positive nature.

Image is a dimension that has received the most attention in the academic literature. Pike (2002, 2007) and Gallarza, Saura and García (2002) have reviewed the extensive literature on tourism image. By their count, over 140 papers have been published on the subject. Image was initially viewed as encompassing all the other brand dimensions (Ritchie and Ritchie 1998), but this view is changing. "Image formation is not branding, albeit the former constitutes the core of the latter. Image building is one step closer, but there still remains a critical missing link: the brand identity" (Cai 2002:722). Images refer to the attributes or benefits one expects a destination to possess. They are formed on many different levels and throughout one's lifetime

(Gartner 1993a, 1993b). Because of the high risk factor when choosing a destination one knows very little about, images are used to create awareness. There is no money back guarantee for tourists, and therefore, destinations use images extensively in their promotional literature to gain awareness for the attributes and benefits that set them apart from competitors. The same are also used to counteract negative attributes that may have been acquired through media awareness. Creating and projecting images is a staple of destination promotion.

Loyalty refers to repeat visitation or in the case of singular products repeat purchase. It can be of either the behavioral or attitudinal variety. Behavioral loyalty may be due to a number of reasons. Business travel to a particular destination does not involve free choice. Such tourists go to where their business or customers are located, but this does not necessarily mean they would return given a choice. Awareness of the destination is a given, but the image dimension may be weak as its attributes may not be important in the decision process for these tourists. Behavioral loyalty in this case affects brand equity only to the extent that the destination can maintain a healthy business community. Behavioral loyalty may also arise from past travel and be tied to tradition. For example, the lake-based resorts in the United States thrived for years on selling week long holidays. There were few if any opportunities for stays less than a week. The reason for this business model was based on traditional vacation patterns that were continued by succeeding generations. If parents took their children to the same resort each year, this tradition was often passed down to the next generation. However, the pattern appears to be fading as smaller lake-based resorts have declined in number with most now offering flexible stay options.

Nonetheless, this type of behavioral loyalty should not be discounted as an emotional attachment to a particular resort. In this case, it is an essential ingredient in brand development and enhancement of its equity. Other forms of behavioral loyalty are tied to financial investments in a particular place. Second home or property ownership (such as time share) is a good example of this type of behavioral loyalty. Due to the financial commitment made in a particular place, loyalty will result. Attitudinal loyalty, on the contrary, is making a choice based on attributes and benefits to be obtained from travel to a particular place modified with ones attitudes toward those benefits. For example, if a destination is of the sun, sand, and sea variety, those not wishing to spend time in the sun or on a beach would possess negative attitudes toward these particular attributes. Destinations that possess attributes and benefits that match tourists' expectations have the potential to score high on the attitudinal loyalty dimension. The loyalty concept has been extensively investigated within the marketing literature. By contrast, destination loyalty has rarely been studied. Oppermann (2000) argued that loyalty should not be neglected when examining destination brands.

Quality is a very subjective term, but it can be operationalized through a variety of scale measures, as can all the other brand equity dimensions (Konecnik and Gartner 2007). Since quality is so subjective, it was often subsumed in the image dimension (Pike 2002). As a distinct variable, it has been investigated by Fick and Ritchie (1991), Keane (1997), Murphy, Pritchard and Smith (2000), and Weiermair and Fuchs (1999). It can be viewed as simply meeting or exceeding expectations. Destinations that are comprised of different stakeholders and businesses have a much more difficult time delivering consistent quality over time. Maintaining quality levels is a prerequisite for enhancing product brand equity and it should be for destinations. However, since they do not control service quality for individual businesses, it makes the task more difficult. Destinations that have quality resources, such as a National Park or some other unique natural feature, have a much easier time building brand equity through the quality dimension than those that must differentiate based on service quality alone.

Best defined as return on expenditure, value is the brand equity dimension most recently uncovered (Tasci et al 2007b). It has often been viewed as a component of quality reflected through the price one pays for a product. The importance of price has been recognized by other authors investigating the destination development phenomenon (Baloglu and Mangaloglu 2001; Crompton 1979; Echtner and Ritchie 1993). Hence, price is seen as one of the important extrinsic quality cues, but it is not always synonymous with quality. Value is a subjective measure; this differs from quality in the sense that value can be tied to the cost of accessing some desired attributes (such as sun) rather than the quality of the services. For example, lodging quality and customer service may be poor, but value is still obtained by the low cost required to reach and stay at the destination. Packaged tours are often driven by value rather than quality service. Extant literature is sparse on destination brand equity dimensions. It is entirely possible that others can be identified, isolated, and tested. The criteria for establishing brand dimensions used by Konecnik and Gartner (2007) and Tasci et al (2007b) were that scales used to isolate dimensions must show independence from each other. Operationalizing dimensions through scale measurements is a necessary precondition to isolating additional dimensions.

Building Brand Equity

Destination brand equity is not a direct monetary value as for branded commodity products, but rather the valuation of the overall effect of tourist behavior including length of stay, expenditure level, and tourist arrivals. Destinations are branded by name that gives the potential tourists an indication of its meaning and value. This information is used in the travel decision process. If, as has been hypothesized, brand equity has a number of dimensions, they should be able to be recognized and evaluated by both potential and current tourists. There should also be separation between the dimensions. In other words, when operationalized, they should have little correlation among themselves. This is the situation found in the studies conducted by Konecnik and Gartner (2007) and Tasci et al (2007b). Therefore, building brand equity starts with understanding the importance and influence of each dimension to a particular market. Here is where the evidence is still being assembled. Apart from the two studies mentioned above, there is very little in the literature to support this claim but even less to refute it.

Accepting that different dimensions may be affecting destination brand equity allows for a testable model to be developed. First, the concepts of repeat and renewal visitation must be addressed. Repeat visitation is defined as traveling to a particular destination more than once. Renewal is the recruitment of new tourists, as previous ones, either repeat or first time, decide to frequent other destinations. Recognizing that both of these concepts are fluid and may change from one reporting period to the next, there should be a long-term average that clearly shows repeat and renewal trends. To maintain stable or increasing growth, the renewal market must equal or exceed the loss from the repeat market. When both show increases, a destination may be in a long-term growth cycle.

Brand equity dimensions should affect the renewal and repeat markets in different ways. For first-time tourists (members of the renewal market), the dimensions of awareness and image would seem to be the most important. Obviously, without awareness, a destination is very unlikely to be chosen. Due to the inability to "pre-test" the destination, image would be used to inform. For the repeat market, awareness should become less important. The dimensions of image to reinforce destination attributes, loyalty, quality, and value should be more important. Value and quality may also be very vital, and even more so than image for the renewal market, as Konecnik and Gartner (2007) found that one market in particular scored higher on quality than image. Therefore, the effect of each dimension on different markets should be understood. It is only through this insight that destinations can be effectively branded for each market through its image dimension, which remains as the central core of brand equity. Building brand equity cannot be done without a thorough understanding of how markets, which may be geographically identified, relate to the different dimensions of brand equity. It should also be noted that same geographic markets may not be homogenous when it comes to each dimension. There are segments within markets that may see the importance of brand equity dimensions differently. This has been borne out by the numerous studies that have dissected markets based on geography, demographics, and psychographics.

Brand Equity Examples

Turkey provides an excellent example of how brand equity dimensions are influenced by destination brand (its name). A recent study by Tasci, Gartner and Cavusgil (2007a) examined the effect of its name on the image dimension. The study was operationalized by splitting a sample into three groups. The first group was shown a series of pictures that were from locations in Turkey, but its name was not disclosed. They were asked to rate these images on a scale. A second group was provided the same pictures plus some music that once again highlighted Turkey without the respondents knowing the images were from Turkey. The third group was shown the exact same pictures as the first group but this time the brand "Turkey" was identified throughout. On almost every attribute, those who knew it was Turkey gave significantly lower favorable scores than the groups that did not know their country identity. Although many reasons could be provided for this finding, the fact remains that Turkeys' brand was valued lower than a generic brand.

Turkey entered in a major phase of tourism developments in the early 1990s with assistance from the World Bank and foreign direct investment. Resorts are found throughout the western and southwestern Aegean and Mediterranean coastlines. Many can be accessed through regional airports with tourists being picked up and taken to the western style destinations. The language of tourists is spoken, and foreign currency such as dollars and euros are freely taken and exchanged. One strategy employed, consciously, is to remove the foreign feel of the place and the potential negative influence of the brand as much as possible from tourists' space. Another resort area that has successfully used this strategy is Eilat, Israel, located on the Red Sea. Its promotional images are branded with the name Eilat but not Israel. A regional airport connects Eilat to many European cities, and charter airlines operate between Europe and the resort. There is no information available regarding how many tourists do not know they are in Israel when they enter

Eilat, but the number is very likely low. The value then of promoting Eilat and not Israel is in the awareness dimension. Thinking about a trip to this destination removes to some extent any potential negative bias that comes with the brand Israel.

Tourist arrivals in Turkey were on an upward trajectory from 1998 until 2005, moving it into the top 10 in the world with respect to arrivals and receipts. One could argue that almost all the news coming from that part of the world since 2005 has been negative, thus depressing the value of the brand name. Tourist arrivals and receipts have shown declines in recent years, all indications of brand effect on the equity. In addition to those that come with enclave development (environmental bubble), coping strategies have included second-home development and the offer of incredibly low hotel packages, especially when compared to some other Mediterranean basin destinations. Turkish resorts focus on the value dimension, as evidenced by increasingly reliance on tour operators for mass tourism at beach resort destinations. The strategy of second home development leads to increasing the loyalty dimension.

The second example is Mallorca, which is part of the Balearic island chain of Spain. A number of years ago, it was decided to embrace the mass tourism model for the island. An international airport was built with an annual capacity of over 20 million passengers. Tourism has always been a part of the island. Its beautiful landscape and seashore attracts wealthy tourists seeking second homes. These homes on the island differ from those found in other destinations in that they are not mass-produced subdivisions but rather single houses scattered across the island. But for the majority of tourists, a stay in one of the all-inclusive hotels is usually a staple. During the height of the tourism season, narrow mountain roads are often crowded with tour busses.

It appears that the brand dimensions most important to Mallorca are different for their various markets. Awareness for the renewal market is through images developed and distributed by official government tourism office. However, it is also done, most effectively, by tour operators who sell the island. The awareness, image, and value dimensions appear to be operational for this market. The more upscale market is most likely to be affected by the quality and loyalty dimensions. This brings up an interesting question that deserves investigation: do the different markets complement or compete with each other? If the public resources are in limited supply and the number of tourists using these sites is high, does this serve to lower the quality of the destination. If so then, those markets most inclined to see the quality dimension as critical to their destination choice may opt to relocate. The majority of tourists to the island today are buying packages from tour operators, which is a fairly strong indication of the value dimension's importance. This also allows for a comparison with Turkish seaside destinations. On almost every value and quality dimension, its resorts would be viewed as equal as or better than the resorts on Mallorca. Climatic characteristics are similar and service quality better, at each price level, for the resorts in Turkey vs. those found on Mallorca. Yet, Mallorca receives more tourists and a much larger tourism expenditure than Turkey does from tourism at its beach resorts. One could surmise from this that Mallorca of Spain has a better brand than Turkey.

When mass market development is the staple of a destination, another issue is the long-term control over brand identity. Mallorca tourism office engages in image promotion, which is often used by tour operators for selling their packages. However, tour operators who have a vested interest in a destination, such as occurs through block bookings, will also spend a substantial amount of money to develop brand dimensions of places that support their business. This often means a reliance on the image and value dimensions once awareness is established. The form of development that occurs when tour operators control tourist flows to a destination is uni-directional—once this becomes the model, it is often impossible for a destination, even if it wants to, to back away from mass tourism development. Too many economic linkages would be severed if this were the case. Mass tourism focuses on the value dimension of brand equity, thereby reducing the importance of other dimensions such as image and quality. Does this then mean that more tourists are needed to equal the expenditure that would come from fewer tourists who place higher importance on quality and loyalty? None of this is known as the research is silent on many of the issues raised in the chapter. However, it is worth noting the relationships that may result as more destinations continually develop for tourism.

CONCLUSION

Destination branding is a rather new but fertile area of research. Although the marketing literature is ripe with branding studies, most of them relate to consumer products. Since consumer products and tourism products differ on many levels, it is not possible to easily transfer knowledge from consumer product literature into the understanding of destination branding. Foremost among them is the concept of brand equity.

This chapter attempted to explore the dimensions that make up destination brand equity. It differs from its consumer product variety in that there is no way to sell a destination to capture the monetary value of the brand. This is frequently done with consumer products as companies buy brands because of the equity inherent in the name. However, even though destination brand equity cannot be captured directly in the marketplace, it can be captured indirectly. It manifests itself by affecting the number of tourists that choose to visit a destination, their length of stay, and the amount they have to or are willing to spend upon arrival.

Understanding brand equity requires that brand dimensions be isolated and assessed. These dimensions may be the same ones operational for consumer product brands. As the complexity increases, it is more likely different dimensions will be associated with different markets. Destination brands may be the most complex of all, as they consist of services provided by different and often competing stakeholders, local climatic conditions, access costs and convenience, host culture receptiveness including laws and customs, and a variety of other factors that are difficult to isolate and identify.

This chapter presents a discussion of destination brand equity and its dimensions. Due to the dearth of literature on the subject, it is only a starting point, but it provides a theoretical base from which to assess the importance of each brand equity dimension. Awareness is a critical dimension for the renewal market. Awareness is often enhanced through the use of destination images. These two dimensions are important to any destination that wants to expand its customer base or replace those tourists who will not return. For the repeat market, awareness is a given, but images are still strong reminders used to either elevate the level of awareness or keep destinations in the minds of past tourists. The repeat market should also be affected by the quality and loyalty dimensions. The latter is enhanced by the development of second home markets and, to a lesser extent, by time share development. Quality may be a perceptual concept for the renewal market, but it is more of an assessed concept for repeaters. If quality is a brand equity dimension important to a particular market, then both the destination's natural attributes and the service quality performance should be examined. Value most likely affects both renewal and repeat markets. Expressed by destination access price, it may be an important consideration for first-timers just as it is for repeaters who have experienced the "value" of a destination. It is also a brand equity dimension that many mass destinations rely on for maintaining or increasing its number of tourists. However, there could be a problem with over-reliance on the value dimension, especially if tour operators are the controlling force in the distribution channel. Mass market tour operators often rely on the value dimension to increase their customer base. This seems to have served a number of destination well, but there has been no research undertaken that can be used to determine if destinations possessing markets that focus on different dimensions compete or complement each other. What does appear clear is that the reliance on a mass tourism tour operator model does reduce the ability for a destination to manage the dimensions of its brand.

Turkey and Mallorca of Spain were used as examples in this chapter. The Turkey example indicates that a negative brand image may result in decreased brand equity over a "generic" destination. Some of the consequences of a negative brand image (i.e., decreased tourist arrivals, reduced revenue) seem to be affecting Turkey. This becomes especially clear when compared to a competitor, Mallorca. By almost every measure, a holiday in Mallorca is much more expensive than a holiday at one of the Turkish beach resorts. Yet, Mallorca continues to attract more tourists indicating that the value dimension is being overcome, for Turkey, by other dimensions (e.g., image, quality). Unfortunately, there is no study that examines the brand Mallorca in terms of market acceptance and perception; therefore, much of the discussion for this destination remains theoretical.

The lack of research on branding has not stopped destinations from attempting to brand themselves. As Pride (2007) pointed out, their attempt usually means a tagline be adopted to distance one destination from another without really identifying what the destination stands for except a claim of difference. What is known from the previous research is that destination brands have different dimensions that together determine brand equity. There is enough evidence to suggest that understanding how different dimensions relate to different markets and segments within markets is the right way to begin a destination branding strategy.

Chapter 5

A TWO-DIMENSIONAL APPROACH TO BRANDING
Integrating Identity and Equity

Maja Konecnik Ruzzier
University of Ljubljana, Slovenia

Mitja Ruzzier
University of Primorska, Slovenia

Abridgement: This chapter integrates brand identity and equity as a two-dimensional approach to destination branding. By incorporating the supply- and demand-side perspectives, the approach enables different destination stakeholders to be included in this process. Drawing on general branding and marketing literature, the study presents a three-part framework for building and implementing a destination brand. It illustrates consumer-based equity as consisting of the four dimensions: awareness, image, perceived quality, and loyalty. The chapter also offers a critical synthesis of destination image studies and recognizes the important research advancement from image to branding. **Keywords:** identity; equity; image; branding.

Tourism Branding: Communities in Action
Bridging Tourism Theory and Practice, Volume 1, 65–73
Copyright © 2009 by Emerald Group Publishing Limited
All rights of reproduction in any form reserved
ISSN: 2042-1443/doi:10.1108/S2042-1443(2009)0000001007

INTRODUCTION

Branding has been around for many decades, but its importance is growing rapidly in the 21st century. The concept was originally developed for products, and its principles primarily apply to products. More recently, they are also being transferred and applied to services and organizations (de Chernatony 1999). New findings have shown that a destination can be branded and that its main principles can be used at this level. This chapter follows ideas discussed in studies by Cai (2002) and Morgan and Pritchard (2002). At the same time, it also illustrates that considerable care should be taken in transferring general branding principles to a destination context. The premise is that an approach that is too commercial and not adapted to the needs of destinations might spoil place characteristics such as social relationships, its history, and geography. These characteristics are essential and can be used to construct identity and, in turn, contribute to distinguishing a place from its competitors (Konecnik and Go 2008). The purpose of this chapter is to synthesize and critically review previous findings on tourism destination branding. These findings are also compared with those from general marketing and management literature. Drawing on the review and comparison, the chapter undertakes an integration of identity and equity concepts and introduces a two-dimensional approach to destination branding. The two dimensions represent the supply and demand perspectives, respectively.

SUPPLY AND DEMAND DIMENSIONS

The phenomenon of destination branding was only introduced to tourism literature a few years ago (Gnoth 1998). However, in a relatively short period, the topic has attracted the attention of many researchers and practitioners (Anholt 2003; Cai 2002; Morgan and Pritchard 2002). One reason for this may lie in the fact that destination branding has been partly covered under the alternative label of destination image (Ritchie and Ritchie 1998). Studies of image are abundant and can be traced back to the early 1970s when Hunt (1975) examined it as a development factor (Cai 2002).

Advances in Destination Branding Research

Destination image has become one of the prevalent topics in the tourism literature (Gallarza, Saura and García 2002; Pike 2002). The study of it has its roots in the 1970s when the first papers on the topic stressed its importance in tourists' behavioral process of selecting and evaluating a destination (Gunn 1972; Hunt 1975). Since then, the topic has attracted enormous interest. Pike (2002) identified 142 papers that directly or indirectly investigated destination image topics. There is a diversity of opinions on destination image. However, authors agree that it may be analyzed from different perspectives and composed of a variety of individual perceptions relating to various product attributes. Gunn (1972) referred to two levels of image as being organic and induced. Fakeye and Crompton (1991) developed a model to describe the relationships between organic, induced, and complex images that incorporated experiences at destinations. Goodrich (1978) pointed out that primary image was formed by a visit, and the secondary one was formed by information received from external sources. Phelps' (1986) study also referred to the same two levels of being primary and secondary. Milman and Pizam (1995) suggested that a destination's image has three components: the product (quality and variety of attractions, price, uniqueness); the behavior and attitude of employees who come in direct contact with tourists; and the environment such as the weather, the quality and type of accommodation, or physical safety. Finally, in investigating measurement techniques, Echtner and Ritchie (1993) suggested an image framework consisting of three continuums: attribute to holistic, functional to psychological, and common to unique.

Empirical studies have employed different approaches and measures in conceptualization. Image has largely been operationalized as comprising of the cognitive, affective, and conative components (Gartner 1993a). Analyses have involved multiple attribute-based variables to capture the cognitive component of image that refers to beliefs and knowledge about the entity (Boulding 1956; Gartner 1989, 1993a). Echtner and Ritchie (1993) classified all attribute-based variables within functional (or more tangible) and psychological (or more abstract) characteristics. Empirical studies have also investigated the affective component of image, which refers to feelings about destinations (Baloglu and Brinberg 1997; Ward and Russell 1981) and mirrors the benefit category of brand associations (Cai 2002). The conative image component has been considered a combination of images developed during the cognitive stage and evaluated during the affective stage (Gartner 1993a). This component mirrors the attitude type of associations (Keller 1993) and represents the overall evaluation of a brand and the basis for actions and behavior. Cai (2002) undertook a comparison of both theoretical typologies: Gartner's (1993a) image components and Keller's (1993) types of brand associations. The many different types of analyses indicate that the concept is a complex and multidimensional construct. In the comprehensive overview of previous work on the topic by Gallarza et al (2002), image is considered to have complex, multiple, relativistic, and dynamic features.

Abundant work has been done insofar as image is treated as solely as a concept in the destination selection process. Previous work does not give a clear idea about its role and importance in branding. There has been no significant effort to distinguish between the image and the branding functions. Consequently, words such as "brand" and "branding" appear in many image studies. In several cases, they are used inconsistently as a synonym for image. Cai (2002) points out that inaccurate wording is also evident in the special issue of the *Journal of Vacation Marketing* (1999) dedicated to "destination branding," where the authors of its leading paper (Nickerson and Moisey 1999) define branding more or less in terms of image. For the first time in the tourism literature, Cai's (2002:722) work clearly highlights the difference between image formation process and its branding in that "image formation is not branding, albeit the former constitutes the core of the latter. Image-building is one step closer, but there still remains a critical missing link: the brand identity." The importance of it is also evident in Cai's definition whereby the aim of destination branding is, when selecting a consistent mix of elements, in the first place to identify and then distinguish a destination through positive image building. By introducing identity concept at the destination level, Cai's work overcomes the shortfalls of previous image studies and is therefore the most comprehensive to date in the literature, which marks the beginning of academic inquiry into the realm of destination branding.

In this pioneering work, Cai (2002) also proposes a conceptual branding model that centers on building an identity through spreading activation, which results from dynamic linkages among the brand element mix, image building, brand associations, and marketing activities. The process starts by choosing one or more elements to serve as trademarkable devices that distinctly identify the destination and begin the formation of strong and consistent associations that reflect the attribute, affective, and attitude components of an image. Probably, the biggest advantage of the model is that image formation goes beyond the tourist-oriented approach to encompass what image a destination management organization wants to project through each of the associations. In this way, the model stresses the importance of other stakeholders or interest groups of a destination, not just tourists. This treatment is a big step forward for brand development because previous marketing strategies mostly emphasize those characteristics that have been recognized by tourists. This could be a serious problem, especially in situations where image is not representative of what a destination has to offer. Given that destination management organizations send those signals to their target markets, which in their opinion are the most unique for the destination, it is possible to assess the gap between the perceived and the projected. The assessment then provides an input for building the desired image that is consistent with the brand identity and through marketing programs, marketing communications, and marketing secondary associations. At the same time, Cai's model specifies that spreading activation takes place in the four conditions of an existing organic image, existing induced image, destination size and composition, and positioning and the target market.

Cai's model considers the role of the marketing function but does not go into detail on how to build and develop a brand identity for a specific destination on one hand and how to measure its equity on the other. So that a destination can be treated as a brand, its identity should encompass all vital functions of competitive and sustainable development underpinned by different stakeholders. After that, marketing function should project a desirable image to potential tourists and evaluate how it is perceived. Where a gap between the perceived and projected image exists, proper marketing strategies should be used to close that gap. The two-dimensional approach to destination branding is presented in this chapter as a combination of developing and building brand identity, spreading it to target markets, and evaluating the perceived image in target markets. Accordingly, image is expanded to brand equity. This approach is illustrated in Figure 1. Brand identity is a necessary condition for evaluating destinations from customers' perspective. In addition, in light of de Chernatony's (1999) reminder that modern brand analysis should treat both the identity and the equity as interrelated, they are examined and presented as such in this chapter.

Figure 1 A Two-Dimensional Approach to Destination Branding.

Brand Identity: Supply Dimension

The literature has introduced brand identity as an important conceptualization (Aaker and Joachimsthaler 2000; de Chernatony 1999; Ind 1997;
Kapferer 1997). There is a diversity of opinions in this regard. However, these
authors agree that brand identity development is a theoretical concept that is
best understood from the supply-side perspective. This means that the identity
concept incorporates the perspectives of internal interest groups on a brand,
such as managers, employees, and other internal stakeholders. On the
contrary, the research stream more or less ignores the identity concept, which,
according to Cai (2002), Pride (2002), and Konecnik and Go (2008), is a vital
element that must also be investigated within the destination branding
content. The identity in Figure 1 has its roots in the theoretical representation
and interpretation of the identity concept in the brand leadership model by
Aaker and Joachimsthaler (2000). This model is by far the most
comprehensive to date in the general branding literature. Not only is the
nature of identity development given but their systematic and strategic
analyses as well as the post-brand implementation processes are also included.

Aaker and Joachimsthaler's model is informative for conducting a
strategic analysis for destination brand identity. The analysis comprises
three main steps: tourist analysis, competitor analysis, and self-analysis. First,
a destination must conduct a systematic tourist analysis. It should focus on
identifying relevant new trends and developing a thorough understanding of
tourists' motivation for travel (Fodness 1994; Middleton and Clarke 2001).
This step should involve marketing research, in particular an evaluation of
appropriate destination target markets and target groups. Second, a
destination should carry out a competitor analysis. It needs insights into its
competitors' advantages and disadvantages to improve its own competitiveness, for example, by capitalizing on what is simultaneously an opportunity
to respond to existing tourist niche markets that the rival destinations have so
far not observed. Third, a destination should also systematically prepare a
self-analysis with the aim to recognize its true position in the market.
Destination managers should respect the interests and wishes of different
stakeholders and manage them through a cooperative approach rather than a
competitive one (Buhalis 2000).

A destination identity should clearly incorporate its unique characteristics.
As Aaker and Joachimsthaler (2000) suggest, 6–12 dimensions should be
considered to adequately describe the aspirations of a particular brand. At
least one of these dimensions must differentiate the destination from
competing ones. Although they can vary from one destination to another,

they can mostly be presented through four brand characteristics: as a product, a symbol, an organization, and as a person. A destination brand should incorporate not only product and symbol characteristics but also represent it as both an organization and a personality. Modern tourists want to experience "a sense of place" when visiting a destination. Experiential and symbolic benefits therefore play just as important a role as functional benefits (Keller 1993) in developing a brand identity. Investigating the specific characteristics of the brand as an organization should address the destination's culture, its local people, and their relationship with each other and with tourists. The main feature of brand identity arises from the fact that different stakeholder groups are a vital part of forming a brand, and different social, historical, cultural, and political relationships exist among them.

The concept of destination brand identity as described above was applied in a study for Slovenia. Although Slovenia became an independent country only in 1991, its history and culture date back many centuries. Up until 2003, no consensus had been reached on what constitutes Slovenia's identity despite considerable interest in brand development, especially on the part of the Slovenian Tourist Board. The study, conducted in 2003, represented the first significant effort toward developing an identity of Slovenia as a destination. Besides documentation and archival records, the most important data came from interviews with leading Slovenian opinion makers. A systematic approach to Slovenia's brand identity development was ensured. The findings of the study were reported in Konecnik (2005) and Konecnik and Go (2008).

Brand Equity: Demand Dimension

General marketing literature has investigated the demand-side perspective on the branding phenomenon through customers' evaluation of brand equity (Aaker 1991; Keller 1993; Yoo and Donthu 2001). Although tourists' perspective on brand has been operationalized with a variety of different measures, the concept of customer-based brand equity has attracted the most interest during the past few years (Barwise 1993; Vazquez, Del Rio and Iglesias 2002). Within this concept, several different dimensions have been explored. Most notably are those from Aaker (1991) and Keller's (1993), which include awareness, image, quality, and loyalty.

Previous research on destination branding from tourists' perspective is mostly grounded on image, which is largely presented as a combination of many attribute-based variables. None of the recent image literature explicitly mentions the existence of a quality dimension, although previous analyses of destination image (Baker and Crompton 2000; Baloglu and McCleary

1999a) employed some variables (price) that in general brand studies have been recognized as quality measures. In tourism development literature, a few articles covered the topic of perceived quality (Fick and Ritchie 1991; Murphy, Prichard and Smith 2000; Weiermair and Fuchs 1999). Little research has focused on the investigation of the dimensions of destination awareness and loyalty. This has mostly been examined within the process of destination selection (Goodall 1993; Woodside and Lysonski 1989). Awareness is treated as a first and necessary step leading to visiting a destination, but not as a sufficient one (Milman and Pizam 1995). Oppermann (2000) in his seminal work on loyalty argues that its dimension should not be neglected when examining a destination's selection and performance. Some previous studies on repeat visitation have partially incorporated the loyalty dimension (Bigné, Sánchez and Sánchez 2001; Gitelson and Crompton 1984; Kozak 2001).

Following Aaker (1991) and Keller (1993), tourists' evaluation of a destination can be understood as customer-based brand equity that consists of awareness, image, perceived quality, and loyalty dimensions (Figure 2). However, originally developed for products, the application of customer-based equity in destination context must take into special consideration its unique characteristics when image and perceived quality dimensions are conceptualized and operationalized. The customer-based brand equity of destinations was empirically examined in a study on Slovenia and Austria brands. The study investigated the perspective of two groups of tourists from Germany and Croatia. The results show that there is a relationship between image, awareness, quality, and loyalty and that they are important in a destination evaluation and can be expressed as composing the customer-based brand equity of destinations. The study's findings were also consistent with numerous previous findings that image dimension was the most important in the evaluation process. The full results of these investigations were reported in the works by Konecnik (2005) and Konecnik and Gartner (2007).

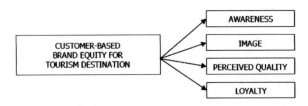

Figure 2 Customer-Based Brand Equity of Tourism Destination.

CONCLUSION

The branding concept has attracted great interest among researchers and practitioners and is being transferred from the investigation of products to services and organizations. Only recently has it been applied to destinations. This chapter undertook a review of previous research and recognized that the academic movement from destination image to branding was made by Cai (2002), although some may argue that destination branding started over 30 years ago when image research was initiated. In his work, Cai (2002) introduced the concept of brand identity and for the first time in scientific literature stressed a clear difference between the two concepts of destination image and branding.

The chapter proposed a two-dimensional approach to destination branding: identity and equity. They represent the supply- and demand-side perspectives from different stakeholder groups. Both dimensions are interrelated. Aaker and Joachimsthaler's (2000) brand leadership model was the foundation for the presentation of the dimension of identity. The works by Aaker (1991) and Keller (1993) provided the underpinning for the four dimensions of the consumer-based equity for destination brands. They are awareness, image, perceived quality, and loyalty. In practice, destination branding is often equated with visual identity and slogans, although the nature of it is much more complex. While destination managers and marketers are essential for brand building, host community plays a vital role in the strategic process. Various stakeholder groups should understand and participate in the process of brand identity building. The participation and involvement of community residents is essential so as to bring about a systematic approach to brand development and its implementation.

Chapter 6

COLLABORATIVE DESTINATION BRANDING

OunJoung Park, Liping A. Cai and Xinran Y. Lehto
Purdue University, USA

Abridgement: Collaboration has become a key paradigm in community-based tourism literature. Yet, it has not been well understood in destination branding. This chapter delineates a conceptual model to better describe and explain the nature and dynamism of collaborative branding for destinations. The model is based on a review of theoretical constructs of interorganizational collaboration process and the reconciliation of two product branding models. It suggests that the model begins in a context of environmental forces and evolves sequentially through the phrases of problem-setting, direction-setting, implementation, evaluation, and outcome. **Keywords:** collaboration process; double vortex model; consumer-based brand equity model; collaborative branding.

INTRODUCTION

As pressures continue to rise for accountability to their stakeholders, destination marketing organizations (DMOs) strive for greater return on investment through aggressive marketing programs. More and more of them

Tourism Branding: Communities in Action
Bridging Tourism Theory and Practice, Volume 1, 75–86
Copyright © 2009 by Emerald Group Publishing Limited
All rights of reproduction in any form reserved
ISSN: 2042-1443/doi:10.1108/S2042-1443(2009)0000001008

have joined the bandwagon of creating catchy slogans in the name of destination branding. Evidence is scarce, however, that such practices have ever involved community stakeholders. The pursuit of momentary gain may be responsible for the loss of unique selling proposition and long-term benefits to destination communities (Miller and Henthorne 2006). The uniqueness of a destination created by the united vision of a local community can provide the greatest intrinsic benefit to tourists (Gartner 1989). For branding to yield its expected outcome, a DMO's strategy should be rooted not only in a genuinely unique local experience for tourists but also in a shared vision of a diverse community (Bramwell and Sharman 1999; Reed 1997).

DMOs are hampered by various challenges in engaging stakeholders in the overall branding process and appealing to tourists at the same time. They are under pressure to reconcile local and regional interests while promoting their brand identities in a way that is acceptable to a range of public and private sector constituencies (Kotler, Haider and Rein 1993). They also have to confront the culture clash between public and private sectors, both of which possess highly differentiated value systems (Morgan, Pritchard and Piggott 2003). As a result, DMO and community stakeholders have not established an entirely satisfactory partnership for developing destination brands (de Araujo and Bramwell 2002). Moreover, DMOs of small destinations often contend with limited budgets and a lack of manpower to develop differentiated branding strategies to compete with larger urban destinations (Morgan and Pritchard 2005). Within this context, doubt has been cast over how DMOs can establish a sustainable brand identity while achieving a balance between the perspectives of tourists and a diverse array of community stakeholders.

The role of residents has been examined extensively in image studies (Lawson, Williams, Young and Cossens 1998; Prentice and Hudson 1993; Ryan and Montgomery 1994; Schroeder 1996), in their attitudes toward tourism (Ap and Crompton 1993; King, Pizam and Milman 1993; Pearce, Moscardo and Ross 1996), and in other community-related literature. However, there has been little investigation of resident involvement in community-based branding. Furthermore, the concept of branding has not been studied and practiced as vigorously in tourism as in the general marketing field (Cai 2002). The theoretical paradigms for collaboration issues have not fully explained the nature of networks among destination organizations (Wang and Fesenmaier 2007) and not yet been applied to destination branding. Drawing from the extant literature, this chapter proposes a conceptual model of collaborative branding for destinations. This model serves a dual purpose of bringing together the differing perspectives of tourists and stakeholders and providing a better understanding of the strategic importance of collaboration and guidance for community-based branding initiatives. The proposed model incorporates the theoretical constructs of interorganizational collaboration processes and branding concepts in general marketing literature. Previous studies related to collaboration process (Gray 1985; Jamal and Getz 1995; McCann and Chiles 1983; Selin and Chavez 1995; Wang and Fesenmaier 2007) are examined in conjunction with the synthesis of the double vortex (de Chernatony and Riley 1998) and consumer-based brand equity (CBBE) (Keller 2003) models.

COMMUNITY-BASED COLLABORATIVE BRANDING

Academic research concerning communities and tourism began in the 1970s with the advocacy platform that for the most part promotes the virtues of tourism development. In the 1980s, the second platform emerged. Described as "cautionary" by Jafari (1990), it highlights the negative impacts of tourism on host communities. The third platform, represented by studies in the 1990s, reveals a different perspective that communities are positive about tourism and supportive of its continued growth. Ap and Crompton (1993) and King et al (1993) present similar evidence that, despite the high levels of development and contact with tourists, local residents remain very positive in their reactions and attitudes toward tourism. Recognizing these tendencies, pioneering studies generate the fourth platform of community-based tourism that focuses more on developing theoretical foundations. Emerging theories have sought to integrate existing research findings (Dann, Nash and Pearce 1988; Pearce et al 1996). Burr (1991) summarizes four theoretical approaches to community-based tourism. They are the human ecological approach, the social systems approach, the interactional approach, and the critical approach.

The main issue in understanding relationship between community and tourism centers on how local stakeholders communicate and interact with each other and how this dynamic process of influence can be successfully managed. However, achieving coordination among local governments, residents, and industries is a challenging task and requires development of new mechanisms to incorporate the diverse elements of the tourism system (Jamal and Getz 1995). To overcome this challenge, collaborative relationships rooted in interorganizational theory are becoming a key research paradigm in community-based literature that covers such topics as partnership, stakeholder involvement, and shared decisionmaking.

Collaboration in Tourism

According to Jamal and Getz (1995:188), collaboration in a community-based tourism context is "a process of joint decisionmaking among autonomous key stakeholders of an inter-organizational community tourism domain to resolve planning problems of the domain and/or to manage issues related to the planning and development of the domain." This definition indicates the most straightforward aspect of collaboration that occurs in the interorganizational domain (Lawrence, Phillips and Hardy 1999) and yields optimum balance of interests (Reed 1997). In his seminal text on community-based tourism, Murphy (1985) articulates the principles of collaboration in tourism that community involvement in tourism planning and development can result in a shared vision and that destination distinctiveness can be created by focusing on the community's heritage and culture in the development of tourism products. Subsequent studies further reinforce the argument that local stakeholders who concur with tourism goals and objectives will be equally happy with the outcomes, which in turn help to achieve sustainable development and a sense of place (Simpson 2001; Walsh, Jamrozy and Burr 2001). However, the typically ambiguous, complex, and dynamic structure of collaboration presents some challenges that require practitioners to engage in a continuous process of nurturing (Huxham and Vangen 2000).

Gray (1985) proposes a three-stage model in which interorganizational collaboration develops through the process of problem setting, direction setting, and implementation. This model has evolved and been applied in two ways. The studies by Jamal and Getz (1995) and de Araujo and Bramwell (2002) are the most representative cases that apply the model deductively without modification. On the contrary, Selin and Chavez (1995) and Wang and Fesenmaier (2007) propose extended versions, named evolutionally partnerships model and marketing alliance formation, respectively. While mirror the original three stages in Gray's model, these researchers detailed the process by adding the preconditions and outcomes steps. Preconditions include various environmental forces that influence actual collaborative relationships such as crisis, competition, and organization network. Notice-ably, Wang and Fesenmaier separate the evaluation step from the implementation stage. Outcomes occurring in the last step indicate visible and tangible benefits, as well as any changes resulting from implementation of a collaboration plan. Selin and Chavez classify the outcomes into programs, impacts, and derived benefits, whereas Wang and Fesenmaier view them from the perspectives of strategy, learning, and social capital (Park, Lehto and Morrison 2008). The rest of the steps are commonly found in earlier models.

Wang and Fesenmaier employ a different terminology, though. They describe specific steps as assembling, ordering, and structuring, instead of problem setting, direction setting, and implementation.

Although these interorganizational collaboration process models have been adapted both conceptually (Jamal and Getz 1995; Selin and Chavez 1995; Wang and Fesenmaier 2007) and empirically (Aas, Ladkin and Fletcher 2005; de Araujo and Bramwell 2002; Park et al 2008; Vernon, Essex, Pinder and Curry 2005) to the studies on planning, development, and management of community-based tourism, there has yet to be applied to destination branding. This chapter fills the gap by proposing a five-stage process model of community-based collaborative branding (Table 1).

First, preconditions influencing current brand strategy should be analyzed and grouped into major environmental categories such as crisis, competition, and organization networks. In the problem-setting stage, the common issues and problems of current branding strategy are identified through brainstorming among key stakeholders. Next, direction is set through identifying and appreciating a sense of common goals, objectives, and action plan for the new branding strategy while ensuring a balance of power among the stakeholders. After direction setting, selected ideas are implemented into action items, and a suitable organization is established to institutionalize working relationships and assign goals and responsibilities to each stakeholder. Evaluations assess whether the predefined vision, goals, objectives, and each stakeholder's responsibilities have been achieved through the entire branding process. Finally, outcomes produced by implementing the new branding strategy are grouped into increased brand equity, enhanced collaborative initiatives among stakeholders, and capital-oriented return on investment in terms of human, finance, and social resources.

Reconciling the Perspectives of Stakeholders and Tourists

The importance of destination image has been extensively acknowledged and has engendered a growing body of research (Gallarza et al 2002). According to Gartner (1993a, 1993b), projected images do change and can be manipulated. He argues that those two facts make image assessment and development essential for destinations that increasingly rely on tourism for their economic well-being. Although image has been a core component of destination branding, it should be considered as one step, not branding itself, in forming a community's brand identity (Cai 2002). Studies of the subject have become an active area of research, but the debate continues as

Table 1. A Collaboration Process for Community-Based Branding

Stages	Actions
Stage I Precondition	Crisis/competition/organization network influencing the current brand strategy
Stage II Problem setting	Identify convener Convene stakeholders Define problems/issues of the existing branding strategy Identify and legitimize stakeholders Build commitment to collaborate by raising awareness of interdependence Address stakeholder concerns Ensure availability of adequate resources to allow collaboration to proceed with key stakeholders present
Stage III Direction setting	Collect and share information Appreciate shared values; enhance perceived interdependence Ensure power distributed among several stakeholders Establish rules and agenda for direction setting Organize subgroups if required; list alternatives Discuss various options Select appropriate solutions Arrive at shared vision/goal/objectives for the new branding strategy Streamline detail branding strategy through consensus
Stage IV Implementation	Formalize legal structure for institutionalizing process Assign roles and responsibilities Discuss means of implementing and monitoring solutions, shared vision, plan, or strategy Design monitoring and control system to collaboration decisions Implement branding strategy/action tools
Stage V Evaluation	Assess predefined values/goals/objectives Evaluate detailed branding strategy/action tools Evaluate responsibilities Document evaluated results Follow-up Benchmark
Stage VI Outcomes	Programmatic outcome: increased brand equity Collaborative outcome: enhanced collaborative initiatives among stakeholders Capital-oriented outcomes: return on investment in terms of human, financial, and social

Adapted from de Araujo and Bramwell (2002); Gray (1985); Jamal and Getz (1995); Selin and Chavez (1995); Wang and Fesenmaier (2007).

to whether accepted general branding principles can be transferred to a destination context (Gallarza et al 2002). Therefore, it is meaningful to explore different models and investigate an appropriate approach to destination branding that extends beyond image domain.

In building brand equity, the most debated issue is whether the process should center on the perspective of community stakeholders or tourists There have been a few independent empirical studies from the perspective of stakeholders (Morgan et al 2003) and tourists (Gallarza et al 2002). This chapter compares two existing models that represent the two respective perspectives. They are the double vortex model by de Chernatony and Riley (1998), and the CBBE model by Keller (1993). The latter mainly reinforces the continuous cognitive steps that consumers experience in the process of responding to a brand. The steps include awareness, performance and imagery, judgments and feelings, and resonance. These sequential dimensions logically represent how consumers aware of, think, feel, and act with respect to a brand. The model assumes that building a strong brand in the mind of consumers should involve each of the steps. Meanwhile, a corporate brand represents an organization and reflects its heritage, values, culture, people, and strategy (Aaker 2004), which are developed at the organizational level (Knox and Bickerton 2003) and require managing interactions with multiple stakeholders (Balmer and Gray 2003; Hatch and Schultz 2003; Knox and Bickerton 2003). These organizational values, however, are often excluded from the branding process as a basis for differentiation among corporations (de Chernatony and Riley 1998).

Recognizing the need for more inclusiveness, de Chernatony and Riley (1998) proposed a double vortex model. It considers the perceptions of brand managers and consumers simultaneously. The main logic is that brands are conceived inside organizations, but their success is decided by consumer perceptions. Two vortexes are specified. One demonstrates that corporate managers build brands by reflecting the vision, mission, and values of the firm and its stakeholders, and then blending them with its culture and heritage. This strategic direction is then implemented by incorporating several resourcing elements (naming policy, functional capability, service, risk reducer, personality, legal device, and communicator) that are needed to develop the brand. The importance of each of the elements in a spinning vortex varies when they encounter new environments such as different types of product and consumer segments, resulting in their being closer or further from each other. The second vortex shows how consumers respond to the firm's projected brand. Their perceptions of the brand could be considered in terms of their rational and emotional confidence in the brand. That is, the more consumers' confidence increases, the more favorably they react to the brand. Finally, the overall consumer response to it should augment its value for its stakeholders.

Compared to the CBBE model that stresses a consumer-based product, the double vortex model pays attention to the organization, particularly its stakeholders, and then links consumer value to stakeholder value. The former proposes a more detailed and systematic process of consumer perception than the other. In the CBBE model brand awareness is the first stage, in which consumers recognize or recall it. Consumers then move to the next level of recognizing its attributes (performance) and shaping images (imagery) about it. Then they attach emotional meaning (feelings and judgments) to the brand. Loyalty, which is the ultimate goal in the CBBE model, can be finally formed through brand resonance. The double vortex model, on the contrary, starts with consumer perceptions of brand image (imagery) without the awareness stage, followed by rational performance (performance) and emotional match (feelings and judgments). In this sense, the CBBE model provides a more logical flow for understanding consumers' experience. However, the double vortex model is more dynamic by taking into consideration external factors. As a firm's strategies enter new environments and consumers gain more experiences, the implementation trajectory of a brand changes. In comparison, the CBBE model is more static because it places emphasis on the consumer's cognitive process without consideration of such external factors. Although the two models use different labels for the same steps and place them in different stages, they share commonality in the ultimate goal and the interpretations given to the specific steps. For example, imagery in the CBBE model can be understood as consumer perception in the double vortex model and so can "emotional psycho-social match" to "feeling and judgment." "Brand resonance" parallels "response relationship" in the double vortex model because they are interpreted as the stage where consumers bond positively to the brand.

For successful destination branding, organizational and customer-based perspectives should be linked more coherently. Application of the four steps of the CBBE model with respect to destination branding makes it possible for this study to go beyond the image-oriented approach that has been used extensively in literature. However, to close the gap between the projected and the perceived destination brand, simply adopting the model may not be the optimal solution because stakeholder perspective is excluded in the four steps. Therefore, integrating the two models would make it possible to produce a more consistent brand identity. Local uniqueness is created when

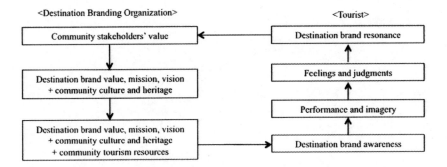

Figure 1 Reconciling Double Vortex and CBBE Models.

tourists are made aware of, benefit from, and are emotionally attached to a harmonized, consistent, and genuine experience. That is, consensus and collaboration among community stakeholders are prerequisite to project local authenticity to the market. Figure 1 demonstrates how the CBBE and double vortex models can be reconciled for destination branding. First, stakeholders' value should be the source of the values, mission, and vision of any destination brand. Then the brand is blended with community culture and heritage and based on local tourism resources. Next, tourists' loyalty is built toward the brand through experiencing the whole process of its awareness, perceived benefits of its performance and image, and feelings and judgments. As a result, their loyalty to the brand corresponds to stakeholders' value. The consistency bridges the perceptual gap between tourists and the community.

The Collaborative Model

The reconciliation of the two existing models, coupled with the concepts of collaboration process, results in the proposed model for community-based collaborative branding. The model presented in Figure 2 shows how each step of the collaboration process in Table 1 parallels the elements in Figure 1. The model integrates the essence of the double vortex (de Chernatony and Riley 1998) and CBBE (Keller 1993) models and the collaboration process synthesized from the work of de Araujo and Bramwell (2002), Gray (1985), Jamal and Getz (1995), Selin and Chavez (1995), and Wang and Fesenmaier (2007). The following discussion centers on the recursive components: recognizing preconditions, identifying problems in current branding strategy,

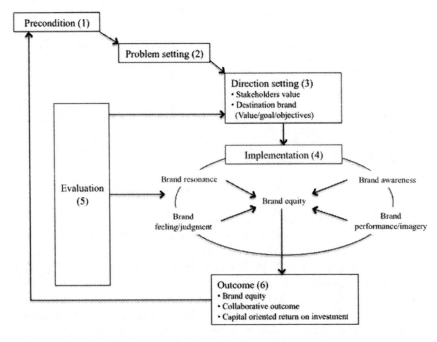

Figure 2 Collaborative Destination Branding.

defining directions rooted in stakeholders' value, implementing tourist-based brand equity strategies, evaluating the performance of the newly proposed branding strategy at each step, and analyzing outcomes of the new brand strategy.

Precondition. DMOs measure impacts of external environmental changes on tourism through collective partnerships among inter-agencies at national, state, and local levels. For example, unexpected crises such as natural disasters, terrorist attacks, and outbreaks of contagious flu are investigated to understand how much the changes disrupt residents' lives and cause serious economic damage. In addition, internal factors are measured such as organizational restructuring, budget condition, community suspicion regarding marketing budget, and regulatory and political influence in the operational activities. These antecedents directly or indirectly cause problems with the current branding strategy.

Problem Setting. Various community interest groups appreciate the interdependencies that exist among them and begin to realize the necessity of collective action to solve problems. The problems in current branding efforts can be identified through brainstorming among stakeholders in public forums or workshops. Consensus on common interests will be generated through addressing their concerns about logos, symbols, slogans, advertising and promotion channels, perceived image, and tourists' reactions. Furthermore, tourists' perceptions of their experience can be measured. For instance, an image study is often conducted to identify the gap among projected, perceived, and desired images. Problem identification should also include a series of studies that survey local stakeholder groups and tourists.

Direction Setting. Once problems of current branding strategy are identified, a new or revised strategy is established. First, stakeholders establish vision, short- and long-term goals, and objectives that they can expect from the new strategy. Directions of branding programs including logos, symbols, and slogans, and communication message and channels can be streamlined to build brand equity. In addition, DMOs should specify goals for enhancing relationships between private and public sectors by refining channels of communication and developing new media for information exchange. Evaluation mechanisms are also established at this stage.

Implementation. The next important procedure is implementing branding programs designed for each step of awareness, performance and imagery, judgments and feelings, and resonance. The ultimate goal of program implementation is to establish or increase genuine brand equity for a destination. Stakeholders should participate in this step through their assigned roles and responsibilities.

Evaluation. To monitor ongoing progress and ensure compliance with collaborative decisions, stakeholders should be involved in the evaluation step. Through sharing opinions and feedback on each step, participants can revise branding programs to increase tourists' awareness and generate more positive emotional responses from them. Moreover, evaluation makes it possible to recognize what tourists really expect from their experience and strengthen their intention to revisit and the effects of word-of-mouth marketing. In addition, participants can evaluate whether predefined directions and their responsibilities have been followed through.

Outcomes. Upon completion of implementation and evaluation of branding programs, outcomes can be assessed in terms of increased brand equity, collaborative initiatives among stakeholders, and their performance levels regarding their responsibilities. The driving issues from the outcomes can be a starting point to identify problems while considering environmental influences.

CONCLUSION

Destination banding at the community level is a complex task for DMOs. Many forces can create frictions among stakeholder groups and render a collaboration initiative ineffective. These include a general lack of financial and human resources, competing or opposing interests among stakeholder groups, unequal power relations, and insufficient understanding of tourism and destination marketing (Aas et al 2005; Bramwell and Sharman 1999; de Araujo and Bramwell 2002; Reed 1997; Williams, Penrose and Hawkes 1998). Moreover, the lack of shared core values among various stakeholders makes it difficult to create a consistent brand identity that can appeal to a destination's tourists. At the same time, tourists become increasingly sophisticated, and expect that there be a mind behind the destination brand and that its promise be kept by whomever they come in contact with. Recognizing these challenges, a model of community-based collaborative destination branding is proposed in this chapter. The model reconciles the double vortex and CBBE models and introduces an integrative approach to building destination brand equity by drawing on the perspectives of both community stakeholders and tourists. A collective and conscious vision from stakeholders should be the source of the promise put forth by the community. A destination brand is more than a slogan and an icon. Collaborative approach among stakeholders can offer a competitively attractive proposition. In this sense, the proposed model can be a guideline to practice collaborative branding using a systematic and collaborative process. The model, however, calls for its validations through empirical investigations.

PART II

FROM THEORIES TO PRACTICES

Chapter 7

TOURISM BRANDING IN A SOCIAL EXCHANGE SYSTEM

Liping A. Cai
Purdue University, USA

Abridgement: This chapter adopts a sociological perspective to examine the phenomenon of destination branding. Invoking the social exchange theory as the foundation and its complex exchange system as its framework, the chapter elaborates the uniqueness of rural destination as a social structure rather than a market or organizational entity. A branding model for rural destinations is proposed and illustrated through a case study. The model advocates a community-based approach to image research as a platform on which the branding process takes place. The chapter reports the comparative findings on the image as projected by a destination marketing organization, perceived by current and potential tourists, and desired by local residents. By highlighting the role of host community's participation in tourism branding, the study informs its definition as a continuing process to create affective experiences through building a unique identity and sustaining a consistent image that emotionally bond with residents and resonate with tourists. **Keywords:** tourism branding model; community-based; destination image; social exchange.

Tourism Branding: Communities in Action
Bridging Tourism Theory and Practice, Volume 1, 89–104
Copyright © 2009 by Emerald Group Publishing Limited
All rights of reproduction in any form reserved
ISSN: 2042-1443/doi:10.1108/S2042-1443(2009)0000001009

INTRODUCTION

As an academic inquiry, destination branding is a relatively new field. In the 1999 special issue of a journal, Nickerson and Moisey (1999) considered branding of a state as "what images people have of the state and what kind of relationship they have with it" (p. 217). A paper by Hall (1999) included the definition of a brand in general marketing terms. Instead of defining what it was, Hall (1999) stated its core objective as "producing a consistent, focused communication strategy" (p. 230). Two other papers (Westwood, Morgan, Pritchard and Ineson 1999; Williams and Palmer 1999) made not only some references to branding concept, but also in general marketing terms and without direct application to destinations. One non-academic paper (Crockett and Wood 1999) illustrated the process of developing a brand for Western Australia from the practitioners' perspective. The study stopped short of defining destination branding.

An emerging body of literature on destination branding has been introduced since the special issue on the topic. Researchers have reported the practices of it (Hall 2002; Martinovic 2002), and examined a wide array of challenges (d'Hauteserre 2001; Papadopoulos and Heslop 2002). Konecnik and Gartner (2007) applied Keller's concept of customer-based brand equity to destination image. There have been attempts to formulate a formal definition (Blain, Levy and Ritchie 2005; Cai 2002, Foley and Fahy 2004; Hankinson 2004, 2005), with Cai accompanying his with a cooperative model for rural destinations. The purpose of this chapter is to conceptualize a model of tourism branding through a case study. Differentiated from branding literature to date, the chapter approaches the marketing concept from a sociological perspective. Specifically, it founds the proposed model on the tenets of social exchange theory.

A SOCIOLOGICAL PERSPECTIVE

In a seminal review, sociologist Richard Emerson (1976) concluded that social exchange theory can be thought of as "developing the conceptual tools needed ... to deal with exactly those topics that economics theory has trouble with: market imperfections" (p. 359). A most troublesome market imperfection for economists is the exchange between interdependent actors in a social structure where long-term relations among actors are involved. In other words, economics theory is concerned with a short-run, cross-sectional game of single market transactions between buyers and sellers, whereas a sociological perspective of exchange takes a longitudinal view of such relations over the long-run and among interdependent actors. Branding as a contemporary marketing concept aims at achieving added value by cultivating customers' loyalty. With long-term relationship building as a primacy of branding activities, social exchange theory provides a solid framework within which the study and practice of it should take place. The sociological perspective of exchange is in particular inimitable for tourism branding because it must deal with the relationship not just between buyers and sellers as typical with consumer goods, but among multiple inter-dependent actors in a community destination.

Destination Actors in an Imperfect Social Structure

A community becomes a destination once tourism is accepted as an economic activity. Its attractiveness lies in the fact that the "seed money" through the economic multiplier effect comes from tourists—people living outside the community. Like any business wanting more customers, a destination is naturally inclined to strive for more arrivals. However, unlike other businesses, a destination is unique in several ways. First, its offerings are largely intangible. Tourists as buyers purchase an experience and bring home a memory. As such, they cannot "test drive" it before making a purchase decision. Second, the production and consumption of the destination offerings take place simultaneously. It is extremely perishable. In fact, it has no shelf life. Third, the supply chain is both horizontal and vertical. It involves an array of customer contact points that encompasses almost anyone that tourists come in contact with. Fourth, a destination does not have a well-defined organizational structure as a typical business does. Its only distinct function is marketing carried out by a destination marketing organization (DMO). There are no clearly delineated human resource and customer service functions that support marketing activities.

Although these unique aspects present management and marketing challenges for all destinations, those in rural areas are at a greater disadvantage due to differences of perceptions and expectations between urban- and rural-bound tourists. By analogy, an urban destination can be regarded as a large bureaucratic corporation, whereas a rural setting is an equivalent to a small cozy family business. One important feature of the latter is of being local, being rooted in its scenery and culture. Rural-bound tourists are in search of a personalized response to their need for physical, emotional, and social appreciation in a simpler environment, such as countryside, nature, and rural way of life. In this simpler environment, they expect a greater sense of community and a warmer expression of local hospitality. For a rural destination that does not have community support for tourism, a singular focus on external marketing, as is typically practiced by DMOs, fails to meet such expectations, even if tourists are initially attracted to it.

Be it urban or rural, a destination is a market. Economics theory of market deals with many actors "by references to impersonal criteria which disregard personal ties and social ends in favor of an immediate maximization principle of profitmaking" (Firth 1967:5), and by assuming an aggregate behavior of all other actors. This approach works well "in circumstances involving a large number of economic units" (Coddington 1968:2), as in the case of an urban destination. However, the economics theory of market fails in the situation involving the much stronger interdependence of a small number of actors in a social structure. Social exchange theory is formed specifically "toward the analysis of such real but imperfect social structures—that is, social structures involving fairly long-term relations between people" (Emerson 1976:351). A rural community destination is typical of such structure.

Social exchange theory has been recognized as a major influence on the understanding of relationships in marketing (Araujo and Easton 1996). Bagozzi (1975) posited that marketing be conceptualized as consisting of three types of exchanges: restricted, generalized, and complex. Their delineation is determined by the number of social actors and directional characteristics in the exchange process. The most advanced type of the three is complex exchange, which involves at least three social actors and multi-directional relationships in marketing activities.

> Complex exchange refers to a system of mutual relationships between at least three parties. Each social actor is involved in at least one direct exchange, while the entire system is organized by an interconnecting web of relationships. (Bagozzi 1975:33)

A community destination is characterized by such a system, within which tourism can be seen as an economic activity that is generated and maintained by the complex exchanges among tourists, residents, businesses, and a DMO. Interpretations of complex exchange varied in the general marketing literature in the late 1960s (Luck 1969) and 1970s (Carman 1973;

Kotler 1972). However, there has been little dispute since then that an exchange can be both of a tangible and intangible nature. Although most exchanges in a market place are characterized by the transfer of a product or service for money, underlining each "lies in the social and psychological significance of the experience, feelings, and meanings of the parties" (Bagozzi 1975:36).

The sociological understanding of complex exchange beyond the utilitarian and physical functions has inspired numerous contemporary concepts, such as relationship, experiential, and permission marketing. These, largely founded on sociological perspectives, have challenged the traditional "marketing mix" framework, because the "4Ps" of it "in many cases may not fully describe modern marketing programs" (Keller 2003:237). Although the impact of each individual concept has been fragmented, they together have brought about significant paradigm shifts in thinking and practice. A manifestation of such shifts is the concept and practice of branding as a strategic platform for marketing, although examples are abundant that many remain committed to constraining it as a tactical tool of marketing. In tourism, "our knowledge of destination branding remains poorly understood and [it] is often misunderstood by practitioners" (Blain et al 2005:328). This unfortunate reality will persist, unless the study and practice of branding for community destinations are founded on a theoretical framework, such as social exchange theory, that explicitly recognizes and accommodates the long-term relationships and interdependence of destination actors.

Destination Image

Cohen (1984) conducted a review of approaches, issues, and findings of the sociology of tourism. Despite abundant literature in the field, he concluded that "[few] studies deal specifically ... with the nature and dynamics of the tourist-local relationship" (p. 379), which consists of three dimensions: people's perceptions, interactions, and attitudes. These dimensions are essential for tourist experience at a rural community destination. The tourists' perceptions determine destination choice, affect their attitude toward the locals, and influence future visit intention. The tourist—local interactions form relationships, which in turn modify their attitude toward each other.

Albeit in the absence of a sociological perspective, scholars have spared no efforts in studying how tourists perceive destinations, typically in the form of image and from the angle of understanding their decision making.

Different from consumer goods and other tangible products, tourists are not able to try out the destination before making a choice (Eby, Molnar and Cai 1999:55; Gartner 1989:16). As a bundle of products and services, purchase of a destination mix has an inherent uncertainty and is usually expensive. The complexity of the decision process on the part of tourists therefore "involves greater risk and extensive information search, and depends on tourists' mental construct of what a potential destination has to offer relative to their needs" (Cai 2002).

The first destination image studies appeared about three decades ago (Pike and Ryan 2004), with an increasing recognition of the role and influence of image in tourists' buying behavior and satisfaction. Gallarza et al (2002) attempted to synthesize image variables and dimensions that had been explored sporadically from 1971 to 1999. Explaining Mazanec's (1994) work, they pointed out that

> [I]n any image study, relationships between variables are set out in three dimensions: the subject's perceptions are measured (1st dimension) around objects or destinations (2nd dimension) and with respect to certain attributes or characteristics (3rd dimension). (Gallarza et al 2002:62)

With few exceptions, however, the prevalent approach to destination image studies is nested in scrutinizing the perceptions of the subject (tourists) about the objects (destination) and their attributes. Among many others works in this stream, Echtner and Ritchie (1991) stressed the necessity to separate visitors' and non-visitors' images. Beerli and Martín (2004) addressed the need for differentiating between first time and repeat tourists. Litvin and Ling (2001) classified consumers into potential, prospective, one-time, and repeat visitors.

To the extent that the knowledge of how tourists perceive a destination is valuable to a DMO, its branding utility is severely limited without contrasting their perceptions with the projected image. Some researchers have examined the mismatch between perceived and projected image and its effect on overall destination image and tourists' satisfaction (Andreu, Bigne and Cooper 2000; Chon 1990; Hu and Ritchie 1993; Ryan 1994). Whether the projected image reflects the desire of the host community remains unexplored. The extant literature on destination image remains cocooned within the domain of its own. The study of destination branding calls for a deliberate scrutiny of the differences of destination image between what is perceived by tourists and what is projected by the DMO. Furthermore, what types of image community stakeholders desire to communicate to tourists must also be integrated in studying and practicing the branding of it as a destination. Two distinct groups of stakeholders are businesses which directly serve various needs of tourists, and residents who, in interaction with their customers, communicate an overall hospitality and impact the affective experience of tourists.

Given the significant role of destination image in determining tourists' choice (Lee O'Leary and Hong 2002), it is only appropriate that most studies to date have examined tourists' image as their central thesis. In practice, as Blain et al found out, image was considered by DMO respondents as the most important rationale for destination branding. What has been missing in both academic inquiries and in industry applications is the explicit consideration of the destination image that the locals desire of their community. A broader sociological perceptive such as social exchange theory offers a timely platform to advance the branding research and practice.

The significance of invoking social exchange theory to form the theoretical framework for the study and practice of branding is profound in three ways. First, the theory's component of complex exchange accepts both overt and covert types of coordination of actors' activities. Overt coordination typically occurs in a firm or a clearly defined distribution channel. Covert coordination, on the other hand, occurs in relatively unconscious systems of social and economic relationships. As such, second, the theory explicitly recognizes residents, together with businesses, as an actor in the exchange process and system. Third, when applied to marketing, "there is definitely an exchange in social marketing relationships" (Bagozzi 1975:38), and the exchange involves the transfer of tangible goods, as well as intangible and symbolic meaning of experiences and feelings.

As actors in a system where experience at a destination is exchanged and consumed, residents and businesses must participate in branding which, among other objectives, is to attract the actor of tourists to the system. The study of it must explicitly inform the role of host community in the branding process. In particular, this chapter contends that, in examining a destination image as a central thesis of branding, the image that host community desires to communicate to the actor of tourists should be investigated integrally. The case of Harrison County, USA, illustrates how this was accomplished.

The Case Study

Harrison County is located in the southern part of the state of Indiana in the United States. The marketing of it as a destination is charged to the

Harrison County Convention and Visitors Bureau (HCCVB). For years, this body presented the community under the banner of "Scenic Southern Indiana—Historic Corydon." Situated along the Ohio River, the terrain of southern Indiana is more diverse than that of the northern part of the state. Corydon is the county seat, and was the first capital of the state. Graphical representation of the banner (flag) was autumn foliage and the first state capital building. The banner was used consistently in the destination marketing materials, which also featured caverns and caves in the region and a casino boat docking on the shore of the Ohio River. The image of the destination as projected by HCCVB was "historic, scenic, outdoor, and entertaining."

In 2004 HCCVB sanctioned a series of research contracts, one of which was a comprehensive image study aimed at developing a destination brand. This was conducted in three phases. During the first phase, focus groups were conducted with the participation of local residents and business owners or operators. They were moderated to gauge participants' general sense of the county as a unique place to live and a place to visit, as well as its strengths and weaknesses as a destination. Each focus group was concluded with a summary session during which participants were asked to recommend an image statement that could best capture the essence of the place, and present it to the market. These sessions were video and audio-taped and transcribed. The second phase was the gathering of data from tourists and potential tourists on their perceptions of the county as a destination. The data were collected through personal interviews with the former and phone interviews with the latter.

The survey instrument was developed following the review of academic literature on image, appraisal of HCCVB marketing materials, and interview with its staff. The results of a concurrent tourist profile study were also consulted. The instrument included a 26-item measurement scale of image. The sample consisted of 463 tourists and 83 potential tourists. The sub-sample of the former was drawn through random interceptions at the destination and the latter from those who had been exposed to HCCVB marketing materials but had never been to Harrison County. The third phase consisted of data analysis, reporting of results, and dissemination of the findings to various stakeholders groups through town hall meetings, seminars, and other public events.

Desired Image. The analysis of the focus group transcripts was aided with CATegory PACkage to identify the most significant words in text strings and determine the patterns of similarity based on the way they were used in

Table 1. Host Community's Desired Image

Ranking	Significant Words	Ranking	Significant Words
1	Downtown Corydon, the square	6	Friendly
2	Home, hometown, family, community	7	Caesars Casino
3	Slower pace, relaxing	8	Caves
4	Historic	9	Rural, rolling hills
5	Step back in time nostalgic, quaint	10	Scenic, charming

the transcripts. This analysis was aimed at understanding what type of image the host community desired to present to tourists (Table 1). The significant words in Table 1 reflected the participants' consensus on the strength of the area as a destination. These significant words also made up the key terms in various image statements they recommended as their desired message for HCCVB to present to tourists. The participants tended to emphasize more on the intangible than the tangible attributes as the primary appeal to tourists. One participant's view on the area's weakness as a destination was shared by many that "… Someone said you can come and visit the capital building, but it will make no sense to stay overnight. Some things need to be developed to encourage people to come and stay for more than 10 minutes." Residents seemed to deliberately refrain themselves from citing Caesars Casino as a unique attraction of the area, although it was mentioned often as a draw. There was no hesitation on the part of the business focus group to mention the casino.

Perceived Image. The analysis of the survey data from actual and potential tourists aided the understanding of how they perceived the area as a destination. The application of exploratory factor analysis resulted in five components of perceived image. They were quality of facilities, overall attractiveness, affective appeal, variety of attractions, and casino draw. All components showed acceptable levels of reliability of over 0.8. The component of "quality of facilities" refers to respondents' perceptions on the quality of lodging and food, information provision, and accessibility. The "overall attractiveness" refers to their perceptions on the area's scenery, rural view, outdoor recreation, historical heritage, and small town characteristics. The "affective appeal" refers to the respondents' affective assessment of the place as a destination. The scale items loaded on this component included warm and friendly people, peaceful and relaxed mood, favorite, ideal, and daytrip/weekend destination, and "my type of destination." The "variety of attractions" involves respondents' perception about specific attractions in the area including local crafts, antique shopping, festivals, and caves. The "casino draw" component refers to the uniqueness and appeal as the area's attraction. Significant differences of the perceive image were found between tourists and potential tourists for each of the five image components (Table 2). An immediate observation was that the rankings of the five image components were in exact reverse orders. The rankings were based on the standardized mean scores of the factors, interpreted as the strength of image components.

An item-by-item comparison, part of which is shown in Table 3, confirmed the component differences in Table 2. The top five perceptual items of tourists were mostly in the image component of affective appeal which was the highest ranking in Table 2. In contrast, only one of the top five perceptual items of potential tourists was in the affective component. Both groups scored high on this affective appeal item, "People are warm and friendly." One overall attractiveness item of "The area is nestled in beautiful nature and scenery" was ranked fifth by both groups. It was also noted that potential tourists held stronger perceptions than their counterparts in all instances, including those not listed in Table 3. The differences of the 26 perceptual scores were significant at 0.001.

The Community-Based Branding Model

In general terms, brand image and awareness constitute brand knowledge, from which equity develops. Various definitions of destination branding

Table 2. Components of Perceived Image

Component/Item	Tourists		Potential Tourists	
	Ranking	Mean	Ranking	Mean
Affective appeal	1	0.056215	5	−0.31358
Quality of facilities	2	−0.01831	4	0.102143
Overall attractiveness	3	−0.04464	3	0.249029
Casino draw	4	−0.06777	2	0.378056
Variety of attractions	5	−0.12663	1	0.706378

Table 3. Top Five Perceptions

Ranking	Perception	Score
Tourists		
1	The overall mood of the area is peaceful and relaxed	8.44
2	People are warm and friendly	8.40
3	The area is ideal for weekend trips	8.07
4	The area is ideal for day trips	7.97
5	The area is nestled in beautiful nature and scenery	7.97
Potential Tourists		
1	People are warm and friendly	9.34
2	The area is rich in history and heritage	9.25
3	Visitor information is readily available	9.20
4	The area offers affordable accommodation choices	9.14
5	The area is nestled in beautiful nature and scenery	9.12

have been proposed (Blain et al 2005; Cai 2002; Foley and Fahy 2004; Hankinson 2004, 2005). They all recognize, to varying degrees, that image plays a central and integral role due to its determining influence on consumers' pre-visitation decisions or choices from a set of competitive locations. The findings from the case of Harrison County beg for an answer to the question: whose image is it?

The case brings to focus the two golden rules of service quality applied elsewhere in the tourism system—service failure occurs when expectation exceeds perception and customers' perception is the reality. The potential tourists' perception was tantamount to the expectation. In all its marketing materials before the study, HCCVB projected the area as "historic, scenic, outdoor, and entertaining." To the extent that its marketing materials might or might not be entirely responsible for setting up the expectation, the tourists were disappointed at least in one aspect. In their eyes, the area's history and heritage were after all not that abundant. The area did live up to the expectation for its scenic beauty. However, the tourists were most impressed with the area's affective appeal, such as the overall mood of peacefulness and relaxation, and the warm and friendly people. Did it mean that HCCVB should accept the tourists' perception as reality?

It did, but not without a coordinated effort to reconcile perceived image of tourists with the desired one of the host community as an integral part of its branding process that ensued immediately after the completion of the study. Instead of rushing to sanction its advertising agency to create its brand with various elements, HCCVB held town hall meetings to disseminate the findings of the image and other concurrent studies. Seminars and workshops were conducted for community leaders and other destination actors. Other public events such as National Tourism Week were devoted to bringing together all stakeholders to educate and appreciate the process of branding their community. HCCVB's approach to branding is illustrated in Figure 1.

The desired image, together with images of actual and potential tourists, forms a tripod branding platform in Figure 1. The solidness and stableness of the platform depends on the strength of each, its relative position, and the balance of all. Built on the host community's consensus, HCCVB identified "Indiana's Hometown" as its brand name, "This Is Indiana" as its initial slogan, and graphic design featuring Corydon and Indiana's first capital building as its logo. Working together, these brand elements project an affective image that emotionally appeals to rural-bound tourists who search for simple originality, sense of community, and genuine hospitality of one's home town. This is a significant departure from HCCVB's previous emphasis on a lineup of its scenery, history, and other specific attractions.

The HCCVB staff and community leaders were convinced through the image study that the totality of tourists' experience is what will satisfy them and cultivate their loyalty to the brand, and such experience must be

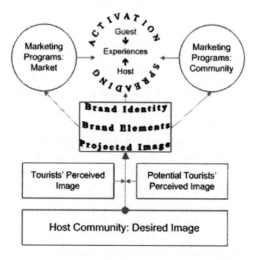

Figure 1 Community-Based Tourism Branding.

sustained consistently across all brand contacts and overtime. Therefore, marketing programs to build and maintain its brand identity should explicitly include the participation of the host community. An educational DVD was crafted for community-wide circulation to effectively start its internal marketing before the presentation of its new brand to the external market.

Although not in the graphic illustration, the community-based model of branding recognizes the extant understanding of destination image as consisting of cognitive or attribute, affective, and conative or attitude components (Cai 2002; Gartner 1993a, 1993b). The model specifies that image be examined from the multi-faceted perspectives of tourists, potential markets, and host community. Furthermore, image is not a brand. It is the foundation to articulate a brand identity through expressions of its elements such as name, slogan, graphics, or their combination. For it to be strong and brand identity to be favorable, branding—the commitment of actions—must take place. Thus, the model puts forward the definition of tourism branding as a continuing process to create affective experiences through building a unique identity and sustaining a consistent image that emotionally bond with residents and resonate with tourists. As much of the world is shifting from a service to an experience economy in which consumers' decision making become more emotionally than rationally oriented, the currency of the proposed definition of tourism branding should inform both the research and practice of it.

The community-based model and definition of tourism branding extend, and are modified from, existing destination branding models and definitions. In addition to the inclusion of experiences, the current model and definition emphasize the role of host community. The use of "sustaining" and "consistent" in the definition is to signify the psychological concept of spreading activation (for the discussion of the concept's relevance to branding, see Anderson 1983:29; Cai 2002:723; Keller 1998:93). These improvements deem it necessary to replace the term of destination branding with that of tourism branding. The former is too limiting to encompass the role of community stakeholders in this process. Industry practices focusing on creative advertising to impress tourists with catchy slogans have also degraded the former term.

CONCLUSION

The importance of residents' role in destination success has long been recognized in tourism studies. In the past 30 years, tourism researchers have constantly examined such community issues as residents' attitudes toward tourism. Accordingly, it is widely believed that tourism must have the support of the host community (Lankford 1994; Murphy 1985). However, research work has unequivocally found that support is not always there. In fact, support only constitutes one pole of a continuum of host community's attitudes. The other pole is opposition. Depending on the stage of the destination lifecycle, the distribution of residents on this "love–hate" continuum varies. Studies agree on some factors that underlie different attitudes, including attachment to the community (McCool and Martin 1994), level of knowledge about tourism and the local economy (Davis, Allen and Cosenza 1988), level of contact with tourists (Akis, Peristianis and Warner 1996), and perceived ability to influence tourism planning decisions (Lankford 1994).

Krippendorf (1987) points out that the social effects of tourism on local communities are so significant that they must be studied before anything else. Mathieson and Wall (1982) argue that although many studies make passing reference to the existence of social impacts, most cast little light on their nature or the means for their investigation. Research should be "directed more explicitly at determining the perceptions and attitudes of the host population; and *unless local inhabitants are contacted*, it may not be possible to identify the real significance of any change" (Brunt and Courtney 1999).

The case of Harrison County highlights the need for and benefits from invoking the social exchange theory to study and practice tourism branding. Residents as an actor of exchange should not only participate in the planning and development of tourism, but should also inform and be informed of how their community is presented to tourists. They are the ones who not only deliver the experience expected by tourists, but more importantly are part of the experience in the social exchange of both tangibles and intangibles. A Gallup 2001 survey of 6,000 customers strongly suggests that

> Employees who deal with customers not only represent the brand but, in the perceptions of customers, become the brand. Employees have the power, by dint of actual service and sometimes by mere attitude and body language, to add to or subtract from brand value. Attention must be paid to the subtraction side, because customers have the memory of elephants when it comes to disappointments and unmet

expectations. Positive memories may fade, but resentments can last a life time. (McEwen 2001:4)

In tourism branding terms, residents are *de facto* employees of the destination enterprise.

Framing the study and practice of branding in social exchange theory advances the application of it in tourism research in general. The theory was implied in the literature as early as in the 1960s. Since the 1990s, it has been widely adopted to explore residents' perceptions and attitudes toward tourism (Ap 1990; Lindberg and Johnson 1997; McGehee and Andereck 2004). Sutton (1967) regarded exchange as a social characteristic that defines the touring encounter, and the social interactions between hosts and guests. The interactions "may provide either an opportunity for rewarding and satisfying exchanges, or it may stimulate and reinforce impulses to exploitation on the part of the host and, to suspicion and resentment on the part of the visitor" (Sutton 1967:220). Sutton erred, however, in grouping all locals in the category of catering to tourists' needs and wishes and in restricting these needs and wishes to tangible and functional exchanges. As aforementioned, social exchange theory has evolved to accommodate emotional and symbolic exchanges among multiple social actors.

Social exchange theory as applied to tourism branding brings to question the validity of the basic traits of host–guest encounter, a concept prominent in the earlier sociological reference to tourism studies, as exemplified by Sutton's work. Cohen (1984) summarized the traits as "... essentially transitory, nonrepetitive and asymmetrical; the participants are oriented toward achieving immediate gratification rather than toward maintaining a continuous relationship" (p. 379). This understanding of host–guest encounter is entrenched in economics theory which assumes short-term, transaction-based gains by and between the dyad of buyers and sellers or tourists and locals. The case study in this chapter suggests that the basic traits of the encounter need not take place. Tourists perceived the community as warm and friendly, and locals genuinely desired to present their community as such. More importantly, the chapter shows that the tenets of social exchange theory can not only provide a theoretical framework to study contemporary marketing issues such as branding, but also offer a conceptual tool to guide marketing practices in an environment characterized by the pursuit of long-term relationships among multiple stakeholders.

Acknowledgement

The data used in the case study were drawn from a research project sanctioned by the Harrison County Convention and Visitors' Bureau, Indiana, USA, and conducted by the faculty and graduate students affiliated with the Purdue Tourism and Hospitality Research Center, Purdue University. The author is indebted to James Epperson, Xinran Lehto, Joseph Ismail, and the center's graduate students for their contribution to the project.

Chapter 8

LINKING LOCAL AND CULINARY CUISINES WITH DESTINATION BRANDING

Yi-Chin Lin
National Kaohsiung Hospitality College, Taiwan

Abridgement: This chapter examines residents' attitudes toward the use of local cuisine and culinary establishments in developing a destination brand. Analyses were based on a sample of residents in Taiwan. Three distinctive groups were identified: "indifferent," "ambivalent," and "supportive." Residents belonging to the latter category had the most interest in being involved in promoting culinary cuisine to international tourists. The ambivalent group was conservative in making recommendations to international tourists about local food. The indifferent members had a low level of support for using culinary tourism. Generally, residents were likely to recommend snacks at local night markets and seafood-based cuisine at Chinese restaurants to international tourists. The chapter concludes with a discussion of implications for developing effective destination branding strategies through culinary tourism. **Keywords:** resident; cuisine; culinary establishment.

Tourism Branding: Communities in Action
Bridging Tourism Theory and Practice, Volume 1, 105–118
Copyright © 2009 by Emerald Group Publishing Limited
All rights of reproduction in any form reserved
ISSN: 2042-1443/doi:10.1108/S2042-1443(2009)0000001010

INTRODUCTION

Destination marketing organizations (DMOs) are increasingly seeking to gain a competitive advantage by featuring their cuisines as attractions to international tourists. In Asia, cuisines have become a new marketing tool of differentiation adopted by such competing destinations as Taiwan, Macao, Singapore, Hong Kong, and mainland China (Kivela and Crotts 2006). Several recent studies have indicated the possibility of using food to develop a tourism brand (Hashimoto and Telfer 2006; Tellström, Gustafsson and Mossberg 2006). Bell (2007) suggested that building food and drink hospitality spaces as public social sites was useful in branding and promoting a place. As an integral part of destination offerings, local cuisine and culinary establishments are now recognized as important for marketing and branding a destination.

Researchers have observed that destination marketing success requires the building of good relationships between the host community residents and DMOs (Dwyer and Kim 2003; Pérez and Nadal 2005). Gibson and Davidson (2004) indicated that locals are critical to the achievement of destination marketing. Residents and other key stakeholders in host communities should be involved in the planning and decision-making process of tourism development (Ap and Crompton 1998; Jamal and Getz 1995; Sheehan and Ritchie 2005). Successful destination marketing activities not only depend on the integration of marketing functions, the quality of infrastructure, facilities and services, and the attractiveness of destinations but also require support and involvement of locals and their hospitality toward tourists (Gursoy and Kendall 2006; Kim and Petrick 2005; Skinner 2005).

According to a 2006 survey (Taiwan Tourism Bureau 2007), food and friendly residents were rated as the top attractions in Taiwan by inbound tourists. The majority of arrivals were from Hong Kong and Macau, South East Asia, Japan, and the United States. In addition, Kaohsiung City, located in the south, was the third most visited city in Taiwan. Traditionally known as a major industrial center and an international harbor, the city is improving its attractions in an effort to brand itself as a more appealing destination. There are several famous night markets for international tourists to taste a variety of local snacks while enjoying Taiwanese cultural dining areas. Cijin Island, on the western side of Kaohsiung City, is a popular location for tourists to sample the seafood-based cuisine. A review of literature has revealed little prior work on residents' attitudes toward the use of local cuisine and culinary establishments as attractions to brand a destination. This chapter attempts to fill the gap through a case study of Kaohsiung City and in the context of destination branding.

CUISINE AND DESTINATION BRANDING

Culinary tourism has emerged as an increasingly important component of destination marketing (Hashimoto and Telfer 2006; Long 2004). It has been used in explaining the phenomenon of using local cuisine as an instrument for fostering tourism at a specific destination, and can be defined as

> [T]he intentional, exploratory participation by tourists in the foodways of an other—participation including the consumption, preparation, and presentation of a food item, cuisine, meal system, or eating style considered to belong to a culinary system not one's own. (Long 2004:20–21)

By exploring foods new to them, tourists experience the local culture. By sharing their culture with tourists through this medium, local residents make it a representation of destination identity.

Long's (2004) viewpoint on culinary tourism mirrors the "push" and "pull" concept of tourist motivations proposed by Dann (1977). Push factors refer to internal forces and include social-psychological motives that drive a person's desires to travel. Pull factors refer to external forces that influence a person's tourism decision-making. Typically, these external factors are described as attractions designed, developed, and managed for motivating tourists to seek out and visit destinations where they are located. Attractions usually consist of a number of attributes of a "non-home" place that can pull individuals away from their familiar environment to observe, to participate in, and to experience (Lew 1987). In line of this view, local cuisine can be perceived as a "pull factor." It can be used in marketing and branding a specific destination (Boyne Hall and Williams 2003; Cohen and Avieli 2004; du Rand, Heath and Alberts 2003; Frochot 2003; Kivela and Johns 2003).

du Rand et al (2003) suggested that food can contribute to the development and competitiveness of a destination through agricultural activity, authentic exploitation, attraction enhancement, empowerment, pride generation, and branding identity. Cohen and Avieli (2004) argued that culinary establishments can contribute to the development of local cuisine to become popular attractions. They indicated several local Thailand restaurants as their examples. Sparks, Wildman and Bowen (2001) also stated that restaurants constitute an important part of tourism products/ attractions; are important to tourists' overall satisfaction with a destination; act as key factors influencing tourists' behavior and the host culture; and as such restaurants can be a part of destination image through their own reputations. A study by Josiam, Mattson and Sullivan (2004) showed that tourists to the Historaunt (Mickey's Dining Car) were motivated by local history, culture, and scenery. New eating experience is suggested as the key factor in attracting tourists. Hjalager and Richards (2002) and Long (2004) indicated that tourists generally show great pleasure in trying and tasting local food and dishes, because a particular cuisine is relevant to the host culture and embodies local culinary skills and techniques (Long 2004). Several studies further illustrated that different types of culinary establishments can also become appealing attractions, such as food vendors and shops, food and beverage outlets, farms, wineries, and culinary culture exhibitions (Bessière 1998; Mitchell and Hall 2003; Timothy and Wall 1997). Local cuisine and different culinary establishments can provide tourists with a wide array of opportunities to experience the culture of a specific destination.

Nield, Kozak, and LeGrys (2000) conducted a survey at the Black Sea resorts of Romania and found that quality of food, value of money, variety of dishes, attractiveness of surrounding, and presentation of food were the significant attributes influencing tourists' overall dining experiences and satisfaction. Likewise, Kivela and Johns (2003) analyzed tourists' discourses in relation to their dining experiences in Hong Kong and found that some of respondents traveled in search of gastronomy. Many selected Hong Kong because of their past local dining experiences. They concluded that food quality, the authenticity of local dishes, service quality, dining experiences, benefit sought, and appealing physical environment are important to tourists' total culinary experiences. Food can be a symbol, a sign of communion, a class marker, and an emblem of a specific region (Bessière 1998). These symbolic characteristics are composed of the nature, culture, and identity of a place. Consistent with this understanding of food, Frochot (2003) asserted that local cuisine and culinary establishments can be used to strengthen the identity of a destination in order to differentiate it from others on the global competitive marketplaces.

Residents' Attitudes

Stakeholders can be influenced by, or may influence, the outcome of tourism activities as performed by DMOs. Residents are considered as one of the salient stakeholders (Choi and Sirakaya 2006; Sheehan and Ritchie 2005). Several studies have examined the extent of their collaboration, power sharing, and decision-making process (Reed 1997; Sheehan and Ritchie 2005). For example, how destination developers and planners interact with locals and take residents' opinions into account when making decisions (MacKay and Campbell 2004; Gursoy and Kendall 2006). The coordination and cooperation of different stakeholders is considered to be the core competency of DMOs in achieving success in marketing their communities.

Researchers indicated that friendly encounters between residents and tourists are important to a positive destination image, to generate positive word-of-mouth communications, and to ensure local business and tourism activities success (Snaith and Haley 1999; Perdue, Long and Kang 1999). Seaton and Palmer (1997) and Young, Corsun, and Baloglu (2007) found that locals' opinions and suggestions were important to tourists' activities. Specifically, the content and quality of residents' word-of-mouth communications are influential on tourists' decisionmaking and essential for promoting local products, activities, and attractions. DMOs can implement internal marketing strategies to raise public awareness of destination activities, to gain support from the host communities, and thus to increase local involvement (Gursoy and Kendall 2006). For example, locals' support for tourism activities can be achieved by highlighting the economic benefits that host communities gained from business growth, increased job opportunities (Tosun 2002), and tourists' expenditure on local products and services (Ritchie and Inkari 2006). It is suggested that residents benefiting from tourism are more likely to engage in supportive behavior (Gursoy and Kendall 2006; Gursoy and Rutherford 2004). They are more likely to recommend what they perceive as valuable and meaningful to tourists.

Lockie (2001) indicated that local cuisine can be linked to individuals' senses of self and place. Residents' preference for their own food can also reflect their support for local economy, because gastronomy is usually associated with a destination's historic past, culture, and social and natural environment that residents usually take pride in. Restaurants are the spaces in which local culinary culture is produced and performed (Bell 2007). A distinctive style of cuisine can not only represent a group's history of reciprocal relations in society, but also stimulate individuals' perceptions of in-group and out-group memberships based on their race, class, age, and gender (Alexander 2000; Mintz and Du Bois 2002). Thus, local cuisine and culinary establishments can lead tourists to experience a unique gastronomy culture of a particular region. In this sense, local cuisine has potentials to enhance tourism development, strengthen local economy, foster the hospitality of a particular destination (du Rand et al 2003), and establish an identity of its brand.

The main purpose of the study reported in this chapter was to empirically examine residents' attitudes toward the use of local cuisine and culinary establishments in destination branding through a segmentation analysis. In general, segmentation studies are to examine characteristics and features of distinct groupings within a sample. Cluster analysis is one of the most common statistical tools for exploring the underlying structure of a given data set. Rather than assessing respondents' general responses to research questions, segmentation analysis allows researchers to explicitly examine respondents' perceptions and opinions by identifying their unique characteristics. More and more studies concerning residents' opinions have utilized the segmentation method (Pérez and Nadal 2005; Zhang, Inbakaran and Jackson 2006). It becomes essential in understanding residents' perceptions of and attitudes toward tourism activities. Williams and Lawson (2001) suggested that the advantage of the method is that it can facilitate the implementation of tourism strategies. The objectives of the study are to segment residents based on their attitudes toward perceived attractiveness, quality, and benefits of using local cuisine and culinary establishments in destination branding; and to understand the level of their interest promoting local cuisine and culinary establishments to international tourists.

Study Methods

A convenience sampling method was used in this study. The survey timeframe was from April 20 to May 10, 2007. A total of 550 questionnaires were distributed to Kaohsiung City residents above 18 years of age with a least one-year residency. First, questionnaires were delivered to students' parents through six different local schools (one elementary school, two junior high schools, and three high schools). Responses were returned in sealed envelopes to a contact person and collected by researchers. Additionally, onsite surveys were conducted at different locations of the city, such as supermarkets and shopping malls, to reach local residents. Participants were asked to fill in a self-administrated survey. Overall, 483 valid questionnaires were obtained, representing an 87.8% response rate. The survey instrument used in this study consists of five main sections: residents' demographic information, dining behavior, attitudes toward local cuisine and culinary establishments, the interest of promoting local cuisine and culinary establishments to international tourists, and recommendations of local cuisine and culinary establishments. Demographic characteristics included the length of residency, gender, marital status, age, occupation, education, and monthly income. These variables, except age, were measured as categorical variables. Respondents were asked to report their current age.

Items related to dining behavior included frequency of dining out, selection of dining places, and the expenditure on dining out.

Residents' attitudes toward using local cuisine and culinary establishments in destination marketing were measured with 16 items by using a 5-point Likert scale (from 1 = strongly disagree to 5 = strongly agree). Three main concepts were included: perceived attractiveness of local cuisine and culinary establishments; perceived quality of the quality of local cuisine and culinary establishments when making recommendations to international tourists; and perceived benefits that may arise from the development of culinary tourism. Respondents' interest of promoting local cuisine and culinary establishments to international tourists was assessed by six items based on a 5-point Likert scale (from 1 = strongly disagree to 5 = strongly agree). Data were analyzed using the SPSS 12.0 for Windows. Descriptive statistics were first used to profile the characteristics of the sampled residents. Principle components analysis using varimax rotation was first conducted to examine the hypothesized structure of the items. Four distinct factors emerged, accounting for 66.15% of the variance. Reliability tests which that Cronbach alpha values were performed on all factors to test their respective internal consistency.

Cluster analyses were performed on the resultant factors to identify groups of residents. A two-stage cluster procedure was adopted in this study. In the first step, hierarchical cluster analyses with average linkage method were used to detect the number of clusters. At the second step, the number of clusters determined in the preliminary analysis was used in K-means clustering. To further validate the groupings resulting from the cluster analyses, discriminant analyses were conducted on the cluster memberships. One-way ANOVA analyses with Student–Newman–Keuls (S–N–K) tests were employed to differentiate group differences in terms of residents' characteristics, attitudes toward local cuisine and culinary establishments, and the interest of promoting local cuisine and culinary establishments to international tourists. Study respondents were asked to write down at least one local dish with dining places that they would like to recommend to international tourists. A content analysis approach was adopted and respondents' opinions were classified into five categories: snack at night markets and food vendors, Chinese and local cuisines at Chinese restaurants, fusion cuisine at fusion restaurants, international cuisine at exotic restaurants, and delicate cuisine at fine dining restaurants. In order to gain a better understanding of residents' suggestions, data were then examined based on the groups that resulted from cluster analyses.

Study Findings

Most respondents (58.6%) lived in the city for more than 15 years and were approximately 35.15 years of age. Of the total sample, 46% were male and 53.8% female. More than half of the respondents were married (56.5%); about three-fourth of them (75%) had at least a bachelor degree; and almost half of them (46%) had a monthly income of US$1,000 or more. In addition, about 28.2% of respondents were students, 26.9% were officers, and 21.2% were business managers or sales persons. Respondents reported that they had eaten more frequently at night markets (76.8%) and fusion restaurants (50.1%). Approximately half of the respondents stated that their average weekly dining-out spending was under $30. Results also illustrated that residents had a high frequency of dining out behavior (Table 1).

The respondents' attitudes in relation to quality and attractiveness of local cuisine and culinary establishments are presented in Table 2. Results revealed that the top five positive responses are a prevalence of high-quality cuisine for international tourists ($M = 3.35$); a prevalence of high-quality culinary establishments for international tourists ($M = 3.17$); a prevalence of high-quality foodservice for international tourists ($M = 3.14$); local cuisine is attractive ($M = 3.07$); and there is an uniqueness of local cuisine to attract international tourists ($M = 3.04$). Regarding their recommendations, residents' primarily suggested cuisine at night markets and food vendors ($M = 3.74$), at fine dining restaurants ($M = 3.63$), and at Chinese restaurants ($M = 3.62$).

As presented in Table 3, 16 attitude items yielded three factors, which explained about 66.15% of variance. These three factors were labeled, respectively, as "benefits of culinary tourism development ($\partial = .91$)," "quality of foodservice management ($\partial = .87$)," and "attractiveness of local cuisine and culinary establishments ($\partial = .84$)." The total internal consistency was 0.86. The Kaiser–Meyer–Olkin measure of sampling adequacy was high at 0.85 and the Bartlett test of sphericity was 4548.34, p-value $= 0.000$, indicating an appropriate sample for factor analysis.

Three distinctive groups were revealed by the two-stage cluster analyses and supported by follow-up discriminant analyses (Table 4). Cluster 1 was named as "supportive residents" ($n = 138$), cluster 2 was named as "ambivalent residents" ($n = 145$), and cluster 3 was named as "indifferent residents" ($n = 200$). Two canonical discriminant functions were calculated. Function 1: Wilk's Lamada $= .176$, Chi-square $= 832.87$, df $= 6$, p-value $= .000$; Function 2: Wilk's Lamada $= .494$, Chi-square $= 337.90$, df $= 2$, p-value $= .000$. The classification matrices of respondents indicated that 97.7% of 483 cases were correctly classified. Based on the three specified groups of respondents, group differences in demographic variables, attitudes toward local cuisine and

Table 1. Residents' Dining Behavior

Variables	Percentage
Weekly frequency of dining out	
Breakfast	
More than 5 times	44.3
1–4 times	37.1
None	18.6
Lunch	
More than 5 times	46.4
1–4 times	42.5
None	11.1
Dinner	
More than 5 times	34.2
1–4 times	53.0
None	12.8
Snack	
More than 5 times	12.0
1–4 times	60.3
None	27.7
Main dining places	
Night markets, food vendors	76.8
Chinese restaurants	38.4
Fusion restaurants	50.1
Exotic restaurants	30.2
Fine dining restaurants	16.4
Weekly expenditure	
Under $30	50.4
31–60	29.4
61–100	8.5
101–130	6.0
131–160	2.5
Above 160	3.1

culinary establishments, and the interest of promoting the same to international tourists were performed using one-way ANOVA with S–N–K tests.

Results of one-way ANOVA analyses indicated that all factors of residents' attitudes toward local cuisine and culinary establishments were significantly different among the three groups. The indifferent residents do not consider the possible benefits gained from culinary tourism development.

Table 2. Top Ranked Residents' Attitudes and Recommendations

	Rank	Items	Mean	SD
Attitudes	1	A prevalence of high-quality cuisine for international tourists	3.35	.97
	2	A prevalence of high-quality culinary establishments for international tourists	3.17	.94
	3	A prevalence of high-quality foodservice for international tourists	3.14	.94
	4	Local cuisine is attractive	3.07	.92
	5	An uniqueness of local cuisine to attract international tourists	3.04	.98
Recommendations	1	Night markets and food vendors	3.74	.87
	2	Fine dining restaurants	3.63	.87
	3	Chinese restaurants	3.62	.80
	4	Exotic restaurants	3.51	.87
	5	Fusion restaurants	3.49	.83

They tend to have more negative attitudes than the ambivalent and supportive respondents. Additionally, the indifferent residents are reluctant to engage in activities relevant to promoting local cuisine and culinary establishments. In their perception, they may only have limited abilities to capture international tourists' attention. The supportive residents hold more positive attitudes toward local cuisine, culinary establishments, and gastronomy tourism development than the other two clusters; and the ambivalent residents are supportive of such development than the indifferent group.

Content analyses revealed that both the ambivalent and supportive groups, approximately 60% of the respondents, are more likely to recommend different types of local cuisine and culinary establishments to international tourists than the indifferent group. All these three groups prefer to suggest snacks at night markets and seafood at Chinese restaurants, although members in the indifferent group are not as highly

Table 3. Results of Factor Analysis

Factors of Attitudes	Factor Loading	Eigen Value	Variance Explained	Mean
Benefits (Cronbach's ∂ = 0.91)		4.25	26.58%	
Enhance overall tourism development	.89			4.11
Provide job opportunities	.87			4.06
Enhance economic development	.84			4.05
Local culinary establishments can become residents' recreational places	.83			4.18
Local cuisine and establishment can become tourism attractions	.78			4.07
Increase city awareness	.77			4.12
Quality (Cronbach's ∂ = 0.87)		3.31	20.66%	
A prevalence of high-quality culinary establishments for international tourists	.87			3.17
A prevalence of high-quality foodservice for international tourists	.85			3.14
Adequate English-speaking service environment such as menu, food product brand name, and food labeling	.79			2.91
Adequate English-speaking service employees	.70			2.83
A prevalence of high-quality cuisine for international tourists	.67			3.35
Attractiveness (Cronbach's ∂ = 0.84)		3.02	18.90%	
Adequate local culinary culture information	.83			2.75
Attractive local culinary campaigns	.81			2.92
Appealing local culinary culture attractions	.79			2.69

Table 3 (*Continued*)

Factors of Attitudes	Factor Loading	Eigen Value	Variance Explained	Mean
Local cuisine is attractive	.68			3.07
An uniqueness of local cuisine to attract international tourists	.59			3.04
Total variance explained			66.15%	

Table 4. One-Way ANOVA Tests among Three Clusters

	Means			F-Value	Sig.	Student–Newman–Keuls test
	Cluster 1 ($n = 138$)	Cluster 2 ($n = 145$)	Cluster 3 ($n = 200$)			
Perceived benefit	3.52	4.35	4.32	147.85	.00	2, 3 > 1[a]
Perceived quality	2.55	3.02	3.50	79.01	.00	3 > 2 > 1
Perceived attractiveness	2.66	2.20	3.56	418.55	.00	3 > 1 > 2
Recommend night markets and food vendors	3.35	3.47	4.02	26.83	.00	3 > 2 > 1
Recommend Chinese restaurants	3.30	3.65	3.83	19.28	.00	3 > 2 > 1
Recommend fusion restaurants	3.15	3.43	3.78	27.06	.00	3 > 2 > 1
Recommend exotic restaurants	3.20	3.53	3.71	15.04	.00	2, 3 > 1
Recommend fine dining restaurants	3.28	3.70	3.82	17.59	.00	2, 3 > 1
Involvement in local culinary culture development	2.98	3.36	3.66	27.61	.00	3 > 2 > 1
Proud to introduce local culinary culture	3.23	3.81	4.02	45.21	.00	3 > 2 > 1

[a]1 = indifferent cluster, 2 = ambivalent cluster, 3 = supportive cluster.

interested in participating in culinary tourism development. In other words, various kinds of snacks at night markets and seafood-based cuisine at Chinese seafood restaurants could be considered as representative local cuisine and culinary establishments of Kaohsiung City as perceived by locals, and used in branding the city with the culinary tourism theme.

Previous studies asserted that residents' attitudes toward tourism development were associated with their characteristics such as length of residency and education level (Teye, Sönmez and Sirakaya 2002). Further statistical analyses were performed to examine whether these three groups were significantly different in their demographic characteristics. Results illustrated that they were not. Most of them had a least a bachelor degree and had lived in the city for more than 15 years. Thus, in this study, attitude differences among the three groups are not related to their demographic characteristics, but are associated with perceived benefits, quality, and attractiveness of culinary tourism development.

CONCLUSION

Culinary tourism is recognized as a way to perform local culinary culture, stimulate tourism demand, and enhance destination competitiveness. This chapter reports on a study that examined residents' attitudes toward and their feelings about the use of local cuisine and culinary establishments to brand a destination and what they would like to recommend to international tourists in support of destination's gastronomy. By segmenting residents' attitudes toward the use of local cuisine and culinary establishments in destination branding, three distinct groups of residents are identified. Although these groups are similar in terms of age, gender, educational level, and length of residency, they have significantly different attitudes in using local cuisine and culinary establishments to brand the city to international tourists. By identifying specific groups of residents' attitudes toward culinary tourism development, results of the study provides the basis for a more focused approach to the planning and implementation of destination branding strategies through fostering the development of culinary tourism. Forming such an identity and creating a more appropriate image related to local food can attract the intended markets, and at the same time benefit culinary tourism development. The findings of the study confirm that snacks at local night markets and seafood-based cuisine at Chinese restaurants can serve as the important elements for building a destination brand for Kaohsiung City. Additionally, the study's findings suggest that local culinary establishments need to improve and strengthen their English-speaking services, including employees, menus, signs, and food labeling.

Prior research found that the assessment of locals' attitudes toward and perceptions of tourism is more useful than the analysis of residents' characteristics (Williams and Lawson 2001). Tourism officials and destination marketing managers with a better understanding of specific groups of residents' attitudes and perceptions are likely to achieve greater support from the locals. In particular, it is suggested that internal marketing techniques can be used to inform host communities and residents about DMOs' goals (Gursoy and Kendall 2006) and destination branding strategies. The major advantage of such approach is that it may maximize DMOs' marketing communications effectiveness. That is, the important brand message and the brand commitment of a specific tourism destination can be properly delivered to tourists by local residents. The findings of the study reported in this chapter should facilitate tourism marketing agencies of Kaohsiung City in such endeavors. They need to recognize that local cuisine and culinary establishments should be appealing to residents first. Their attitudes cannot be overlooked in the process of branding a destination. Local culinary businesses and entrepreneurs have to work together to improve the quality of local dishes, foodservice facilities, and dining environment. Moreover, local foodservice managers at all levels must fully recognize the need for improving their employees English-speaking abilities.

The study represents a beginning step toward examining residents' support for destination branding in relation to culinary tourism. As a case study, the utility of its findings may be limited by its geographic scope and the chosen methodology. Selected variables used in this investigation may not capture all attitudes of residents with respect to the use of local cuisine and culinary establishments in destination branding. Future studies should consider the use of different approaches, including qualitative techniques, to map out causal relationships between residents' attitudes and their word-of-mouth communications. For culinary tourism to play a more productive role in the success of branding destinations, there is also the need to investigate the effect of residents' attitude and their recommendations on tourists' attitudes and behavior.

Acknowledgement

This study was partially supported by the Teaching Excellence Project (KHCR 9) and by the National Science Council Project (NSC 96-2914-I-328-002-A1). The author thanks Mei-Jung Wang, David Goodman, and David Wolff for their valuable comments on the study's questionnaire.

Chapter 9

SPANISH HOLIDAY BRANDS:
Comparative Analysis of 10 Destinations

Josep-Francesc Valls, Vicenta Sierra,
Miguel Angel Bañuelos and Ignacio Ochoa
Escuela Superior Administración y Dirección de Empresas, Spain

Abridgement: This chapter analyzes the attribute associations, supplied by experts, of top 10 destination brands in Spain. Using a sample of respondents that represents the domestic tourist population, the study examined how they perceive the importance of each of the attributes when selecting a holiday destination. They are rated for all the 10 brands as a whole and for each individually. Comparisons are made between each and the average of all other brands. The application of multidimensional scale method resulted in five distinct groups or competitive sets based on the similarities and disparities of tourists' ratings of these attributes. For each, the study suggests how these sets are perceived as a whole and in comparison with each other. The chapter offers meaningful relationships between the respondents' demographic and socioeconomic characteristics and their perceived importance of the destination brands' attributes. **Keywords:** brand image; brand building; Spanish destinations.

Tourism Branding: Communities in Action
Bridging Tourism Theory and Practice, Volume 1, 119–131
Copyright © 2009 by Emerald Group Publishing Limited
All rights of reproduction in any form reserved
ISSN: 2042-1443/doi:10.1108/S2042-1443(2009)0000001011

INTRODUCTION

Brand building as a scientific objective has undergone important changes over the past few years. Brands have gone from being considered just another product element to being managed as a strategic asset. The classic brand management model is based on having a team in charge of preparing a marketing plan and coordinating with sales and production. From the classic point of view, the brand refers to many things: a product offer from a known source (Kotler, Jain and Maesincee 2002), a product adding new dimensions and differentiating it from other goods and services aimed at satisfying the same need (Keller 2003), an intangible yet critical component of what a company means, a set of promises, and a source of value added for consumers. Kapferer (1997) identifies eight brand functions: identification, practice, assurance, optimization, characterization, continuity, hedonism, and ethics.

BRANDING AS A STRATEGIC ASSET

Aaker and Joachimsthaler (2000) describe a transition from the classic model to a new one. This new model, concurrently with operative elements, emphasizes strategy and has, as a result, a much broader playing field. It is based on sales and brand identity—and, beyond the latter, on experience (Keller 2003). The identity and experience referred to by Keller (2003) leads to a brand equity concept, which was first introduced by Farquhar (1989). Based on his proposal, the conceptualization of brand equity has been enriched by new perspectives. Lassar, Mittal and Sharma (1995) identified five dimensions of brand equity: performance, value, social image, credibility, and commitment. Aaker and Joachimsthaler (2000) considered brand equity as being made up by the assets related to the brand name or symbol, which add or take away value from a product or service. As such, the assets they refer to are notoriety, perceived quality, brand associations, and brand loyalty. Another important perspective is that a brand's power is in the mind of consumers, in everything they have learnt, sensed, seen, and heard about the brand over time. Therefore, brand equity has been associated with profitability and differential effect observed in consumer response after discovering the brand as measured by its notoriety and image (Keller 1993).

In 2002, Davis and Dunn referred to a holistic concept that consists of all employees at all levels of the corporation working cohesively and consistently to support the promises the brand makes to all its audiences. They understood that brand building must be tackled from a strategic perspective and as a long-term process. They argued that this focus was possible when, among other things, the business was aligned with the brand strategy, and management assumed a serious and explicit commitment to build it. In fact, many companies already recognize that their brands are, along with their clients and human resources, their most important assets. This strategic-level thinking allows them to manage the brand as an indispensable requirement to obtain clients and profit. Dealing specifically with destination brands, Gnoth (2002a, 2002b) identifies them as umbrella brands that permit leveraging everything generated underneath. Like Papadopoulos and Heslop (2002), Gnoth sees the tourism industry as a system in which the experiences afforded by destinations as well as by their products and services must be included. As such, he proposes a destination brand development model consisting of four levels. They are the main attraction, the basic tourist services that provide the experience, other industries that contribute to tourism at the destination with primary and secondary products, and other products and services that leverage their image along with that of the destination. All four levels allow for the definitive and semantic expression of the experience provided.

Bedbury and Fenichell (2003) interpret branding as a portfolio of meanings. A brand is a psychological concept and results from a synoptic process within consumers' mind in the shape of content sponges, images, sensations, and experiences. At the same time, it must be able to contain relevant values for each intended audiences. The destination, as a supplier of experiences, synthesizes all of these values. The experiential marketing concept (Schmitt 1999) typifies brands as an integral and holistic experience, which can be created by cultivating sensorial, affective, and creative relation-ships, as along with a lifestyle. Bearing in mind the classic and contemporary conceptions as well as the conditioning factors projected by the competitive environment, a destination brand is perceived to be a global, stable, and high value-added support mechanism. It is fixed in people's minds, identifying and representing the products, values, feelings, experiences, lifestyles, and business groups that make up the destination in such a way as to clearly differentiate it from the competition. It brings it closer to its various audiences, offering them reliable information. It is the external reflection captured by the target audience of everything specific to that destination, including qualities and attributes that may be traced to its roots and its most intimate aspects. It is a bridge making the destination intelligible, suggestive, and an accomplice for the target audience. As destinations have become ample spaces in which to have experiences and fulfill tourists' needs, brands must respond accordingly. Satisfying the needs is no longer generic, standardized, and universal. It has to be specific, personalized, and particular. The destination brand must be closely linked to the relevant values of its consumers.

Consumers analyze brands both rationally and emotionally (Urde 1999). It is important to balance the values and meanings a brand wants to embody with those its audience interprets and perceives it possessing. However, despite the brand being a strategic platform to interact with customers, it cannot become an unconditional response to everything demanded by customers, since not everything that they want is necessarily what is best to build a strong brand (Urde 1999). According to Keller's (2003) model, building a strong brand implies four sequential steps: ensuring that the public identifies and relates it to a product category or specific need (brand identity); strengthening its meaning in consumers' mind by means of the strategic linking of tangible and intangible associations with certain properties (brand meaning); evoking consumer response regarding its identification and meaning (brand response); and converting this response into an intense, active, and loyal relationship between it and consumers (brand relationships).

Study Objectives and Methods

This chapter reports a study that focused on the first of the brand equity steps. To ensure that tourists identify a destination brand and relate it to its competitive set, its building process begins at two distinct levels: selecting the most noteworthy attributes with which tourists identify the whole, and understanding their preference structure and comparative vision they have regarding the competing destinations. After this first step, brand building requires a strategy that takes into consideration three factors: the value offered (functional, emotional, and differentiating), brand architecture (based on segmentation), and communication plan (bearing in mind its positioning, strategy, creativity, and investment).

The study has two objectives. First, it identifies important attributes of 10 destination brands in Spain and examines the degree of importance attached to the attributes by for Spaniards when they choose these destinations for their holiday needs. In branding terms, these attributes are the associations that tourists perceive of the destination brands. Second, it compares the 10 brands with regard to these associations. The brands are Andalusia, Catalonia, Valencia, Galicia, the Basque Country, the Balearic Islands, the

Canary Islands, Castilla-La Mancha, Castilla-Leon, and Madrid. Given that brand equity arises from the target audience's mental perception, a qualitative study involving tourism experts was first conducted to allow the identification of possible brand associations and to explore their meanings for tourists. The experts were presented with an open list detailing an exhaustive number of attributes, of which 13 were chosen and were grouped into two categories: eight relating to theme and setting and five relating to infrastructure and services. A quantitative study then followed with a survey of 1,154 telephone interviews. Respondents came from Madrid (290), Andalusia (230), Catalonia (230), Valencia (135), Castilla-Leon (115), and the Basque Country (100). The respondents from these regions represent 70% of all domestic tourists in Spain. The data was analyzed using SPSS/PC and the Answer Tree application.

The subsample for each region is proportional to its percentage of the actual Spanish population. The sample's age is broken down as follows: 20–30 (241), 30–40 (252), 40–50 (215), 50–60 (175), and 60–75 years old (217). The age distribution is proportional to that of all Spain. The respondents' average income is $1,700 per month. Both in the entire sample and in each subsample, there is a 1:1 ratio between men and women. Only those respondents who have taken a holiday in the last three years are taken into account. All types of holiday travel are considered, except for weekend getaways to holiday homes. Each respondent in the survey was first asked to rate the importance of the 13 attributes when choosing a destination (from $0 =$ not at all important to $10 =$ most important). They were then asked to rate 3 of the 10 destinations ($0 =$ terrible, $10 =$ optimal). Although the objective was to analyze tourists' perception regarding these destinations, it was decided to only ask about three, given the difficulty of keeping the respondents' attention and their ability to discriminate. Each of the destinations was presented as one whole brand and compared to the other nine. The study did not take into account the quality and quantity of smaller destinations or sub-brands within each of the 10 brands.

Comparative Appraisal of Individual Brands

Figure 1 presents the average ratings of importance for the 13 attributes. They are grouped by theme and setting and by infrastructure and services. The scale used ranges from 0 to 10. Figure 1 shows that the hospitality of local residents tops the list for Spanish tourists when choosing a destination brand, followed by good weather, gastronomic offering, and cultural offering. In Table 1, each of the attribute was associated with a profile of

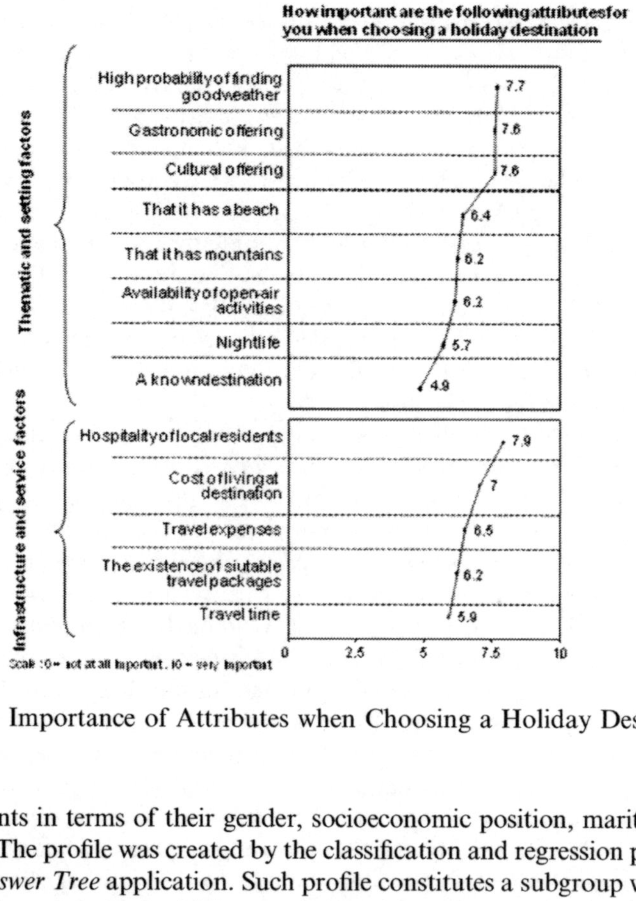

How important are the following attributes for you when choosing a holiday destination

Thematic and setting factors

- High probability of finding good weather — 7.7
- Gastronomic offering — 7.6
- Cultural offering — 7.6
- That it has a beach — 6.4
- That it has mountains — 6.2
- Availability of open-air activities — 6.2
- Nightlife — 5.7
- A known destination — 4.9

Infrastructure and service factors

- Hospitality of local residents — 7.9
- Cost of living at destination — 7
- Travel expenses — 6.5
- The existence of siutable travel packages — 6.2
- Travel time — 5.9

Scale : 0 = not at all important. 10 = very important

Figure 1 Importance of Attributes when Choosing a Holiday Destination.

respondents in terms of their gender, socioeconomic position, marital status, and age. The profile was created by the classification and regression procedure in the *Answer Tree* application. Such profile constitutes a subgroup within the sample that gives it the highest rating and has the most appreciation for the attribute. For example, the global mean for "night life" attribute is 5.72, but for single respondents under the age of 30, regardless of gender and social class, the importance of this attribute rises to 7.43.

The respondents' rating of each attribute for each brand was also analyzed and compared with the average of all other nine brands. Andalusia scores higher than the average for beach (6.9 vs. 6.4), mountains (6.9 vs. 6.4), open-air activities (6.5 vs. 6.1), night life (6.8 vs. 5.7), and known destination (6.4 vs. 4.9). It is very close to the average in terms of travel packages (6.2 vs. 6.3) and travel time (5.9 vs. 6.0) but is below the average for high probability of finding a good climate (7.1 vs. 7.7), gastronomic offering (7.1 vs. 7.6), cultural offering (7.2 vs. 7.6), hospitality

Table 1. Brand Attributes with a Profile of the Highest Rating

Global Mean		A Profile of the Highest Rating
Travel time	5.91	Married → Female → between 40 and 50 years: Mean = 6.77 ($n = 77$)
Travel packages	6.20	Middle class → Female → Under 30 years: Mean = 6.86 ($n = 76$)
Travel expenses	6.49	Middle class → Single → Under 30 years: Mean = 7.06 ($n = 89$)
Cost of living at destination	7.03	Under 30 years → Female: Mean = 7.65 ($n = 96$)
Hospitality of local residents	7.92	Married → Middle Class → between 40 and 50 years: Mean = 8.38 ($n = 73$)
Known destination	4.88	Over 30 years → Married: Mean = 5.29 ($n = 533$)
Night life	5.72	Single → Under 30 years: Mean = 7.43 ($n = 150$)
Open-air activities	6.15	Under 40 years → Single : Mean = 6.79 ($n = 234$) Between 30 and 40 years → Married → Female: Mean = 6.82 ($n = 122$)
Mountains	6.24	Over 30 years → Middle class → Female: Mean = 6.66 ($n = 195$)
Beach	6.45	Female → Over 50 years: Mean = 7.14 ($n = 96$)
Cultural offering	7.61	Over 40 years → Female → Middle class: Mean = 8.02 ($n = 111$)
Gastronomic offering	7.61	Married → Over 50 years : Mean = 7.82 ($n = 186$) Married → Middle Class → Between 30 and 60 years → Female: Mean = 7.83 ($n = 195$)
High probability of good weather	7.69	Middle class → Female → Married: Mean = 8.04 ($n = 275$) Upper and upper middle class → Over 50 years: Mean = 8.02 ($n = 93$)

of local residents (7.6 vs. 7.9), cost of living (6.2 vs. 7), and travel expenses (6.1 vs. 6.5). Valencia scores higher than the average for mountains (6.2 vs. 6.0), open-air activities (6.5 vs. 6.3), night life (7 vs. 5.7), known destination (6.6 vs. 4.9), travel packages (6.5 vs. 6.2), and travel time (6.3 vs. 5.9).

It almost equals the average for beach (6.4 vs. 6.6) and is below the average in terms of good weather (7.4 vs. 7.7), gastronomic offering (7.1 vs. 7.6), cultural offering (6.8 vs. 7.6), hospitality (7.1 vs. 7.9), cost of living (6.3 vs. 7.0), and travel expenses (6.1 vs. 6.5).

Castilla-La Mancha is generally very close to the average for most of the attributes. It scores higher than the average in terms of known destination (6.0 vs. 4.9) and travel time (6.5 vs. 5.9). It is slightly below the average in terms of good weather (6.4 vs. 7.7), gastronomic offering (7.4 vs. 7.6), cultural offering (7.1 vs. 7.6), hospitality (7.6 vs. 7.9), cost of living (6.4 vs. 7.9), travel expenses (6.3 vs. 6.5), and travel packages (5.5 vs. 6.2). Madrid scores higher than the average for cultural offering (8.2 vs. 7.6), mountains (6.7 vs. 6.2), open-air activities (6.4 vs. 6.2), night life (7.6 vs. 5.7), known destination (7.0 vs. 4.9), travel packages (6.4 vs. 6.2), and travel time (6.9 vs. 5.9); it is below the average for good weather (6.4 vs. 7.7), hospitality (7.5 vs. 7.9), cost of living (6.0 vs. 7.0), and travel expenses (6.2 vs. 6.5). The Canary Islands score higher than the average in terms of good weather (8.0 vs. 7.7), beach (7.1 vs. 6.4), mountains (6.8 vs. 6.2), open-air activities (6, 8 vs. 6.2), night life (7.0 vs. 5.7), known destination (5.6 vs. 4.9), travel packages (6.7 vs. 6.2), and travel time (6.1 vs. 5.9). It falls below the average in terms of gastronomic offering (6.6 vs. 7.6), cultural offering (6.3 vs. 7.6), hospitality (7.5 vs. 7.9), cost of living (6.1 vs. 7.0), and travel expenses (5.9 vs. 6.1).

Castilla-Leon scores higher than the average for mountains (6.8 vs. 6.2), open-air activities (6.3 vs. 6.2), night life (6.1 vs. 5.7), known desti-nation (5.9 vs. 4.9), and travel time (6.2 vs. 5.9). It almost matches the average for gastronomic offering (7.6 vs. 7.7) but is below the average in terms of good weather (6.4 vs. 7.7), cultural offering (7.3 vs. 7.6), hospitality (7.3 vs. 7.9), cost of living (6.3 vs. 7), travel expenses (6.1 vs. 6.5), and travel packages (5.8 vs. 6.2). Galicia scores higher than the average for gastronomic offering (8.5 vs. 7.6), beach (6.8 vs. 6.4), mountains (7.3 vs. 6.2), open-air activities (6.5 vs. 6.2), night life (6.3 vs. 5.7), and known destination (6.3 vs. 4.9). It almost equals the average in cultural offering (7.6 vs. 7.59), hospitality (8.0 vs. 7.9), travel packages (6.3 vs. 6.2), and travel time (5.9 vs. 5.7). It falls just below the average in terms of good weather (6.6 vs. 7.7).

Catalonia scores higher than the average for mountains (7.2 vs. 6.2), open-air activities (6.7 vs. 6.2), night life (6.8 vs. 5.7), and known destination (6.0 vs. 4.9). It almost equals the average in cultural offering (7.4 vs. 7.6), beach (6.3 vs. 6.4), travel packages (6.3 vs. 6.2), and travel time (6.0 vs. 5.9). It is below the average in terms of good weather (6.8 vs. 7.7), gastronomic offering (7.3 vs. 7.6), hospitality (6.4 vs. 7.9), cost of living (6.1 vs. 7.0), and travel expenses (6.0 vs. 6.5). The Balearic Islands score higher than the average for beach (7.0 vs. 6.4), night life (6.7 vs. 5.7), known destination (5.6 vs. 4.9), and travel time (6.3 vs. 5.9). They almost equal the average for good weather (7.6 vs. 7.7), mountains (6.4 vs. 6.2), open-air activities (6.4 vs. 6.2), and travel packages (6.4 vs. 6.2) and are below the average in terms of gastronomic offering (6.5 vs. 7.6), cultural offering (6.4 vs. 7.6), hospitality (6.8 vs. 7.9), cost of living (5.8 vs. 7.0), and travel expenses (5.6 vs. 6.5). The Basque Country scores higher than the average for gastronomic offering (8.2 vs. 7.6), mountains (7.3 vs. 6.2), and known destination (5.8 vs. 4.9). It almost equals the average in beach (6.6 vs. 6.4), open-air activities (6.4 vs. 6.2), night life (5.9 vs. 5.7), and travel time (6.0 vs. 5.9). It is below the average in terms of good weather (5.9 vs. 7.7), cultural offering (7.0 vs. 7.6), hospitality (7.0 vs. 7.9), cost of living (5, 8 vs. 7.0), travel expenses (5.7 vs. 6.5), and travel packages (5.8 vs. 6.2).

Competitive Sets among the Brands

Multidimensional scaling method and cluster analysis were applied to examine how the 10 brands were similar or different in the totality of the attributes as perceived by tourists. The examination includes 12 of the 13 attributes, omitting that of beach because it is not common among all destinations. The multidimensional scaling technique produces the perceptual map of survey respondents with respect to the 12 attributes by means of generating two orthogonal dimensions (Figure 2). The graphical representation is statistically significant (RSQ = 0.97747 and Stress = 0.06390). The brands closest to each other in Figure 2 are those that survey respondents perceived as similar with respect to the 12 attributes. Five groups emerged: Canary Islands, Balearic Islands, and Valencia; Andalusia and Catalonia; Castilla-La Mancha, Castilla-Leon, and the Basque Country; Madrid; and Galicia. In essence, each of the first three groups constitutes a competitive set of brands. To verify the grouping obtained from the multidimensional scaling, cluster analysis was carried out by means of the Ward Method. The results confirmed the graphic finding.

Table 2 details the average scores of each attribute by the five groups of destinations. A bold-face number is the highest score among the five groups for the attribute (across each row), while an italic number is the lowest score. When they choose the brands in the first group (Canary Islands, Balearic Islands, and Valencia), domestic tourists attach greater importance to beach, good weather, and travel packages than when they choose other four

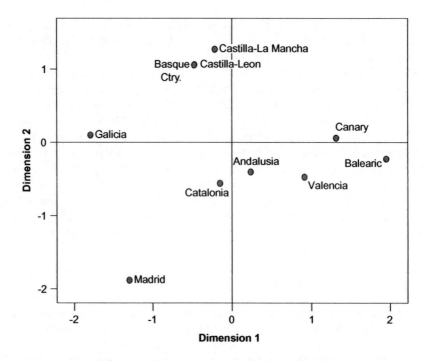

Figure 2 Multidimensional Scaling Results.

groups. For the first group brands, mountains, cultural offering, and gastronomic offering are the least important in the minds of domestic tourists. When they choose destinations in the second (Andalusia and Catalonia) and third (Castilla-La Mancha, Castilla-Leon, and the Basque Country) groups, none of the 12 attributes are perceived as important as when they choose other destinations. Hospitality of locals and open-air activities are actually perceived less important for the second group destinations than for others, and travel packages, known destination, night life, open-air activities, and good weather are the least important for the third group destinations. Several attributes are perceived as more important when choosing Madrid than other destinations. They include travel time, expenses, known destination, night life, and cultural offering. The attribute of cost of living is the least important for Madrid. Cost of living, hospitality of locals, mountains, and gastronomic offering are perceived as more important when choosing Galicia than other destinations; travel time and

Table 2. Groups of Destinations

Attribute	G1	G2	G3	G4	G5
The travel time required to get there	6.25	6.02	6.20	**6.90**	*5.73*
Holiday packages	**6.58**	6.31	*5.71*	6.37	6.28
Travel expenses	5.87	6.06	6.05	**6.23**	*5.96*
Cost of living at the destination	6.06	6.15	6.18	*6.04*	**6.38**
Hospitality of local residents	7.16	*6.99*	7.29	7.51	**7.97**
Known destination	5.92	6.23	*5.90*	**6.98**	6.34
Night life	6.87	6.81	*5.90*	**7.63**	6.30
Open-air activities	6.57	*6.62*	*6.24*	6.37	6.47
Mountains	*6.40*	6.96	6.83	6.73	**7.33**
Cultural offering	*6.48*	7.32	7.16	**8.16**	7.50
Gastronomic offering	*6.72*	7.23	7.72	7.60	**8.54**
High probability of finding good weather	**7.69**	6.94	*6.23*	6.44	6.61
Beach	**6.92**	*6.59*	6.63	.	6.79

G1: Canary Islands, Balearic Islands, and Valencia; G2: Andalusia and Catalonia; G3: Castilla-La Mancha, Castilla-Leon, and Basque Contry; G4: Madrid; G5: Galicia.

expenses are the least important. The generally high importance assigned to gastronomic offering can be explained by the fact that there is no seasonal effect, and it does not exclude other theme-related attributes such as beach, mountains, open-air activities, and cultural offering. It is noted that beach and mountains are mutually exclusive, which explains some of their lower ratings. Within the infrastructure and services categories of attributes, the most highly rated are hospitality of locals and cost of living at destination.

The importance ratings were also analyzed in relation to the respondents' community of origin, age, marital status, and socioeconomic characteristics. In addition to the results given in Table 1, the study found that tourists from Castilla-Leon, Madrid, and the Basque Country give most importance to beach and good weather. The gastronomic offering, while a highly rated attribute in general, is especially highly valued by those from Andalusia and Valencia but least valued by those from Castilla. Tourists from Valencia and Catalonia give less importance to beach but more to mountains than those from other communities. However, this discrepancy between mountains and beach is less pronounced among tourists from Andalusia, most probably due to the region having a greater balance in terms of coastal and inland features. The importance given to infrastructure is similar among respondents from all regions, although there are some exceptions. Those residing in Andalusia are more demanding in terms of all the attributes, while those from Valencia and Castilla are the least. Tourists from Madrid and Catalonia rate the infrastructure and service attributes similarly. The little importance given by Catalonians to travel time is worth noting. Spaniards who live in the outer-lying communities (Basque Country, Andalusia, and Catalonia) give more importance to cost-related attributes such as cost of living at destinations, expenses, and packages. All age groups are in agreement with the three most highly rated attributes: good weather, gastronomic offering, and cultural offering. For the younger audience, night life is the fourth most important attribute after weather, gastronomic offering, and cultural offering. The importance of a known destination is inversely related to age: the younger audience wants to travel to new places, while the older audience prefers places they have already been to. In general, the upper-middle class group gives a slightly lower-than-average rating to every attribute, while the middle class gives a slightly higher-than-average rating. In terms of marital status, singles give greater importance to open-air activities and night life than the married respondents. They are similar in rating other attributes.

CONCLUSION

The first and most important step in branding destinations is to understand how tourists perceive their attributes that are important to their decision-making. This chapter reports a study that examined 13 attributes of 10 destination brands from the perspective of domestic tourists in Spain. The findings include how tourists rate the importance of each of the 13 attributes for all destinations combined (Figure 1) and for each individual destination in comparison with the average of all others. Five distinct groups or competitive sets of destinations are identified based on the similarities and disparities of tourists' ratings of these attributes (Figure 2). The study has also discovered, for each of the attributes, how these groups of destination brands are perceived as a whole and in comparison with each other (Table 2). By linking these findings to tourists' demographic and socio-economic characteristics, the study has revealed the most desirable segment for each attribute (Table 1) and how the importance ratings vary by the respondents' characteristics. The findings form a reliable foundation for these destinations to move to the next stage of building stronger brands for their communities. With the knowledge of its relative strengths and weaknesses in each attribute, a destination can develop a more effective positioning strategy for its brand and target the segments of tourists most appreciative of what the brand has to offer.

Chapter 10

BRANDING SPAIN'S TOURISM MIRACLE (1959–1979)

Julio Aramberri
Drexel University, USA

Abridgement: This chapter aims at casting some doubts on the idea that branding techniques can be easily adopted by destination management organizations. They lack many of the tools that have proved successful in marketing most goods and services. To shed some light on the issue, the chapter focuses on the imaging/branding policies of the Spanish National Tourism Organization between 1959 and 1979. If measured by the inflow of international tourists to the country, they should be deemed extremely well implemented. However, it is difficult to reach this conclusion. The study examines Spanish poster production—one of the most efficient promotional tools of the time—and draws some lessons on how it is possible to be successful in spite of their destination marketing organizations. **Keywords:** branding; Spain; destination marketing organization; posters; cognitive dissonance.

INTRODUCTION

Tourism can make a sizeable contribution to economic growth under the right circumstances. Spain is perhaps the best-known case. Between 1960

Tourism Branding: Communities in Action
Bridging Tourism Theory and Practice, Volume 1, 133–147
Copyright © 2009 by Emerald Group Publishing Limited
All rights of reproduction in any form reserved
ISSN: 2042-1443/doi:10.1108/S2042-1443(2009)0000001012

and today, the country left behind its past as an underdeveloped nation and climbed to a top position in the world economy. One may make a good case that its tourism (both domestic and international) and its impact on several other economic sectors such as agriculture, construction, and transportation played a substantial role in this outcome. Tourism development in Spain came unplanned but was not fortuitous (Galiana and Timón 2006). The country had made a name for itself among many adventurous 19th century tourists. At that time, it vied with some other Mediterranean areas including Greece, Southern Italy, and the Balkans as an unmapped, wild South with its bullfighters, its dusky beauties, and its turbulent lovers prone to sudden outbursts of deadly passion. The country and its people definitely struck a romantic chord in the collective imagery of other more phlegmatic societies of Northern Europe.

However, for all its wild glamour, Spain had been unable to attract big numbers of tourists before the 1960s. The aristocratic and moneyed elites of imperial Russia or of the Austro-Hungarian monarchy would prefer the Venice Lido or Istria for their summer holidays. The British gentry hovered around their own country or closer European destinations. Once the World War I wiped out most of the former, the interwar leisured classes plus the beautiful and "ugly" Americans of the period contributed to the success of the French Côte d'Azur and, in a lower key, to that of the Italian Riviera. Spanish resorts like San Sebastián or Santander were only pale domestic reflections of Nice, Rapallo-Portofino, or Biarritz.

Spain's later tourism success was based on other social groups and on different demands. After the World War II, paid vacations became part of the Western European social compact that has since been known as the Welfare State. With free time in their hands and increasing disposable income in their pockets, millions of Europeans were ready to leave home every year. Many stayed close, but an available fleet of discarded war aircraft made it possible for Northern Europeans to travel much further away to lands where the sun always shone and the atmosphere was warm and energizing (Čavlek 2004; Gaviria 1975, 1996). In some of them, additionally, prices were so favorable that it was often cheaper to spend a vacation there than at home. During the second half of the 20th century, among those destinations the most cost effective in the Mediterranean were found in Spain. It had a price edge over France and Italy and, compared to Greece or the Balkans, it had a head start and was comfortably away from the Iron Curtain that had fallen on Eastern Europe.

In the mid-1950s, after two centuries of decadence, Spain's leading elites were eager to catch up with the wave of economic growth that was swarming all through Western Europe. Until then, all previous attempts to turn the Spanish economy had failed (Velarde 2001). In the 19th century, the country had seen its former vast empire melt away. Since the Napoleonic wars the mainland had been unable to stop internal political turmoil and had reached an economic nadir. Even though modern capitalism made some inroads in Catalonia and in the Basque country, Spanish society had a recessive social structure with an overwhelming majority of peasants; a pesky unfair distribution of land ownership; over-protected industries; small and bureaucratic provincial towns unable to sustain a middle class that could provide an active market for industrial growth; a rigged electoral system that mostly limited the political franchise to the well-to-do; an army trained and ready to fight for the sustainability of this social order; and all of that topped by the iron ideological control of the Catholic church. In a nutshell, Spain was the spitting image of what has been called oligarchic capitalism (Baumol, Litan and Schramm 2007).

Indeed, many forces had opposed this state of affairs over time. The Spanish "long" 19th century (1808–1939) had seen three civil wars, a couple of revolutions, the end and the restoration of the Bourbon monarchy plus its end all over again, two republics, and countless *pronunciamientos* (pronouncements) that reflected an overall decaying economy, growing social tensions, and an increasingly unstable political system. General Franco's dictatorship (1939–1975) made no bones about its determination to sustain the oligarchic structure lock, stock, and barrel (Anderson 1970). The initial period of the regime, until 1959, catered to the interests of traditional elites securing their privileged control of the paltry national market and stifling at the same time any demand for an open economy and for democracy. This period of so-called autarchy came to a dead end in the second half of the 1950s. "By [then] ... problems had reached crisis proportions. There was high level of inflation, the value of the peseta was in decline outside of Spain, and balance-of-payments deficit, coupled with the lack of foreign-exchange reserves, threatened to bankrupt the country" (Salmon 1991:3).

In Spanish history, under similar circumstances, bells usually tolled a temporary end for authoritarian solutions and the beginning of a new cycle of turbulence. However, in post-1945 Europe, the country had new opportunities. Even though Spanish elites had traditionally favored hard-shelled nationalism, they could now perceive that integration in the international economy offered a better chance to preserve their future.

Most Western European countries were registering quick growth by embracing free trade. The Treaty of Rome that gave birth to the European

Economic Community was signed in 1957, and Spanish elites understood that this was the mother of all opportunities to engage in the international bonanza. If further proof was needed, in 1958 France fought recession by opening its markets instead of barricading itself behind penalizing tariffs. Spain, seeing its 1959 foreign exchange reserves go down to US$8 million whereas its debts amounted to nearly $60 million, took good note. In 1959, it implemented a Stabilization Plan (Estefanía 1998; Rodríguez 2007) that became extremely successful. Between 1959 and 1973 "[a]mong the member states of the OECD, only Japan enjoyed faster and more sustained growth ... Spain's gross domestic product, calculated in constant 1970 prices, expanded at an average annual rate of 7.5 percent between 1961 and 1973" (Harrison 1985:144).

The new policy relied amply on the performance of the foreign sector of the Spanish economy. Traditionally the country had been plagued by balance-of-payments deficits that prevented, among other things, machinery imports and technology transfers (Tamames 1968). Now the vicious circle of deficits/low technology/underdevelopment was broken at the root. Not because of overnight improvements in the productivity of agriculture or of manufacturing, but because Spain could now turn to new sources of foreign exchange that would subsequently finance its take-off. The model was not too different from the path to growth followed by other successful developing countries over the past 50 years. It showed, however, that import-substitution and protection of the national market through tariffs, those decades-old staples of economic orthodoxy, could be advantageously replaced by export-led trade and services as the main lever for growth.

In spite of the reluctance of Spanish academics to acknowledge the fact, receipts from incoming foreign tourism played an important role in this development. The Spanish National Tourism Organization (SNTO, used here as shorthand for the many different names it has been given over time) devoted sizeable budgets and displayed an impressive battery of promotional tools, at the time mostly brochures and posters, to reach the proposed end. One might think that, given the outcome, the SNTO strategy duly met its goal. However, a closer look at it should give way to a more nuanced judgment.

BRANDING SPAIN'S MIRACLE

The Spanish case did not follow the same path of other countries in implementing its export-led model for economic development. Inflows of foreign direct investment did not grow significantly until the late 1960s. Foreign credit to Spanish companies passed from $40 to 253 million between 1964 and 1972, whereas foreign direct investment went from $79 to 275 million in the same period. However, foreign investment in real estate was much more impressive—outgrowing foreign direct investment and increasing seven times between 1965 and 1974 (Vidal Villa 1981). A significant, though not easily quantifiable, fraction of these latter inflows financed hotel and residential projects linked to tourism. In total, all kinds of foreign investments increased 26 times between 1959 and 1973 (Harrison 1985).

The Role of Tourism

Two unconventional exports solidified Spanish foreign reserves. One was migrant labor. During the 1960s, between one and two million people left Spain in search of work in Western Europe (Temprano 1981). They were estimated to be around 20% of Spain's agricultural labor force and 12.5% of the industrial working class (Harrison 1985). The amount of their remittances home is not easy to appraise. One source (Fontana and Nadal 1976) reckons that between 1962 and 1971 they covered a yearly average of 7.9% in balance-of-payments deficit. The other largely positive item in foreign exchange was tourism receipts. The 1961 mission of the International Bank for Reconstruction and Development (later known as The World Bank) summarized a number of economic policy objectives, and significantly devoted a whole chapter to the role of international tourism portrayed as an already thriving economic sector. Between 1951 and 1960, both the number of international arrivals and the income derived from their trips had trebled, and according to the mission this was just the beginning. The IBRD's (International Bank for Reconstruction and Development) wide-ranging advice was clear: bet on your main comparative advantages. As opposed to conventional wisdom, those advantages rested for a sizeable part on services, notably in tourism sectors. If the strategy was successful, foreign money would flow in, later helping to jump-start the rest of the economy. Spain's numerous cultural attractions, its beach products, and its price level bode well for laying a wager on tourism, the mission surmised.

In its text, the mission stressed the need to let tourism develop according to market orthodoxy, to modernize its equipments, and to start reducing administrative controls. It also recommended the adoption of an improved statistical system (IBRD 1963). Most of the advice was eagerly embraced by the government and its then minister for Information and Tourism, Manuel

Fraga Iribarne. The guidelines of his tourism policies followed closely on the IBRD's footsteps (Fraga 1964). Over the next 13 years, the IBRD prophecy would quickly fulfill itself. From 1961 to 1973, international tourist flows grew nearly 5 times (to 34.6 million) and receipts over 10 times (to $3 billion), an impressive accomplishment (Harrison 1985:155).

All those foreign receipts helped to cover balance-of-payments deficits in a significant way. The Spanish economic "miracle" thus owed much of its luster to the development of international and domestic tourism; and both have remained as crucial items in its national accounts until today. The new policies did not transpire without a number of tensions among the Spanish economic elites, both within and without the dictatorship. According to Anderson (1970), one could tally three main currents within Franco's camp: establishment falangists, structuralists, and neo-liberals. It was this last group that won the political battle. They were a collection of liberal economists or development technocrats (*desarrollistas* in the Spanish lingo of the times) that had close links to the main financial institutions and to the Catholic, conservative Opus Dei. For them, lingering within the national borders amounted to missing the train of European growth. Protectionism nurtured inefficiency and excessive governmental regulation often hampered the development of industries that produced at a comparative cost advantage. Similar tensions reverberated within the exiled opposition. In the background, however, a silent majority of Spaniards did not disagree with the new social covenant that the dictatorship offered—enjoy the advantages of economic growth and leave political subtleties in our hands. International tourism would help to make Spain truly different (Pack 2006).

How to explain this successful path to a modern economy after so many centuries of stagnation? As has been pointed out, it was due to an export-led model solidly based on the expansion of the tourism industry. Today it would be difficult to deny its appropriateness. However, this success story should not prevent a discussion of its details, especially of the way in which Spain projected its image, or the way in which it tried to brand itself, even if the word could not be found in the language of the time. In a nutshell, the thesis in this chapter will be that the Spanish model thrived in spite of its branding techniques. If accurate, this hypothesis should give some pause to the idea that destination branding has become the decisive tool in tourism success.

The Role of Branding

Branding has an already long history. Many goods were branded centuries ago, but the modern use of the technique dates from the beginning of mass production and consumption, that is, the era conventionally known as Fordism. The recent focus on the subject has been contemporary with the process of globalization—that is, the economic drive in increasing world integration through the reduction of barriers to international flows of capital and labour (Wolf 2004:15). Globalization, therefore, means than a great number of goods are produced for international markets—so customers in different countries and cultures have to be able to identify those products in an environment that becomes more competitive by the day (Kapferer 1994).

There are good reasons for branding, both on the supply and the demand sides (Keller 1998). Above all, brands contribute additional equity to makers of well-branded products—this equity being the difference in price between non-branded or generic goods and branded ones (Aaker 1991). There is a second reason. To some extent brands also allow companies to influence consumer decision making. As long as they maintain a clear level of quality or, as is usually said, provide a satisfactory experience, they can secure loyalty from their customers. The flipside of the coin is that branding requires big investments in promotion, advertising, and crisis control. However, this weakness can be seen as strength when one considers that entry barriers for new competitors also rise.

From the consumer point of view, brands offer definite advantages. In the real world, the textbook rational consumer that gathers huge amounts of information before making a decision does not exist. Satisfactory experiences with a brand, as well as word-of-mouth, advertising, the Web and Web 2.0, and other sources of information, will often lead consumers to conduct their own research and trust the products offered by their provider of choice. Additionally, in many cases consumption of brands offers rewards in terms of status. They create a feeling of belonging to an exclusive group of peers, although not all consumed brands have to be luxury ones. Some authors consider that this emotional link between the brand and the consumer is the most important aspect of the technique. Trust, emotions, and a sense of community are, in their views, the prime consumer mover (Cai 2007).

Branding has been mostly used to sell products and services. In the world of tourism, airlines, hotel chains, tour operators, even travel agents have successfully used branding techniques (Morgan and Pritchard 2000). With an eye on their positive outcomes, other actors have started using them to increase business. Over the past few years, a growing number of destinations have thus tried to establish their own brands. The trend seems to grow by the month and the amounts of money spent follow a steep upside curve. Will branding fulfill the expectations? It has often been stressed that destinations and travel-related companies belong to different bestiaries. To start with, destinations cannot easily extricate themselves from being identified with nation-states (Anholt 2002, 2005, 2006; Lee, Lee and Lee 2005). When asked about where they vacationed last time, many tourists will say China, France, Thailand, or the United States, if they do not wax even more general. "I went to Europe"; "We toured Southeast Asia"; and "Island-hopping in the Caribbean". It is obvious that they did not. They went to some resort, or covered some places in a region, or visited a few towns in a number of countries, but in everyday language they take a shortcut through nations, geographical areas, even continents.

This connection is as vexing as difficult to avoid (Papadopoulos and Heslop 2002). On the one hand, a majority of destinations carry baggage which is not directly related to tourism. Most countries have an image imposed by historical events and their popular interpretation. Resorts in Turkey can be similar to any other elsewhere, but still many tourists feel wary because one of the features they identify the country with is its religion. Seldom political turmoil wreaks havoc in proper tourism areas. However, as in the recent case of Kenya, it can harm incoming flows of international tourists. Most destinations might gain from breaking the association with their national history, but in fact this is an unrealistic expectation. One would sound definitely snobbish telling one's friends: "This summer we are going to Shanxi Province" unless immediately he adds that this is the part of China where Xian is located and that it is where one can see the famous terracotta army in the neighborhood.

Some geographic areas in the world, like the Côte d'Azur in Southern France, have achieved general repute, but they are the exception. For most, name recognition is mostly limited to some markets. Majorca may accommodate 10 million international tourists in one year, but not many people beyond Western Europe would know it. Additionally, destinations do not cater to the same customers. The Northern part of Majorca around Deià may be an elite destination for writers, artists, celebrities, and other jet-setters, so it does not easily mix with the masses that pack El Arenal or Magaluf during the summer. There are many difficult issues trying to create a brand for those two markets (Morgan and Pritchard 2002). Destinations come as a medley of different locations and different products. Their different stakeholders have interests and expectations that are difficult to reconcile.

Finally and significantly, destinations do not have direct control over products, pricing policies, or distribution systems (Prideaux and Cooper 2002). One should acknowledge that, no matter how important customer loyalty can reward brands that provide pleasing experiences, still most tourists' budgets are limited, and they have to reckon with the value their money is buying. There is a difference between acknowledging the emotional tie between customers and brands and concluding that disposable income has disappeared from most people's radars. Inasmuch as destination marketing organizations (DMOs) cannot control most of the marketing's 4Ps—as by definition happens in market-based systems—the talk about the paramount role of emotions in consumer decision making should be toned down. Further, marketers should acknowledge that, because of it, destinations are less amenable to branding than business. The success of Spanish tourism offers counterintuitive evidence to this point of view.

Misguided Branding

The initial boom of mass tourism in Spain (1959–1979) offers a good example on the limits of branding. One can discuss endlessly whether the activities of the specialized Spanish agencies of the time were real branding (which concept had not yet gained the traction it would later) or just image-building (Gartner 1993a, 1993b). Given the fuzziness of both concepts, one should rather take a flexible position. However, whatever the label, SNTO's strategy covered the same bases one expects from branding. It followed a consistent market action, using the best promotional tools of the time, mostly based on distribution of posters and brochures. With limited promotional budgets, they provided a more efficient way to communicate with the target public than expensive advertising campaigns spread thin over many markets by budget strictures. The SNTO also tried to create an emotional bond between (mostly European) consumers and the destination. It took a shot at developing their loyalty so that tourists would make repeated visits to the country. At face value, whether branding or image building, given its economic accomplishments, SNTO's strategy looks extremely successful. However, there are good reasons to doubt the correlation between the plan and its outcome.

The SNTO has recently published a number of volumes containing most of the posters printed since this medium was first used in 1929 (SNTO 2000a, 2000b, 2005) and until 2000. Later on, another volume (SNTO 2007) appeared that contains a bigger number of posters of the same period, including some missing in the previous editions, and covering until 2005. In addition to their documentary interest and artistic value, the now available collection of posters provides a clear view of the communication strategy developed by the SNTO at the time when Spanish mass tourism started its take-off (1959–1979). An analysis of those materials offers a number of significant pointers. Above all, it is clear that the SNTO made a big effort to publicize Spain. From 1959 to 1979, it published a total of 550 posters with an annual average of 21, nearly one poster printed every other week (Figure 1). Indeed, production did not maintain a regular schedule and went in cycles. The time of maximum production was 1965–1969—Minister Fraga's last five years as top executive at the SNTO.

Spain thus tried to create its own branded products. However, what was that brand the SNTO was so eager to create? A couple of basic statistics will make it clear. Taking the distinction between nature- and culture-based posters, one can see a clear bias toward the latter (Figure 2). Of the 550 posters published during the two take-off decades, nearly 80% had culture (monuments, museums, paintings, traditions, and activities) as their main subject. Only in 1973–1974 did natural landscapes get more attention than cultural icons. The trend was obvious—nature was below the SNTO's radar.

When it appeared, however, Spanish communications did not have a clear sense of direction either. Of the 137 nature-based posters, only 89 represented beaches and sea resorts, with only 74 devoted to the Mediterranean, the Balearic Islands, or the Canaries (Figure 3).The rest depicted imposing mountains, snowy landscapes, flowers, forests, dramatic sunsets, and roaming animals. Overall, the sea, the coastline, and the beaches clearly took the rear seat in Spain's image building efforts. Of the

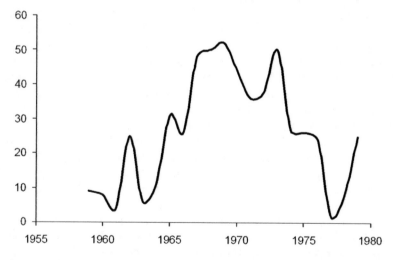

Figure 1 Spanish Tourism Posters (1959–1979). *Source*: SNTO (2007).

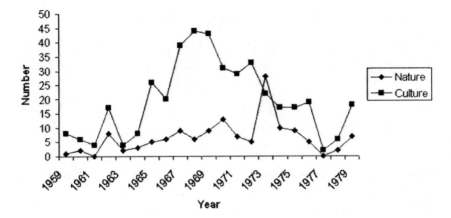

Figure 2 Spanish Posters by Main Subject. *Source*: SNTO (2007).

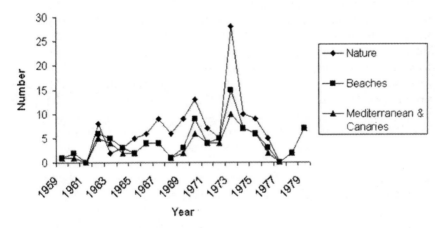

Figure 3 Nature-based Posters. *Source*: SNTO (2007).

total 550 posters of the period, less than 15% associated Spain with sand, sun, and sea.

The SNTO had fallen into the DMO trap (Figure 4). It allowed the brand it wanted to project to overwhelm the image perceived by the target. This is a regular incident that plagues branding, and there is no clear-cut way out of it. Indeed, to some extent, all brands must start with a unilateral statement. Being proposals to the consumer, it is up to the proposer to start the

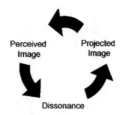

Figure 4 The Destination Marketing Organization Trap.

dialogue. However, if the message and the image are not well calibrated, they will create a degree of dissonance. This danger, as has been pointed out, plagues brands of destinations more easily than other types of brands. They usually have smaller budgets than product brands, meaning that they tend to lag in market research and promotional tools.

In the Spanish case, especially until 1975, the SNTO tried to define itself in a totally unilateral way with no regard for consumer expectations. Contrary to enduring opinion, it is not true that most of its promotion revolved around the political slogan "Spain is different." In fact it was only used in seven posters between 1948 and 1950, never later (SNTO 2005). However, from 1959 to 1975, the SNTO was in denial that its best selling product was the sun and the sea and their consumers were the European middle and lower middle classes. If at all, culture might have been a reasonable bet in the US or the Japanese markets, both of which could find their ration of sun and sea in less remote areas. Those two markets constituted but a small fraction of the overall tourist market. However, the strategy that underpinned Spanish promotion at this time obviously turned its back on the bulk of its consumers. Neither posters nor brochures had them at the top of their list.

A contemporary analysis of Spanish brochures (Febas 1978) had already pointed out such shortcomings. Spanish promotional materials were wanting in at least two aspects. Above all, they were clearly self-referent. Most text and icons forced on audiences the definitions of a communicator that extolled local culture and folklore or put forward highly positive self-evaluations. The addressee was usually cast out of the process. Only 11% of the texts and 20% of the iconic material paid any direct attention to the audience.

Additionally, Spanish posters and brochures prioritized the arts over any other feature. The country was "museumized" and packaged as a place where art (above all, religious art) reigned supreme. It was supposed to epitomize the unchanging features of a Spanish identity beyond time. Arresting churches and abbeys, ascetic saints, and heroic warriors—such was the stuff of an Eternal Spain that required men (not much was said about the role of women) to be half-monks, half-soldiers. In the self-made SNTO symbolic universe, chauvinism and spite for modernity went hand-in-hand.

> Such is the image favored by Spanish brochures, with all their paraphernalia of coats of arms, old monuments ... celebration of the Romanesque and Gothic periods, disregard for everything related with the industrialization and urbanization of the country. This contrasts both with the pro-European economic policies of openness that lie at the base of the Spanish tourist miracle since the Sixties and with the frivolous, exotic and folkloric images tour operators imposed during that time the world over. (Febas 1978:120)

Were incoming tourists really motivated by all that old-age paraphernalia?

When the SNTO started work on its first marketing plan (1985–1986), data showed that international tourists to Spain were not exactly looking for what it was advertising. Over 85% of them spent their vacations on the Mediterranean littoral and the islands (unpublished data from the first Spanish Marketing Plan 1985 known to the author). The projected brand had definitely not seeped deeply into the consumer mind.

However, tourists would come and return to Spain in droves. What happened was obvious. DMOs can project as many images as they want. However, they are neither the sole nor the most important source of information for consumers. In fact, the public is always surrounded by a steady flow of advertising stimuli, educational sources, and interpersonal communication. Those sources can be represented from bottom to top as a pyramid with a solid base in word-of-mouth nowadays greatly enhanced by the operation of Web 2.0, followed by a number of educational sources such as independent advice in travel guides, travel magazines, travel sections, and trade news. They are further topped with the promotional DMO imaging or the specific offers of "travel factories" including airlines, tour operators, and travel counselors. Once the vacation has taken place, past experience may be an additional significant factor in the decision of repeating the destination. Hence, DMOs are but one of the sources of information and not particularly reliable for different reasons, from limited budgets to bureaucratic guidance to inadequate market knowledge. Even the huge presence of DMO web sites in Web 1.0 has not improved their situation. The most they can aim at is to occupy a small place in consumers' evoked set, which is not much. Additionally, a good case can be made that in many instances consumers make tourism decisions on the spur of the moment (Blichfeldt 2005, 2007) and with total lack of awareness of the destination. Therefore, branding may not be as well suited to DMOs as widely anticipated.

CONCLUSION

Between 1959 and 1979, the governments of Spain made a political decision to open the country to the world economy. Tourism was expected to be one of the props of an export-led process of economic growth. The SNTO made a great effort to position the country as a popular destination. During that period, Spain was branded as a magnet for cultural tourism and, to a lesser extent, for nature lovers. However, in all aspects, the SNTO projected an image of the country as an Eternal Spain centered on artistic experiences, above all those derived from religious arts and traditions.

The goal of turning tourism into one of the main sources of foreign exchange was completely successful. In this way, the outcome validated the political strategy. However, as a matter of fact, European tourists, the bulk of foreign incoming flows to the country, clearly voted with their feet away from Eternal Spain. Most were looking for sun and sea family vacations at affordable prices, which were just what foreign tour operators were offering. Their catalogs displayed a number of products, and projected a definite image of beach products that fitted the expectations of many Northern European consumers. Whether they accurately represented the country in their brochures (Dann 1996; Gaviria 1975) was of no consequence.

The complete success of the overall political strategy has precluded a foregone conclusion—the SNTO's branding strategy during the take-off period of mass tourism to Spain (1959–1979) was an unmitigated failure. Indeed, after 1979, under a number of democratic governments, the SNTO has better shaped its communication policies to the tastes of increasingly educated consumers (Gnoth 2002a, 2002b). They have also been quite successful until now. Still, a doubt lingers. Was the Spanish success in the early phase of maturity a product of the new branding exemplified by Joan

Miró's inspired logo, the initial slogan "Everything under the Sun", and attention to the beach and family vacation customer; or just the fact that Spain offered the right experiences at the right price for the right customers? Possibly there cannot be a clear-cut answer to the riddle independently of the circumstances of the context. Taken in isolation, any of the two sides would be misleading. If there is a lesson to draw from the Spanish case, it is that branding always travels a two-way road.

Chapter 11

A PRACTICAL FRAMEWORK FOR DESTINATION BRANDING

Asli D. A. Tasci
Mugla University, Turkey

William C. Gartner
University of Minnesota, USA

Abridgement: Despite the recent academic attention to branding, there seems to be no clear path for authorities to follow in establishing their destinations as distinctive and strategic brands. The purpose of this chapter is to provide a practical framework for destination authorities. Review of relevant literature reveals that branding in a destination context involves development and maintenance of positive image and identity using several elements such as names, logos, slogans, and color. These elements need to be distilled from destination characteristics and they can lead to strong brand equity. A comprehensive research framework with both qualitative and quantitative methods is suggested to assess these brand elements, meanings, and assets for both supply and demand sides of the market. **Keywords:** destination; branding; image; identity; research.

Tourism Branding: Communities in Action
Bridging Tourism Theory and Practice, Volume 1, 149–158
Copyright © 2009 by Emerald Group Publishing Limited
All rights of reproduction in any form reserved
ISSN: 2042-1443/doi:10.1108/S2042-1443(2009)0000001013

INTRODUCTION

Destination branding is rapidly becoming a focal point of management and marketing efforts. It is increasing in importance due to the globally growing need for corporate partnerships to access scarce resources and for more unique and cooperative positioning in a competitive marketplace (Williams, Gill and Chura 2004). Yet, the process of branding for destinations is often more haphazard than strategically planned. The use of strategies and their efficacy has yet to be fully applied and measured for many developing as well as developed destinations.

Researchers started paying attention to brands and branding only recently, but interest in it has accelerated due to the presumed advantages inherent in this strategy. Branding can be simply defined as the use of markers such as names, signs, symbols, etc., to differentiate the products of one seller from another (Kotler 1997). A brand is "what differentiates you and makes you special" (Milligan 1995:39), which is parallel to destination positioning. Kotler and Gertner (2002) postulate that brands not only "differentiate products and represent a promise of value" but also "incite beliefs, evoke emotions and prompt behaviours" (p. 249), which are the desired goals of destination management organizations. They also discuss the potential of country branding and conclude that strong brands can attract not only tourists, but also businesses and investment. Morgan, Pritchard and Piggott (2002) take this a step further by suggesting that branding has become the most powerful marketing tool available to destination marketers due to increased competition and easy substitutability of destination products. They postulate that a brand represents a unique amalgam of both functional and non-functional product characteristics and added values, which, when done correctly, deliver meanings, inextricably linked to conscious or intuitive brand awareness of consumers.

Hankinson (2004) attributes brands as relationships manifested as a match between destination image and consumers' self-image, or between consumers' needs and a brand's symbolic values and functional attributes. The relationship is particularly relevant to service brands due to the interaction between service providers and consumers during the production and delivery. In a similar vein, Williams et al (2004) consider branding as the key to acquiring and enhancing a strategic market position and competitiveness, as well as the mark of a memorable bond or an emotional link between consumers and destinations. Joppe, Martin and Waalen (2001) attribute brand loyalty to a destination's ability in providing tourists with an experience corresponding to their needs and identical with their image of the place. The emotional connection between its brands and their consumers is the desired goal. To achieve such connection, image remains an important element affecting branding strategies.

Awareness about advantages and benefits of branding is not sufficient for successful implementation of it due to the intangible characteristics of tourism products, especially for such multidimensional places as cities, states, and countries. The unique characteristics of products, namely, simultaneous production and consumption, intangibility, perishability, and heterogeneity pose several difficulties for tourism authorities (de Chernatony and Riley 1999). The aim of this chapter is to provide a practical framework for authorities who desire to develop strategic brands.

FROM CONCEPTS TO PRACTICES

In conceptualization of destination brand, notions of image and identity are usually involved. There is a close relationship between brand and image; the former is created through the latter (Cai 2002; Govers 2003; Jensen and Komeliussen 2002; Pritchard and Morgan 2001; Ravinder 2003). Kotler and Gertner (2002) recognize that the image of a country can be activated in the minds of people merely by its name, even when there are no conscious brand management activities. Cai (2002) defines the image of a brand as "perceptions about the place as reflected by the associations held in tourist memory" (p. 723). He distinguishes between image formation and destination branding by arguing that former's formation constitutes the core of branding but is only one dimension. Cai further comments that image building is essential but there still remains a critical missing link: the brand identity, which needs to be fully established.

Blain, Levy and Ritchie (2005) conducted a comprehensive quantitative and qualitative survey of multinational senior executives of 409 destination marketing organizations. It measured the importance and extent of these executives' involvement with respect to several brand elements. They found that although the destination marketing organization executives possessed a conceptual understanding of branding, there was limited involvement in its many aspects. The study revealed brand themes of "identification, differentiation, experience, expectations, image, consolidation, reinforcement, recognition, consistency, brand messages, and emotional response" (p. 336). They offered a definition in the context of destinations that includes using a name, symbol, logo, word mark, or other graphic to readily identify and differentiate a destination; consistently conveying the anticipation of a memorable experience, uniquely associated with the destination; serving to reinforce an emotional connection between tourists and the destination; which should lead to reducing consumer costs and risk (Blain et al 2005).

In a study of assessing branding practices, Pritchard and Morgan (2001) investigated representations of Wales by analyzing branding strategies in the marketing campaigns of the Wales Tourist Board and Welsh local authorities. They conducted a content analysis of brochures, combined with an indepth interview of retired key decision makers, and concluded that Wales' marketing representations used in its branding strategy "are inextricably intertwined with historical, political, and cultural processes and are not solely the outcome of elective marketing practice" (p. 2). They attempted to construct a branding strategy for Wales by using heritage, language, person, myths, legends, and emblems, which were seen as constituting the basic elements of Wales' image.

Similarly, Morgan et al (2002) provided a successful example of "the 100% Pure New Zealand" brand. It was initiated in an effort to double the country's tourism earnings by 2005 and was targeted to tourists in Australia, Japan, the United States, the United Kingdom, Germany, and Singapore. They focused on the UK phase of the branding research, which included focus groups and indepth interviews. Their work demonstrates how a brand's values are identified and incorporated into an emotionally appealing personality, then effectively and efficiently delivered to the target markets, all of which they view as important for successful destination branding. They concluded that marketing research and partnerships facilitated the success of creation and application of "the 100% Pure New Zealand" brand. They pointed out that strong destination brands involve "emotional meaning," "great conversation value," and provide "high anticipation" for potential consumers. Other researchers offered a model with three different foci: functional branding which emphasizes destination's problem solving attributes such as accessibility and reliability, symbolic branding which emphasizes destination's ego-enhancing properties such as family and affiliations with celebrities, and experiential branding which emphasizes a destination's cognitive or affective dimensions such as learning and relaxation (Williams et al 2004).

Cai (2002) also conducted a review of literature and promotional materials along with interviews with destination officials. Through investigating the use of cooperative branding across multiple rural communities with geographic and cultural proximity, Cai proposed a recursive conceptual model, which was applied to seven rural counties in the state of New Mexico in the United States. The findings supported the model, leading to the conclusion that cooperative branding across multiple rural communities is beneficial in projecting a uniform cognitive image for communities with shared destination attributes; strengthening brand associations and their linkages to identity more so for a cooperative region than its constituent member communities; which led to generating greater awareness and favorability toward the functional region than its individual communities.

In another case study, Williams et al (2004) investigated branding applications by Intrawest of Whistler in British Columbia, Canada. They conducted content analysis of marketing information from several sources and identified that branding by Intrawest and a public tourism organization encountered problems in applying Buhalis' (2000) branding principles. They also questioned the suitability of destination branding by suggesting that it stifles unexpected and spontaneous experiences, which are sometimes pursued by tourists. Results of their study lead one to conclude that branding a community as a destination is not about marketing. Although successful attempts stake out a position that appeals to a particular market, branding strategy must also respect the values and goals of the community such that it retains its sense of place (Williams et al 2004).

Caldwell and Freire (2004) conducted an exploratory survey using a sample of multinational students to examine six countries and six regions or cities. They applied the Brand Box Model and concluded that countries, being so diverse, should focus on the emotional or representational dimensions rather than on any tangible/functional features. The smaller the destination becomes (region or city), however, the more brand building should focus on their functional assets. Kotler, Bowen and Makens (2003) go beyond image and add the dimensions of value and quality to the brand concept. They suggest that branding is desirable when tourists can easily identify products with a perception of good value for the price, when the quality and standards can easily be maintained and when there is a large enough demand for the products. The value and quality dimensions relate to the concept of brand equity for a destination, along with loyalty, name awareness, and its link to other associations such as patents, trademarks, and channel relationships (Kotler and Armstrong 1996). For example, country or region of origin of food products, protected by law, is a brand association that has been successfully used to enhance product value.

As can be deduced from the earlier discussions, a destination brand is different from well-known places or places receiving large numbers of tourists. Being well-known does not always include trust, relationship, quality, consumer loyalty, or an emotional attachment as is in the case of a strong brand. A case in point is Iraq. Many people know this country due to its international media coverage. However, the context is of a rather negative political and social conflict which induces concerns of safety and security, thereby reducing intention to visit. However, receiving large number of tourists does not necessarily mean being a successful brand either. Large numbers of people go to certain places for diverse reasons.

One such reason is affordable travel costs. Turkey is such an example. According to the United Nations World Tourism Organization (2007a, 2007b), Turkey received 18.9 million inbound tourists in 2006 and ranked 11th in terms of international arrivals. However, this is mostly due to cheap all-inclusive packages rather than strong brand Turkey. Close distance is another such reason for large numbers of people going to certain places. Ceteris paribus, a destination in Europe is likely to receive more European tourists than one further away, such as Turkey. A more favorable climate, that is usually unavailable at home, is another such factor. For example, the weather of Spain and France is a primary attraction for some Northern European citizens used to a less favorable climate. The existence of ancestral roots is another reason bringing many people from the United States to European destinations. One can argue about the existence of a destination brand when visitation of large numbers of people is induced by a positive relationship with it because it provides values not found in other places, which is rather difficult.

Challenges of Destination Branding

Branding is difficult in tourism because of unique product characteristics (Buhalis 2000; Cai 2002; de Chernatony and Riley 1999; D'Hauteserre 2001; Ekinci 2003; Jensen and Komeliussen 2002). First of all, it is fixed by its name and geographical location (Cai 2002). Second, diverse tangible and intangible attributes are involved in branding a destination, which have to be distilled into an understandable message while keeping the values of involved stakeholders intact (Buhalis 2000). Third, destinations cater to the needs of many different types of tourists. Not everyone thinks alike or wants the same experience. There is no static market position as preferences are constantly shifting (Williams et al 2004). Thus, there is no guarantee that everyone will accept whatever brand development strategy is proposed. Besides, usually a complex decision-making process is involved in tourism consumption. This normally includes some risk assessment whether it is of an emotional, physical, or monetary value in nature, endangering the success potential of a destination brand. Moreover, the politics of destination marketing and limited resources are postulated to contribute to the challenges of branding (Morgan, Pritchard and Pride 2002).

To reduce the impact of these challenges, de Chernatony and Riley (1999) suggest "a consumer-delighting culture" enhanced by internal communication and training. D'Hauteserre (2001) contends that as more destinations turn to branding to create a sense of differentiation from competitors, a comprehensive assessment of all values held in the potential markets must be undertaken to connect its attributes with market values to maximize the destination appeal. Considering such challenges, Buhalis (2000) identifies four principles: collaboration rather than competition among stakeholders; brand's congruence with destination values, including physical and cultural carrying capacity; aligning a brand's strategy with a clearly defined target market; and supporting the destination's vision of development. Kotler and Gertner (2002) define some practical steps and tools of successful country branding. These include projecting a simple, appealing, believable, and distinctive image; defining the attributes forming a basis for strong branding such as natural resources; developing an umbrella concept to cover the country's separate branding activities such as pleasure; a catchy slogan such as "Spain Everything Under the Sun"; visual images or symbols such as Big Ben for London of England; and special events or deeds such as Wimbledon Tennis Tournament for England to increase awareness and reinforce images. Although these tasks are similar to what must be done to develop a successful single product brand, it becomes more complex for destinations as different internal stakeholders, such as hotels must develop their own brands while at the same time buying into that of the destination.

Implications for Strategic Destination Branding

A destination brand, when applied successfully, signals good value, quality, trust, assurance, and anticipation to consumers. This could lead to a more long-term relationship, resulting in repeat purchase and customer loyalty. However, due to the unique characteristics of tourism products aforementioned, branding applications for destinations poses several challenges. Academic research has provided several steps and tools to offset the challenges and achieve successful branding. Some of the most critical can be summarized as collaboration among stakeholders to assure congruence between brand and the physical and social values of the destination; defining a clear target market for the brand; supporting a vision of destination development; projecting a simple, appealing, believable, and distinctive image; defining the attributes forming a basis for strong branding;

developing an umbrella concept to cover the country's separate branding activities; and a catchy slogan, visual images or symbols, and special events to achieve higher levels of awareness.

Most empirical studies conceptualize branding at smaller levels, such as resorts rather than regions and countries. The more amorphous nature of geographically larger destinations complicates the process of distilling essential elements to be used in the brand building strategy. Destination branding is usually examined through case study approaches, and as illustrated in this chapter, carries a decidedly supply-side perspective usually involving focus groups or indepth interviews and/or content analysis of promotional materials. Thus, most such research deals more with how brands are developed by local authorities. This aspect could signal the conceptual difference between brand and its close affiliate: image. Destination image research is mostly conducted with current or potential tourists, a demand-side perspective.

However, developing effective destination brand strategies would require empirical studies involving both the supply- and demand-side. Existing literature supports that branding in a destination context involves development and maintenance of positive image and identity using several elements such as names, signs, logos, designs, symbols, slogans, color, and packages. These elements are distilled from characteristics including, architecture, heritage, language, people, myths, legends, history, politics, culture, and values (Cai 2002; Kotler and Armstrong 1996; Kotler et al 2003; Pritchard and Morgan 2001; Williams et al 2004). The successful distillation of these characteristics, in return, leads to strong brand equity for a destination with high loyalty, name awareness, perceived quality and value, strong brand associations, and other assets such as patents, trademarks, and channel relationships (Kotler and Armstrong 1996; Kotler et al 2003). Using a comprehensive research framework with both qualitative and quantitative methods, these brand elements, meanings, and assets for both sides of the market can be organized in a framework (Figure 1).

The supply-side perspective can be studied by conducting focus groups and indepth interviews with authorities, local stakeholders (including key opinion leaders), and decisio n makers among residents, as well as a content analysis of promotional materials. The demand-side perspective can be revealed through quantitative surveys, focus groups, and indepth interviews of residents and current and potential tourists. Further, content analysis of information from independent sources regarding the destination would provide a fuller picture of the demand-side perspective. This would allow the comparison between the projected brand (including its meanings and assets

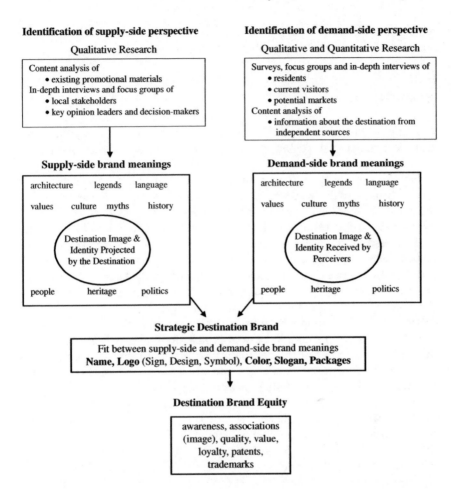

Identification of supply-side perspective

Qualitative Research

Content analysis of
- existing promotional materials

In-depth interviews and focus groups of
- local stakeholders
- key opinion leaders and decision-makers

Identification of demand-side perspective

Qualitative and Quantitative Research

Surveys, focus groups and in-depth interviews of
- residents
- current visitors
- potential markets

Content analysis of
- information about the destination from independent sources

Supply-side brand meanings

architecture   legends   language

values   culture   myths   history

Destination Image & Identity Projected by the Destination

people   heritage   politics

Demand-side brand meanings

architecture   legends   language

values   culture   myths   history

Destination Image & Identity Received by Perceivers

people   heritage   politics

Strategic Destination Brand

Fit between supply-side and demand-side brand meanings
Name, Logo (Sign, Design, Symbol), **Color, Slogan, Packages**

Destination Brand Equity

awareness, associations (image), quality, value, loyalty, patents, trademarks

Figure 1 A Framework for Creating Strategic Destination Brands.

defined by the destination authorities) and the perceived brand (including its meanings and assets defined by tourists). Such comparison facilitates a strategic stance for developing or improving the brand. Theoretically, there would be a fit between the brand projected by authorities and that perceived by its markets. This fit is the basis for selecting a mix of elements to go with the brand. These—be that a name, color, logo or symbol, slogan, and colors—should deliver meaningful messages for consumers. The heritage, language, myths, and legends of destinations should also be coordinated to contribute to the message and ultimately the brand.

CONCLUSION

Branding is difficult but possible for destinations when it is applied in a strategic manner, using market intelligence. To create strong destination brands, a concerted strategy is needed. First, extensive research is needed during the step of generating a brand theme concept, with a democratic approach to hear the voices of all stakeholders, including locals without a direct economic interest in tourism. The suggested framework in Figure 1 can be helpful for authorities in framing their branding activities for any level of destination products. As illustrated in Figure 1, residents are be studied twice, both from supply- and demand-side perspectives. This is purposefully suggested due to the critical role of residents as both providers and consumers of a place. Assessment of their perspective is of utmost importance in developing a successful and strategic brand.

Second, implementing a brand theme requires more than just promotion or making noise, as a trial-and-error approach does not work either. A single voice has to come out of the destination so that the message is uniform. It has to involve promotional activities with a holistic embodying brand theme. An integrated marketing communications approach is needed to achieve that one voice. The same brand theme should permeate public relations, publicity, and advertising (including videos, posters, roadside boards, and direct mailing) and other commercial media. For this reason, an autocratic approach with full cooperation and collaboration is a must during the implementation of the brand strategy. Finally, creating and implementing a strategic destination brand is a continuous endeavor. Considering the changing market conditions and tourists' pursuits of unexpected and spontaneous experiences, the success and fit of destination brands to the needs and expectations should be monitored by longitudinal research; and the brand needs to be tailored accordingly.

PART III

PRACTICAL CASES

Chapter 12

DESTINATION BRAND STRATEGY
The Case of Greece

Alexandros Kouris
Critical Publics-Altervision, Greece

Abridgement: The chapter introduces a model of destination branding
and reports a project that applied the model to examine the current image
of Greece. The project was undertaken on behalf of the Greek national
tourism organization by a binational consortium. Through conducting
primary and secondary research on the public perception and self-
portrayal of Greece, the project team found the current brand image
and identity not to be in accordance with the country's reality. Indeed,
although the brand image elements currently expressed are relevant,
they represent only a small portion of a much larger existing offering.
To that end, the team proposed new branding strategies based on the
model, offering a series of recommendations on how to implement the
strategies. **Keywords:** Greece; re-branding; branding tool; imagery; critical
publics.

INTRODUCTION

As a consequence of the international mobility of people and information
in today's era, competition among destinations is greater than ever before.

Tourism Branding: Communities in Action
Bridging Tourism Theory and Practice, Volume 1, 161–175
Copyright © 2009 by Emerald Group Publishing Limited
All rights of reproduction in any form reserved
ISSN: 2042-1443/doi:10.1108/S2042-1443(2009)0000001014

Destination branding, defined as a process of creating and managing ownable, trustworthy, relevant, unique, and distinctive brand equity, has emerged as an imperative for competitiveness. The trend recognizes the fact that product superiority alone and tactical promotion may not guarantee success. Brand as a concept works on two levels. First, it is how a destination is currently perceived by tourists. Second, it is how destination strategy planners wish to position it to target tourists and other critical internal and external publics. Indeed, brands exist in the minds of tourists and encompass their perceptions and predispositions about the destinations. They are not merely a name or its symbol and logotype, which, in addition to all other identity design and visual elements, are tools to make the brand visible.

If the destination is a country, then its brand should be able to function as an endorsement and not as a product brand. The national endorsement brand should be wide enough to accommodate all its offerings, destinations, products, services, and experiences within its territory. It should furthermore act as a signature of "integrity and reputation" (Travis 2000). To use an analogy, the endorsement brand at country level should be designed to be more like a "multiplex" theater with a large number of cinemas and the ability to offer a number of movies (the national offerings) at the same time. The endorsement brand should be distinctive and relevant to several target groups. This chapter presents such a brand and the development of it through the case of "Destination Greece," a research project that is charged with the task both of determining the current brand image of the country and planning its repositioning so as to better compete in the international marketplace.

RE-BRANDING GREECE

The research project involves, among other techniques, the adaptation and application of brand theory for consumer products to destinations. Aaker (1996) and Aaker (1997) are informative on product perception, brand assets and liabilities, and personality; Travis (2000) on endorsement brands; Ritchie and Ritchie (1998) on equity; Keller (2003) on benefits of positive equity; and Grace and O'Cass (2002) on tourist equity. Vriens and Hofstede (2000) and Sternthal and Tybout (2001) are instructive for the tenets of brand image components, including attributes–benefits interaction, points of difference (PODs), and points of parity (POPs); and Wansink (2003) and Kahle, Poulos and Sukhdial (1988) for feelings and emotional imagery. Kotler and Armstrong's (2005) general brand positioning to destination brands is adapted.

Foundation work for defining how Greece is currently perceived consisted of both primary and secondary research conducted by MRB Hellas, Critical Publics London, and PRC Group—The Management House. The primary research was conducted on the target groups of general traveling population, trade and industry actors, and comprised Target Group Index data analysis, an exit survey, mystery shopping, tour operator and journalist interviews, a travel agent phone survey, and an analysis of European Travel Monitor survey data. The secondary research consisted of an analysis of the perception of Greece and its competitor countries and cases of excellence at national level from both organic and induced sources (Gunn 1988). The former included international publicity, primary reference sources, and postings from bloggers and newsgroup communities. The induced sources included a multitude of official promotional materials produced by Greece and competitors. They were gathered from Greek National Tourism Organization headquarters and offices, and the Internet. Specifically for Greece, the two latest campaigns (2007's "Explore your senses" and 2006's "Live your myth in Greece") were also analyzed. In addition, various groups of stakeholders provided valuable information and inspiration through a series of workshops and personal interviews. Altogether, there were nine taskforces workshops (one for each tourism sector), 12 regional workshops in each of the administrative regions of Greece (all except Thessaly), and 45 personal interviews with key industry players.

Fundamentals of Image Building

There exists a set of positive or negative elements linked with a brand identity, not necessarily all real, that are perceived by tourists. They can be assets or liabilities adding to or subtracting from the value-adding potential of the brand. Destinations with a multitude of brand assets provide a premium to the value provided by products, services, and experiences offered to tourists within the destination region, while those with liabilities reduce its worth. The net effect of the elements to its value-adding potential is brand equity. Image is the meaning of a destination, and is "what the destination is" in the mind of tourists. Building it is the key tool, as it relates to selecting the set of elements to be linked with brand identity. Image building is in essence a process of positioning. Positioning a destination is the act of designing its offer and image so that it occupies a distinct and

valued place in the target tourists' mind (Kotler, Ang, Leong and Tan 1996).
It is a long-term decision for the brand that should not change with every
communication. Leonard (1997:41) mentions that "It takes time to change
perceptions...on-off initiatives have very little impact on attitudes. The basic
message needs to be continually reinforced using different media in different
contexts." The media constitutes mass, social, and human components.
Four concepts determine the brand image of a destination, and at the same
time constitute the sources of potential brand elements. They are destination
performance imagery, emotional imagery, experience imagery, and tourist
imagery, as illustrated in Figure 1.

The first concept involves the features, attributes, and benefits of the
destination's product offering. It is, without doubt, the core of the brand.
It is the compelling reason why tourists decide to select one location over
others, and what they expect to experience during their visit. In branding
terms, the offering may be of the three types representing a hierarchy
from the micro- to macro-level. First, it has features which are functional
and concrete(e.g., the Acropolis or Big Ben, sea and sun, natural beaches,

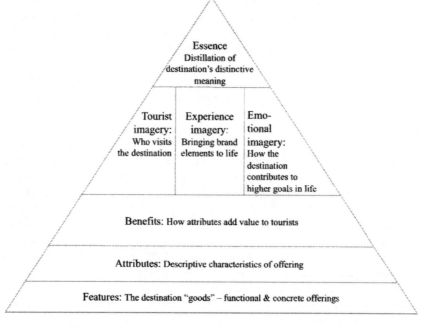

Figure 1 Destination Brand through Image Building.

mountains and lakes, popular hotels, festivals and events, available infrastructure, and unique service offerings). Second, it includes attributes which are descriptive characteristics of the destination offering (e.g., clear blue waters, or the largest variety of islands in Europe). Features support attributes. To demonstrate the relationship between the two, one might use the example of Amsterdam. Presenting the city as a destination, one could select to talk about "progressive urban culture." Features to support this attribute, among others, are the "Stedelijk Museum," or the city's "modern architecture." Finally, attributes support benefits.

Benefits are how attributes add value to tourists' experience. They might explain, for example, that the attribute "clear blue waters" creates a "unique feeling of rejuvenation" to the swimmer, or the attribute "variety of islands" guarantees a "never-ending discovery." Benefits can be functional, emotional, or symbolic. Those most frequently associated with destinations are adventure, discovery, challenge, pleasure, fun, fantasy, escapism, relaxation, rejuvenation care, new experiences, knowledge, romance, immersion, stimulation and happiness, intense emotions, dream fulfillment, cultural edification, indulgence, exploration, freedom, privacy and body, and mind and spirit balance. Features are very important as they are basic elements for the design of attributes and benefits. However, destinations cannot usually build powerful brands just by listing their features.

Destination performance imagery may only be based on attributes and their resulting benefits which characterize its overall offering. It is advisable to separate performance imagery into two categories. The first is PODs that have strong relevance to targeted groups of tourists and are uniquely associated with the destination. These are important attributes and benefits that tourists believe they cannot find in other destinations. They are valuable brand assets adding to the distinctiveness of a destination brand. PODs selected to be part of it should be based on what the location has the ability to deliver with superior value for a prolonged period of time. The second category is POPs that are not uniquely associated with a brand but are nonetheless necessary for a destination offering. Usually, POPs do not add to the competitiveness of a location. They must be present to create a legitimate and credible offering. To use an example from the market of financial services, customers would not easily accept a new service as being a true bank offering unless it has branches and provides saving accounts and deposit boxes. The same idea applies to destinations. For example, basic hospitality infrastructure would be the absolute minimum for a place to attract tourists. POPs are important in positioning new destinations or new offerings to the market of tourists. They are also useful for negating a competitor's POD in an attempt to "break even" in areas where competitors are trying to create an advantage. The imagery of PODs and POPs are usually inspired by the destination's product offering including natural landscapes, landmarks and monuments, and exceptional biodiversity; and by its servicescape and service people including effectiveness, efficiency, and empathy. It is also stimulated by the destination's aesthetic elements including style and design, size and shape, materials and colors, and other sensory aspects such as how it looks, feels, sounds, or smell. Finally, its history and heritage including noteworthy historical events contribute to the imagery as well.

The second concept is destination emotional imagery. Once potential tourists have established a sufficient understanding of product-related, functional attributes, and benefits, it is advantageous to further enhance the meaning of a destination brand. For this to occur, it is necessary to explore deeper and discover how destination PODs relate to tourists' higher values, personal goals, and motivations. Wansink (2003a, 2003b) notes that, in general, consumer purchases are related to seven core values, known as the actualization levels of the Maslow's hierarchy of needs, including sense of belonging, self fulfillment, accomplishment, self esteem, satisfaction, family, and security.

The third concept is destination experience imagery. It aims to bring unique brand elements to life in the imagination of potential tourists to evoke feelings of surprise, movement, anticipation, and relevance. For example, England suggests 12 "unique experiences in special places" that "capture the joy of a holiday in England." To name a few: "Taking a pampering spa break in Bath," "Tracing the footsteps of Robin Hood in Sherwood Forest," and "Finding your own private beach on the Northumbrian coast." Switzerland, on the contrary, promises "authentic nature experiences" such as "swimming in a mountain lake" and "spending the night surrounded by mountains in one of the 156 'huts' of the Swiss Alpine Club." It is important that proposed experiences are real and can easily be enjoyed by the majority of target tourists. It is also essential that new experiences are created and launched every year to keep the brand fresh and exciting.

Finally, there is the concept of tourist imagery. This category of brand elements aims to capture the way people should think about the brand abstractly in terms of who visits the destination and why. The association of such elements becomes possible through the depiction of visual stimuli in the destination's communication. Such visual stimuli might be, first, images of tourists of specific demographic and sociocultural profiles, actual or idealized (youthful lifestyle); and, second, images of situations in which tourists are involved (slices of life suggesting a distinctive destination brand lifestyle). Through such imagery, destinations are able to project their brands' personality, pretty much like human beings. The personality is the set of human characteristics associated with the brand. It includes such characteristics as gender, age, socioeconomic class, as well as human personality traits of warmth and sentimentality. Five dimensions of brand personality have been identified by Aaker (1997): sincerity (such as down to earth, honest, wholesome, and cheerful), excitement (daring, spirited, imaginative, and up-to-date), competence (reliable, intelligent, and successful), sophistication (upper class and charming), and ruggedness (outdoorsy and tough).

To further achieve clarity of a destination's positioning, it is advisable to create a short statement that distils the distinctive meaning, the so-called brand essence. For example, Las Vegas defines its brand essence as "the ultimate entertainment and gaming extravaganza destination." Hong Kong positions itself as "Asia's world city." New Zealand describes its destination as "an adventurous new land and culture on the edge of the Pacific Ocean." Some twenty years ago, Australia launched a very powerful marketing campaign in the United States entitled "Come and say G'Day." This campaign was so effective that it was later included in the Smithsonian Institute's collection of major influences on American culture during the 1980s. The marketers responsible for the campaign defined Australia's brand essence as "civilized adventures in the friendliest place in the world."

Selecting Brand Elements

Selecting which brand elements to link to a destination through image building requires thorough analysis of several parameters. First, "who are the target tourists?" in terms of demographics, lifestyle, travel, holiday and leisure time behavior and attitudes, information habits, and sociocultural values. Second, "who are the competitors?" There is not a single set of competitors to a destination; competitors are different depending on the market sector which destinations aim to attract. Third, "how does the brand compare to competing ones" or what are their similarities and differences? Last, "what are the future trends?" regarding ingredients making up brand elements and influencing tourists' expectations.

Selected elements should pass through three attractiveness and competitiveness tests. First is the "desirability" test. Is the projected attribute, benefit, value, experience, and tourist imagery relevant to the target tourists? Do these satisfy tourists' existing needs and wants? Are they aspirational?

Second is the "deliverability" test. Can brand elements successfully be delivered to tourists through available product offerings? Regarding PODs, is the offering really superior? Third is the "uniqueness" test. The essence is that the destination becomes associated with one or very few sustainable competitive advantages, the PODs that give tourists a compelling reason why to select it over others.

The most important attributes for service offerings are the ones that originate from the core of the service, the experience with the brand, the image of the user (the tourist), the servicescape, and customer-facing employees. The following questions are useful in assessing destination brand imagery. Compared with other destinations suitable for "sea and sun" holidays, for example, how well does this location provide each of the key attributes? How well does it satisfy each of the key benefits? To what extent does it have certain special features? Which are the favorite attractions, products, services, and experiences? How effective and efficient are the services in terms of speed, responsiveness, and so forth? Do they completely satisfy tourists' expectations? How courteous and helpful are the providers of particular services? How stylish do tourists find the destination? How much do they like the look, feel, and other aesthetic aspects? Compared with other destinations suitable for "sea and sun" holidays, for example, with which does this destination competes? Are its prices generally higher, lower, or about the same? Do tourists find experiences relevant to them personally? To what extent do people who tourists admire and respect visit it? How much do tourists like others who visit and/or live here? How well do the following words describe this destination: down-to-earth, honest, daring, up-to-date, reliable, successful, upper class, charming, outdoorsy? How are the appropriate situations in which tourists would visit the place? To what extent does thinking of the destination brings back pleasant memories?

Where is Greece Today?

Until very recently, Greece has been primarily promoted through the brand assets of being an archetypal destination for classical antiquities and summer holidays: that is, where one goes to marvel at the Acropolis and perhaps Delphi or Olympia and to either laze or party away on the beaches of some Aegean or Ionian island. Indeed, both publicity materials produced by the Greek National Tourism Organization and commentary generated by the public at large are feature- and attribute-oriented, conveying the notion of Greece as being the "Cradle of Civilization" and a popular destination for summertime, seaside activities. Elements of the public dialogue also convey negative attributes, or brand liabilities, about the nation, including it being "noisy," "crowded," and "for the masses."

In its conveyance of this rather narrow image of Greece as a brand, the Greek National Tourism Organization's promotional material and advertisements demonstrate inconsistency and a lack of unified voice regarding the projected brand imagery elements. They are characterized by mundane, non-experiential listings of attractions; non-engaging, passive, and postcard-like depictions of features using flawless advertising-type images; and an almost complete absence of diverse and emotion-evoking tourists' imagery. Overall, there has been a lack of integration between Destination Greece's business strategy—mainly regarding its product portfolio and marketing strategy. The inconsistency has inevitably led to disparate, unrelated, and often contradictory promotional activities in an attempt to catch up with the industry's trends and achieve short-term and sometimes personal objectives. In addition, there is no formal brand architecture system to clearly define the way each of the subbrands (or designated regions and sectors brands) relate to the national brand or regulate all communication strategies and tactics. Destination Greece's brand identity system (its signature, typography, tagline, photography, music, tone of voice, and verbal content) as a whole also fell prey to conveying a limited scope of features, attributes, and a narrow brand essence. Elements merely conveyed are those related to the nation's seaside and cultural (antiquities) aspects.

In sum, although Greece certainly has world-leading strengths in the offerings of classical archaeology and seaside activities which, to be sure, have been an important drawcard for the nation up to the present, the sea and the sun have become a commodity, and new competition has arisen. Moreover, tourists nowadays demand experiences, rather than mere visits to monuments, from their travels. To this end, it has become necessary for Greece to expand its brand image (its conceptualization as a destination in the minds of tourists) to increase its market share.

The Road Ahead

The key to a successful brand strategy lies in reaching and convincing the top 10% of opinion-formers, whose options and influence then trickle down to the remaining 90%. These opinion-formers consist of industry decisionmakers, information catalysts (such as journalists and other members of the media), and savvy tourists whose opinions influence their peer group. These top influencers and makers comprise members of the creative class. They are people occupied in creating and applying new knowledge, characterized by "individuality, self-statement, acceptance of difference and the desire for rich multidimensional experiences" (Florida 2002:13), and seeking out "open, diverse communities where difference is welcome and cultural creativity is easily accessed" (Florida and Tinagli 2004:8). They go about their lives with the belief that they are the summation of their lives' stories, and continually crave new experiences which allow them to define themselves in relation to their peers. Indeed, they employ what might be termed the "New Value Formula" (Figure 2) in which they attempt to maximize their amount of experiences (those memorable events becoming stories) per unit of time and money invested.

It thus becomes imperative for Greece to challenge these individuals' preconceived notions about the destination or, put it simply, to get them to "discover the Greece they don't know." Greece can do this using its PODs: its unparalleled diversity. This diversity manifests itself through such features as its 3,000 multidimensional islands, fauna (including the multitude of endangered species in the Dadia forest) and flora that are richer than that of any other European country with more than 6,000 species, with 10% of them found nowhere else in the world (Gay 2004). Indeed, this diversity forms the foundation upon which the nation's new positioning is to be created.

As Greece offers unparalleled, largely unknown, contrasts, and because the creative class seeks new experiences with self-transformational elements, the country can be considered the "infinite experience space" of contrasts in which these unheard-of stories simply unfold. This, indeed, is envisioned as

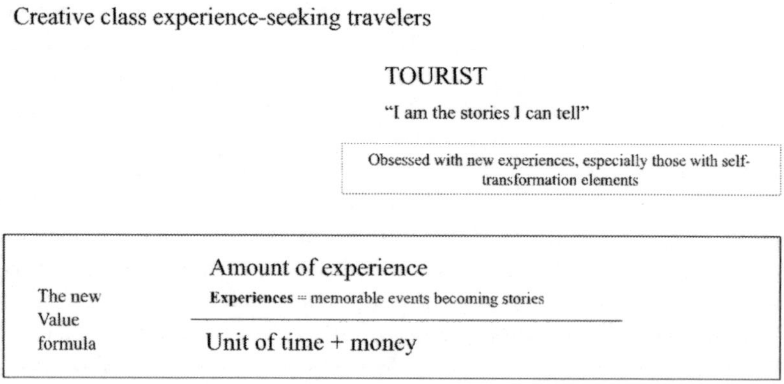

Creative class experience-seeking travelers

TOURIST

"I am the stories I can tell"

Obsessed with new experiences, especially those with self-transformation elements

	Amount of experience
The new Value formula	**Experiences** = memorable events becoming stories
	Unit of time + money

Figure 2 The New Value Formula for the Creative Class.

the new brand essence of Destination Greece. To support this initiative, Greece must challenge tourists' knowledge of the destination by presenting its extraordinary, lesser-known aspects. In essence, the country invites tourists to "discover the Greece you don't know." Believing that no other European destinations can offer its diversity, the project team singled out some key features which have been determined to be "emerging" in Greece: "Hidden Greece," countryside landscapes, Byzantine heritage, mountains, Aegean Chic, and nightlife among them. These features reinforce the notion of the nation being an "infinite experience space" of diversity, and bolster it with such additional elements as "urban culture," "natural products (e.g., wine, olive oil, and mastic)," "differentiated city break ideas," "natural wonders (e.g., Meteora)," "real life and people in Greece," and "luxury products (e.g., hotels, villas, spas, and yachts)." At the same time, current features will continue to be utilized and managed, yet presented in new and surprising ways with experiential dimensions. In doing so, the project team aims to convey a fuller, more accurate picture of the offerings of modern Destination Greece.

In terms of attributes, the project team has gone beyond the widely-known antiquity and seaside-related elements to espouse also the cosmopolitan, contemporary, creative, and authentic aspects of Greece which are "ideal for good life." Furthermore, the range of benefits conferred upon tourists is expanded. Supplementing such existing benefits of cultural edification, relaxation, and romance, the project team has added those of a more experiential nature, including "adventure," "intense emotions," and "body, mind, and spirit balance." These attributes and benefits will be conveyed across a broad spectrum of subbrands representing different tourism sectors within the larger Greece endorsement brand. They include the currently visible sectors of seaside, nautical, and cultural (antiquities); and the currently invisible sectors of countryside, health and wellness, touring, meetings, luxury, and city breaks. Each sector subbrand also carries its own complete model, facilitating the establishment and conveyance of its unique identity both in and of itself and within the larger Destination Greece endorsement brand. Also supporting this initiative, very selective tourist and experience imagery must be invoked. This comprises the depictions of individuals that are employed in promotional materials such as posters and brochures, videos, and internet media. To reinforce the brand essence, this imagery should depict tourists from every walk of life, showing a broad range of ages, ethnic and racial backgrounds, and other demographic criteria. These individuals will be engaged with all of their senses, living moments of joy and surprise in the destination. The experiential, intense atmosphere will be evident, with all images contributing to the storytelling theme.

Experience imagery can be considered the verbal counterpart to tourist imagery. It should, through its diction, "tell" these new stories in beautiful, moving, and real ways. Again, deep and all-sensual experiences must be communicated through evocative verbal imagery. For example, one could craft the following experience imagery based upon the diverse offerings of Samothrace: "Drift away to mysterious Samothrace to explore the tallest mountain in the Aegean and several dramatic waterfalls, wonder at the mystical Sanctuary of the Great Gods, relax in the mineral springs of Loutra and feel the multicultural vibe of the Samothrace World Music Festival." In this way, the creative class and experience-seeking tourists will be drawn to live the distinctive stories they can create only in Greece. In attention to these changes in brand image, Destination Greece should modify its brand identity system of signature, typography, tagline, photography, music, tone of voice, and verbal content so that it accords with the brand image evolution.

Branding Strategies

It remains now for these strategies to become realities. To this end, ten implementation strategies have been developed. Strategy 1 involves creating new "on brand" expressions, that is, expressions that accurately convey aspects of the new brand. Communications should employ the use of color, photography, tone of voice, and narrative according to the new brand image definitions. For example, the colors used in promotional materials should follow those natural colors which derive from Greek landscapes, seascapes, and natural products rather than artificial concoctions. Photography, for its part, should depict individuals engaged in experiences rather than showcasing mere commodities, products, or services. Narratives should use vivid diction, showcase diversity and contrasts at every turn, and employ the tone of a peer-to-peer, discerning tourist voice. Furthermore, thematic concepts such as "Luminous Abandoned Monemvasia" and "Raisins: Warrior's Feast" can be used to better spark interest in the various offerings. The country can create, source, and motivate the development of such content in various media channels. Besides employing conventional tactics, Greece's disseminating of unsigned content and commissioning emblematic publications can be very effective. As consumers are aware that destinations control their own images through dependent sources, they view independent sources as more trustworthy, thus rendering them more valuable for the brand.

Thus far Greece has been examined as a whole, but its perception as whole is in fact only one component of the entire branding strategy. Indeed, Greece, the national brand, functions as an endorsement for nine vertical product positionings: those of the seaside, nautical, culture, Athens and Thessaloniki, nature, touring, wellness, meetings, and luxury sectors, as well as myriad region, city, and cluster brands. This structure comprises Strategy 2, the adoption of a formal brand architecture system. Regions will be able to participate in the promotion of various sectorial offerings according to their particular infrastructure and competencies. It is recommended that, for marketing purposes, these regions assume easy-to-remember and promote names such as "Athens region" instead of Attica, and "Macedonia-Thrace" instead of the various regions of Macedonia and Thrace. These names may well differ from the regions' official administrative names. Last, promotional communications should follow a standard paradigm as regards the use of brand image and identity elements, with each piece of promotional material clearly showcasing the interrelation of sectors, regions, and clusters to the national brand through their signatures.

Turning to direct human-to-human interaction with prospective and current tourists, Strategy 3 involves the empowering of "on-brand" tourist service. As good customer service proves insufficient to meet the demands of the modern consumer, Greece must go beyond this to offer its branded service to tourists. The importance of service people in manifesting the new brand cannot be understated. These individuals serve as direct brand ambassadors during their interaction with tourists. Greek words should be employed for simple greetings whenever possible, with various sensory words and experiential vocabulary (in the English language) used to further reinforce the brand essence. An example of such on-brand communication could be the following: "If you want to experience something truly magical, I recommend 'the Gibraltar of Greece,' Monemvasia, where you can immerse yourself into the ultimate romantic medieval ambience reminiscent of the era of Knights: imagine rambling among Venetian ruins, sampling more delicious cuisine, chatting with the local artists, and taking in a spectacular view from atop the castle!"

Strategy 4 involves aligning communications with the tourist decision process. This comprises the challenge of maintaining their interest during the characteristically attritional process of moving from knowledge of the new brand, to considering it among various available options, to preference, and finally to active intent of traveling there. To do this successfully, Greece must engage in campaigns of messages with successive foci on these stages. Reaching the appropriate audiences for these messages is the objective of Strategy 5, which involves the selection of quality, innovative, influential, and credible media and venues. Tactics here include targeting the creative class, non-traditional and special travel experience and activities, and media and exhibitions, as well as creating "own media."

Strategy 6 delves deeper into promotional possibilities, considering the development of joint offerings and exploitation of promotional opportunities involving significant players that already enjoy strong relations with specific groups of potential tourists. Strategy 7 investigates brand alliance strategies such as co-branding and placement. Strategy 8 involves the undertaking of initiatives to inspire the media community and generate publicity, focusing on the dissemination of "on-brand" messages. Strategy 9 calls for the development of an international promotion opportunities system for Greek tourism service providers. Such a system could comprise industry stakeholders' financial participation as well as quality assurance initiatives. Finally, Strategy 10 addresses tourists' experiences upon entering and exiting the country, calling for such measures as information points, mobile services ,and other means to "leave an aftertaste" of the destination with tourists. With the implementation of these strategic methods, Greece can be successfully rebranded as a tremendously diverse destination for experiential travel, and thus enjoy increased market share for years to come.

CONCLUSION

The chapter presents a model for destination brand through image building, and reports a practical research project that applied the model to study the current state of Destination Greece, analyze the desired image, and provide recommendations of ten implementation strategies. Through primary and secondary research and collaboration with industry stakeholders, the project team determined that Destination Greece comprised a narrow brand image centered upon the seaside and cultural (antiquities) features. Moreover, its brand identity was not in line with recent design trends. It thus became to create a new brand image model for both the overarching Greece endorsement brand and its nine sector/product subbrands. The essence of the new endorsement brand is "A destination of unparalleled, largely-unknown contrasts, creating an infinite experience space, in which unheard-of stories simply unfold." It now appropriately accommodates the breadth and depth of the country's offerings. In addition, the new identity system for Destination Greece both evokes aspects of image evolution while being in concert with modern design trends.

The destination brand model should not be only limited to guiding communication and promotional strategies. It is imperative that product development strategies and public and private investment strategies also use it as a source of inspiration. Moreover, major organizational re-engineering is required. Tourism government institutions at the national and regional levels must transform themselves according to at least four parameters. One is the adoption of less of an introvert political and more of an extrovert sustainable-market vision, reducing their full dependence on the government and state. Two is the creation of the necessary structures to ensure operational efficiency and effectiveness in competitive market environments. Three is the attraction of professional leaders and talent with proven expertise in the areas of marketing and communications. Four is the introduction of new institutions to facilitate the constant decision-making involvement of all tourism-related stakeholders.

Indeed, Greece's effort to reposition itself must start from inside. As tourism experience nowadays is very much about tourists' being part of a destination's real life, Greece needs to initiate programs to inspire leaders and citizens toward fulfilling its new promise. Unfortunately, tourism officials are very much tied to the old sea, sun, and antiquities model, and in this way limit and stereotype their creativity. It is imperative that they change their beliefs and realize that Greece's most valuable assets are "all that's authentic today." The new brand essence disclosed in this chapter is indeed very much aligned with Greece's current authenticity. However, this meaningful authenticity is not always easily accessible to tourists. Greeks themselves need to protect the precious current authenticity assets and help tourists to fulfill their experiential, dream-seeking motivations: in sum, to live his or her "new, unheard-of stories."

Acknowledgement

The author would like to thank all team members for their participation in this project, including Thomas Antoniadis of Critical Publics London and Effie Lazaridou, Kate Alex, and Costis Bastias of Altervision and PRC Group.

Chapter 13

THE COPENHAGEN WAY
Stakeholder-driven Destination Branding

Lars Bernhard Jørgensen
Wonderful Copenhagen, Denmark

Ana María Munar
Copenhagen Business School, Denmark

Abridgement: This chapter examines how the city of Copenhagen, Denmark, has been branding itself as a destination. A broad perspective is adopted to analyze three main issues. They are the relationship between destination branding and the national capacity to insource valuable resources, the need to reframe the concept of branding in a dialogical process with tourists, and the importance of networking centered on host community as a winning business model for cities. The chapter explains how Wonderful Copenhagen (WoCo), the destination management organization, achieves a winning global brand by dealing with various challenges surrounding these issues. The case enlightens the interconnection between branding and national political strategy.
Keywords: destination branding; globalization; policy; network society.

Tourism Branding: Communities in Action
Bridging Tourism Theory and Practice, Volume 1, 177–189
Copyright © 2009 by Emerald Group Publishing Limited
All rights of reproduction in any form reserved
ISSN: 2042-1443/doi:10.1108/S2042-1443(2009)0000001015

INTRODUCTION

During the past decades, globalization processes have reshaped the world and increased the interdependency among individuals, nations, and regions (Giddens 2007). The revolution of information and communication technologies and some main political changes, such as the end of the Cold War, have enhanced a greater interconnectivity worldwide. Besides, such transformations have paved the way to a greater globalization of capital, productivity, and trade (Castells 2001), together with social and cultural aspects impacting on people's lifestyles and social patterns (Beck 2000).

Countries around the world are profoundly affected by these changes. The traditional nation-state's power is contested by global market forces, transnational policymaking, interdependence of changing international economic conjunctures, environmental challenges, and cultural and social movements across frontiers (Held, McGrew, Goldblatt and Perraton 1999). It is in this new context that today's countries face the challenge to remain competitive to provide increased growth and welfare for their citizens. This is not an easy task in a fast moving world that is becoming one large and complex marketplace. In this "flat" world (Friedman 2005), cities—especially big metropolises—are the engines of growth. They are strategic assets for countries as they have become the focal point of growth in this part of the 21st century and are the main providers of knowledge and experience industries.

Today's competition to attract foreign direct investment, tourism, conventions, and global events is more among cities than countries (Van der Berg, Van der Meer, Otgaar and Speller 2008). The importance of the cities in fostering creative production and consumption has been pointed out by other authors interested in the phenomenon of creative economy (Howkins 2001). The analysis by Florida (2002) highlights that labor force in the knowledge and experience industries prefers to live in big cities, as they provide a vast menu of culture, international accessibility, tolerance, and job opportunities. This phenomenon drives corporations to locate in big cities in their search for qualified employees. In services, the trend toward an organization of work, which is more project-based and informal also, demands that firms locate themselves in spatially concentrated labor markets usually found in an urban context (UNCTAD 2008). Furthermore, an analysis of the world population shows that approximately 50% live in urban areas, compared to only 36% in 1970. This percentage is much higher, 74%, for the more developed regions (UN 2008).

A similar trend is seen in European tourism with an improved performance of city destinations when compared to national ones. The number of hits on popular search engines of the Web also tells the same story. On Flickr—one of the popular interactive websites for sharing images—there are more than one million photos of Amsterdam, twice as many as of the Flickr (2008a, 2008b), while Paris has more than three million, which is the same as for all of France (Flickr 2008c, 2008d). The increased importance of the metropolises of the world is also true in the case of Denmark, where the country's capital Copenhagen plays a key strategic role in tourism and international competitiveness.

The strategies of development and growth of today's countries are closely connected to the promotion of their urban areas. This situation calls for them to have a strategy for their big urban centers, which includes a strong and focused city brand. However, this is seldom the case. The most common state of affairs is the absence of a focused city branding strategy at governmental level and also at the level of national tourism agencies, which often have branding strategies focusing on experiences in natural environments and the countryside. However, the consequences of this missing strategy may have different impacts depending on the size of the country. The lack of a coordinated city strategy is especially a challenge for small countries like Denmark, which only have one metropolis, when compared to other larger European countries, such as France or Germany, which have several large mega-cities to benefit from.

In the past few years, there has been an increased interest in place (Anholt 2003) and destination branding (Cai 2002; Konecnik and Gartner 2007; Murphy, Moscardo and Benckendorff 2007; Ooi 2004). In the competitive game among world cities, branding has become crucial both for the future of the tourism industry and for national competitiveness and performance in the global marketplace. However, little is known about the interrelationship among city branding strategies, tourism, and national competitiveness. This chapter analyzes how the city of Copenhagen has been addressing destination branding from a broader perspective in relation to three main issues. They are the relationship between destination branding and the national capacity to insource valuable resources, the need to reframe the concept of branding in a dialogical process with tourists, and the importance of networking including the host community as a winning business model for cities.

SHAPING WONDERFUL COPENHAGEN

Denmark is a Scandinavian country located in the North of Europe with a total population of 5.4 million (Danish Statistics 2008a). The capital city of

Copenhagen, with its 1.8 million residents, hosts most international functions with 75% of conventions, cruise calls, flight arrivals, and other forms of tourism. The number of tourist nights spent in the city reached 8.8 million in 2007. Its share of the European city tourism market is 1.6% (Wonderful Copenhagen 2008a). Its tourism profile is mainly in the areas of meetings, events, city breaks, family trip, and cruises. Copenhagen is the largest cruise destination in Northern Europe (Figure 1).

For the national economy and for Danish tourism, Copenhagen plays a unique role without comparison to other major cities in the country. Visit Denmark, the national tourism organization, has recently conducted a study to examine how blogs portrait the country. It was found that Copenhagen appears in 54% of the over 1,200 references (Visit Denmark 2008). The recognition of the capital city's importance for the national strategy led to

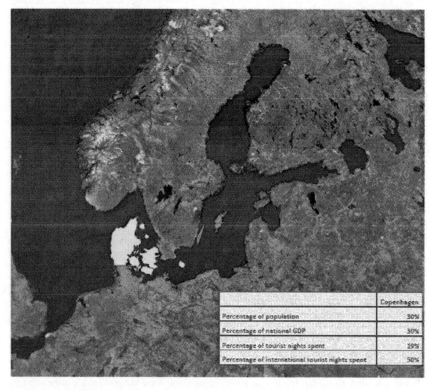

	Copenhagen
Percentage of population	30%
Percentage of national GDP	30%
Percentage of tourist nights spent	19%
Percentage of international tourist nights spent	30%

Figure 1 Facts about Copenhagen. *Source*: Danish Statistics (2008a, 2008b).

the 1989 establishment of the private–public organization Wonderful Copenhagen (WoCo). From its very beginning, the organization aimed to provide an effective and coordinated branding of the destination with its main focus on the international tourism markets. The original idea was to get underway an organization with a down-top matrix structure, including various tourism organizations of the city as stakeholders while receiving strong economic support from the political institutions of the region. However, it was not until the beginning of the 1990s that WoCo started to play a larger strategic role in the enhancement of tourism clusters and networks in the region. In 1991, the Danish Ministry of Industry issued a strategic report entitled "Tourist's Copenhagen" that elaborated the reasons behind the enhancement of WoCo.

The first years of the organization were not easy. WoCo had to face a strong segmentation in the tourism industry of Copenhagen and also the overlapping of competences among many other small tourism organizations of the region. To overcome these challenges, WoCo went through a reorganization of its functions, seeking to achieve larger support from the political actors and market organizations. Its structure consisted of a planning and development department focusing on strategy, a marketing department focusing on marketing, and public relations and a service department coordinating the activities of tourism offices and other functions related to the production and distribution of information material. One of the crucial considerations in this reorganization was to broaden the profile of its stakeholders and the need for a cross-sector partnership strategy. It expanded its activities to include not only the most traditional tourism organizations such as hotels and transport companies but also the representatives of the city's cultural and trade sectors. WoCo realized that the organizations were not focused on the potential of the creative industries and aimed to establish collaborations with those that could contribute to the innovation of the city offering. Furthermore, it decided to strive for an evidence-based policymaking by initiating and developing studies and reports to map the reality of the city and by establishing collaboration with researchers and experts. Finally, WoCo considered its branding and tourism strategies not as isolated initiatives but as a piece of a much larger puzzle in which the policies related to environment, housing, traffic, and transport, and market development also played a major role. The coordination of all the pieces of the puzzle demanded a huge effort of networking and collaboration among many different partners.

The design of the network allowed for different degrees of commitment and involvement, with some major active partners and others that were to be involved on a project base and in a more informal way. The final objective of WoCo was not only to promote the city in a tourism context but also to create awareness of Copenhagen for the benefit of the whole country's competitive advantage. The strategy that it adopted in 1991 laid the foundation for the growth of the organization. Since 1992, WoCo has been the official destination management organization for the greater Copenhagen area. Nowadays, it has approximately 80 employees who work in the main competence areas of communication and marketing, congresses and events, tourist service, and knowledge and innovation. In 2007, WoCo had a budget of about US$25 million, thanks to public and private financial support and its own commercial earnings from projects, marketing campaigns, sponsorships, bookings, and membership fees. Its network counts more than 300 formal member firms within the region and also public and private organizations of other sectors as project partners. WoCo has been addressing the challenge of an increased competition among world cities by focusing on three main issues: the role of tourism and its relation to insourcing, the reframing of branding strategies, and the use of networks and networking as a business model.

Tourism and Insourcing

The globalization agenda has for a long time focused on the issue of outsourcing. This has also been the case in Northern Europe as the region has to face the outsourcing of jobs and tasks to other more competitive regions in the world, which in most cases could benefit from much lower salaries. This has raised the question of how a country like Denmark is supposed to compete in a global market. There is no easy answer to this question. However, one of the strategies has to do with strengthening of those competences in the labor force needed to succeed in the knowledge and experience economy.

The knowledge economy (Drucker 1992) demands of a country to be able to nurture and attract knowledge workers. Besides, the advancement of what has been called the experience economy (Pine and Gilmore 1999), a concept that describes ongoing changes from the consumption and production of mass products and services to that of experiences, demands of organizations enhanced competences related to creativity and innovation. In the industrial age, it was important to insource raw materials and other hardware as basis for the adding of value to products. Today, the need for developed economies is much more to insource software such as talented people, expats, experts, and students, who in turn may help to attract the international functions in organizations such as company headquarters or research labs. The insourcing of these valuable resources is extremely important, as they are the basis of creating jobs and business, establishing networks, fulfilling branding strategies, and community building. Therefore, it is as well important to secure the flow of knowledge workers through events, conventions, and transport facilities, some of the areas that traditionally have been related to the tourism industry.

Insourcing is also becoming more important due to the increase in the fragmentation and flexibility of the value chains. This means that large companies search the world and locate their specialized functions at the most convenient place. The managers of these departments do not have any special attachment to the location and do not show any long-term strategic interest in the development of the city. They are in most cases just temporarily based to run the site, hotel, or other business unit. Therefore, one main challenge for WoCo comes from encouraging the participation and active involvement in its network of tourism managers of international companies that do not have a personal attachment to Copenhagen and that only see the city as a temporal placement in their career. To become competitive, cities need to invest in their quality of life, their internal and external accessibility, the quality of public services, and their image and identity. These cannot be achieved without a clear political support. The previously explained dynamics of globalization demands strong political support of initiatives aiming to attract those valuable resources if the city is to remain attractive as a location to locate business activities, produce knowledge, or attract tourists. The lack of involvement of global businesses in city development and promotion has to be compensated by a stronger commitment from the public authorities. The relationship to policymakers is crucial for city tourism. WoCo strategy builds on the awareness that the measures needed to develop the city are not being solely taken by the market forces.

Copenhagen in particular has also several disadvantages related to its relatively small size when compared to other capitals. The city has a narrow critical mass and suffers from lack of visibility. Furthermore, it does not contain a large labor market. Therefore, to become visible, it needs to increase its efforts and inventiveness. This reckoning has resulted in a type of strategy promoted by WoCo, which focuses not on size but on smart solutions. As an example, Copenhagen has managed to become the largest cruise destination of Northern Europe because it has been able to provide coordinated good business solutions to the cruise sector. However, these types of initiatives are not being provided by the market alone, they need to be driven and organized by the community. The importance of public involvement is not new. There are several international examples of how the public authorities' involvement in the branding and image building of a destination combined with city development has made a difference. Some of them are Barcelona, Singapore, Valencia, and Dubai. These cities have gained momentum, thanks to the development of mega events, which have turned out to be a vehicle for creating awareness of the city but also have produced a long-lasting legacy, being the perfect justification to boost investment and infrastructure development. Copenhagen has also benefited from this type of events when hosting the "European Capital of Culture" in the year 1996.

Improved accessibility has also been a key issue in the development of the city. In the beginning of the 1990s, Copenhagen realized that it was becoming a peripheral area in Europe. Therefore, a whole political strategy was developed through major public investments in infrastructure that resulted in the establishment of a new airport, two new bridges, one connecting the islands of Fyn and Zealand and one connecting Denmark to Sweden, and the establishment of whole new city area, Ørestad, for community and business development in the surroundings of Copenhagen (Ørestad 2008). The birth of WoCo is the result of that awareness of the need for an agent that can mobilize public and private interests to achieve a better coordination of the initiatives and an improved promotion of the city in the area and scope of tourism. The more the tendencies toward the internationalization of capital and workforce take over, the more there is a need for political involvement and strategy. WoCo tries to face this challenge by focusing on a number of variable resources in the experience economy which are important for the city to improve is attractiveness. These resources are in the areas of conventions and events, cruise tourism, airline transportation, and city breaks.

Reframing Branding

Branding has become extremely popular during the past decade and has won recognition as a tool to improve the competitive advantage of a country (Anholt 2003). In the context of tourism, there have also been developments in the understanding of destination branding giving a major role to community involvement (Ooi 2004). Branding, which has received many different definitions throughout time, is closely related to perception and how the product or the place is perceived by customers. In this sense, there is a close relationship between image and brand of a destination. They are two different concepts, but the brand existence is dependent on the image formation of the destination (Cai 2002). The image of a destination is owned by tourists, and it is permeated by the sociocultural and economic changes that impact their sensitiveness. Destinations compete through the images held in the minds of potential tourists (Baloglu and McCleary 1999a, 1999b). In this context, WoCo understands that branding needs to be reframed so that it will no longer be primarily driven by a logo, a brilliant idea, or a catchy slogan in unidirectional one-way communications.

Branding should increasingly be about showing and experiencing through the involvement of people and of the community. It should have a stronger focus on the dialogical relationship between the customer and the product. This demands a stronger focus on relationship building in branding. In this sense, it can promote tourists' involvement so that the destination becomes part of a lifestyle formation and of their lived identity on their return home (Prentice 2004). In the Copenhagen brand strategy, the vision is to make the people of the world wish to become Copenhageners. The basic selling strategy for the city is not to show amazing and spectacular city images but present a type of lifestyle. However, this cannot be constructed in a laboratory. It is intertwined with the daily life of people in the local community. That Copenhagen's lifestyle is worth promoting can be seen in the latest ranking of quality of life by the British design magazine "Monocle" where Copenhagen ranked number one among the world's 25 top cities (Wonderful Copenhagen 2008b). However, this type of branding strategy, because it is founded on the lifestyle of the residents, implies a lot of small initiatives and coordination. This in turn demands the existence of welfare policies and a whole city model which enhances citizen participation and fosters a creative environment. WoCo can partially contribute to this by developing activities that help the community to feel proud of the city as when media with global reach inform about Copenhagen being visited by famous people from around the world.

Based on small but smart and lifestyle strategies, WoCo develops several initiatives related to branding. Some of them aim at generating awareness by improving interest in Copenhagen and opening a window of opportunity for private organizations to enter or keep their markets. WoCo pursues this goal by providing a platform that displays reasons to travel to Copenhagen. This awareness generation uses as tools the presence in international media and the development of events. Besides, there is a whole strategy to follow up once the awareness has been established. The strategy focuses mainly on business-to-business cooperation facilitating entry into new tourism markets. Some of the initiatives in this area include business trips, analyses of customers needs, and other activities to facilitate meeting with the marketplace.

Nevertheless, WoCo is aware that many traditional branding tools are not enough. Today's consumers are overloaded with information, much of which is perceived as having a low level of legitimacy or being produced with only commercial objectives in mind. Tourists increasingly develop resistance to information overload by only trusting what they have personally experienced or the information provided by friends, colleagues, or relatives. There is tremendous competition among destinations (Kim and Fesenmaier 2008). The main challenge is to win awareness in tourists' minds in a way that it is trustworthy. The development of an image that is based on trust is a key asset in branding. This tendency demands of branding planners a new way of doing things and the implementation of new tools to face the upcoming challenges. These tools need to be developed to show the reality of the destination and not simply to "tell" about it. One of the most appropriate tools is the enhancement of events, as they entail a much higher level of participation which increases the possibility of word-of-mouth effect and may provide a positive storytelling about the city.

A second challenge to traditional branding comes from the development of the Web 2.0 platform. Web 2.0 refers to a second generation of services available on the Web that lets people collaborate and share information online (Carter 2007). The application of the Web 2.0 often allows mass publishing through web-based social software and permits the uploading and downloading of digitalized information by tourists (Munar 2008). In times where the Internet has become the primary means with which destination marketing organizations communicate with tourists (Kim and Fesenmaier 2008), the increase of the tourist-generated content on websites transforms the destination in an open source product which cannot be controlled. Platforms such as Youtube, Myspace, Trip-Advisor, and Flickr have become large universes where customers themselves create, transform, and share the brand. These portals are a challenge but also an opportunity as they offer a unique possibility to understand tourists, get into dialog with them, and get innovative ideas as to the development of tourism products. However, very few companies and destinations have yet understood how to either exploit the new potential or to reframe branding in this new context. One of the ways in which WoCo has tried to meet this development has been by launching a noncommercial interactive site on the corporate website entitled "Your Copenhagen" where tourists can share their experiences (Wonderful Copenhagen 2008c).

Branding is also under transformation by cobranding strategies. For destinations, it can be beneficial to team up with brands that add value to the brand of the city and expand its global reach. Cobranding can be the answer to the lack of resources to market the city globally and a door to new distribution channels outside traditional tourism promotion. WoCo has enhanced these types of cobranding initiatives with cities such as Singapore and Vancouver and with product brands such as MTV, Volkswagen, Forbes, Carlsberg, and other organizations such as the World Energy Council and the United Nations Climate Council. These cobranding activities improved global awareness of Copenhagen, facilitating the city's ability to host businesses and job-generating events such as product launches, awards shows, and business events.

Many global companies are positive toward collaboration with a city brand which may add value to that of the company. However, cobranding strategy has several threats in store. It engenders the possibility of partially losing control over the city brand. The destination branding authority does not have influence on how the partners' brand will develop and if in the long run a partnership could become a negative association. Therefore, partnerships shall be very carefully selected. For example, a partnership with the International Cycling Union is a very positive idea when thinking about the environment- and climate-related issues. Furthermore, it is closely related to the image of Copenhagen as a cycling city. However, the development of doping related scandals in the cycling sport could have an unexpected effect. An event like the Fashion Week is also very positive. It helps to promote the city and relates to the idea of Copenhagen as a design city. However, the debate regarding the extreme thinness of the models and its relation to eating disorders may have an unexpected effect as well, which is difficult to foresee beforehand. All in all, cobranding helps to open the brand to the world at large, but it also entails new risks and challenges.

Widening the Network

In an industrial society, the winning business model is built upon capital and technology. While these are still fundamental production factors, the establishment of strong networks and clusters will become a key factor for competitiveness in the global economy (Porter 1990). This is also true in the case of tourism. A key factor in Copenhagen's success in the past decade to attract tourists, cruise calls, and events lies in the fact that the local stakeholders have learned to work together in networks. Networks are important for several reasons. They enable common ownership and sharing of costs and knowledge, allow for coordinated investments, and build critical mass in international marketing initiatives. Furthermore, studies have pointed toward networks as being able to encourage collaboration and diffusion of good practices, benefit small companies by giving them some of the advantages of the larger ones, and as getting better access to suppliers and helping to develop an infrastructure of professional support services for the benefit of all the stakeholders (UNCTAD 2008).

In tourism, networks are particularly important due to the complexity of its offering. Consumption in this industry does not rely in only one single good or service but in a combination of many different ones. Tourists buy into a product compiled of many different elements: transport, lodging, shopping, and culture, to name just a few. Those cities that are able to achieve excellence in compiling these complex value chains are those that can become "winner cities." Therefore, competitiveness is closely related to the establishment of an innovative and flexible organizational capability. WoCo operates in an environment characterized by many and often conflicting issues and actors, which is also the situation for many other destination management organizations. Therefore, their challenge is to help overcome conflicts of interests to improve the performance of these complex value chains. WoCo pursues cooperation to prevail over the clash of differing goals between actors involved by helping in the establishment and development of networks.

These networks (in other sectors, they are often called clusters) usually do not emerge by themselves. In many cases, they need to be initiated. WoCo organizes several hundred companies—both within and outside tourism—in various networks such cruises, conventions, and events. It helps in the establishment and strengthening network providing companies in these networks with professional services in sales, marketing, service concepts, developing events, and knowledge and strategies. Each of the networks have their own board to create true "ownership" among the participating companies, but they buy all their services at WoCo and thus work together under the same Copenhagen brand umbrella. It allows for a large level of independency in each one of the networks but also demands a general commitment to the main strategy of the organization. Networking is perhaps the single most important role for city development and tourism organizations. As a destination management company, WoCo organizes as many of these networks as the city is capable of nurturing.

CONCLUSION

The case of WoCo helps to examine some of the main challenges faced by today's destination organizations when planning their branding strategies. It shows a model of management which adapts and tries to find new ways in times of constant global changes. This chapter shows how WoCo balances among the need for local engagement, accountability, flexibility, and the direction needed to react to a changing global environment. Branding is seen as a powerful tool with which to deal with issues such as national competitive advantages, competition among cities, attracting talent, knowledge workers, attractiveness of location in times of intensive outsourcing, and offshoring business strategies.

The Copenhagen way to overcome these challenges corresponds to an outward-looking management culture. A model characterized by flexible and hybrid forms of production where local and global, centralized and decentralized, public and private, and tourism and non-tourism sectors merge. The development of WoCo has resulted in the establishment of an organization with a complex matrix structure consisting of many small and bigger partnerships with different levels of commitment and participation. It is an example of a fluid organization whose main assets are trust, knowledge, communication, and a clear sense of direction. WoCo is an organization whose value depends on being able to initiate and develop ideas for the benefit of the community. Its most important asset in brand building is related to the capacity of communicating and being able to convince many different types of stakeholders of the benefits of cooperating. This asset cannot be achieved overnight. It relies upon trust and confidence established by many years of developing projects and partnerships for the city. It has a high level of informal bonds among partners. Its branding strategy is an open platform which supports many stakeholders and their brands under one common umbrella. The chapter shows that this model is not an easy path. It demands a high level of involvement from the community and balance between the individual initiatives of the networks and the general strategy of the organization. Nevertheless, the strength of the value proposition of WoCo is as worthwhile as its capital of trust and will last as long as it is possible to create significant and measurable value for all partners and stakeholders involved. The case of WoCo is also a valuable example of the intersection between city destination branding and national political strategy.

Chapter 14

CONSULTATION BUILDS STRONGER BRANDS

Bill Baker
Total Destination Management, USA

Abridgement: The practice of destination branding for cities has been increasingly adopted by communities of all sizes and has enjoyed success to varying degrees. The focus of many of these branding initiatives has frequently been on the creative elements of logo, tagline, and advertising theme, with only limited consideration for the importance of generating stakeholder support and experience delivery. Active stakeholder engagement, to build the brand from the inside out during its planning process, has been shown to be an important factor in those initiatives that are considered more successful. This chapter highlights the need to engage stakeholders in the brand planning for destinations from the earliest stages. It illustrates a consultative model for destination brand planning, primary with a US case study, along with examples of some other cities. **Keywords:** branding; brand adoption and planning; city brands; consultation; stakeholders.

INTRODUCTION

Many countries, cities, and regions have launched a destination brand strategy with great fanfare, only to see it fall flat. Key stakeholders and

Tourism Branding: Communities in Action
Bridging Tourism Theory and Practice, Volume 1, 191–205
Copyright © 2009 by Emerald Group Publishing Limited
All rights of reproduction in any form reserved
ISSN: 2042-1443/doi:10.1108/S2042-1443(2009)0000001016

tourism partners did not support it because the strategy was developed behind closed doors with little or no consultation with anyone outside of destination marketing organizations (DMOs). They should have been working to avoid this situation by building buy-in and support from the start of the project. The path to reveal a community-based destination brand usually requires the involvement of a multitude of stakeholders and may depart somewhat from that generally followed for branding corporate products and services. One reason for the variation is the composite nature of destinations that are a compilation of many independent and competing businesses, products, and experiences that may be owned and managed by many different organizations with no single management team or brand custodian.

Cities generally have extremely limited marketing budgets compared to the resources at the disposal of many consumer and service brands. Exacerbating the situation is the pressure from city stakeholders and the challenge of developing a simple positioning message that will resonate with many customer groups, yet capture the city's diverse tourism attributes. Although a corporate brand needs approval by a marketing team or board, the destination brand often requires endorsement by the city council and other organizations in which political players may never see eye-to-eye. A problem for many branding initiatives is that important political leaders frequently do not have strong marketing credentials, nor do they have a customer-focused perspective. Yet they can exert considerable influence over the process. This is stressed by Morgan and Pritchard (2002), arguing that if a city brand is to be developed as a coherent entity, the different participants in the process must be conscious of the potentially destructive role of politics. The brand must overcome enmity and rise above politics. The support of the political leaders in small cities is vital and must be nurtured because their endorsement and thorough understanding are two of the most important elements of a branding assignment.

Community-based brands must often withstand a level of political and public debate that consumer brands rarely have to undergo. A city brand must be able to stand the test of time, public discourse, political scrutiny, media questions, and the analysis of marketing partners. The best way to insulate the brand from this scrutiny is to generate community and partner buy-in and involvement from the beginning through an open consultative process. For most cities, the challenge is to orchestrate cohesive brand messages and experiences through the commitment of many local players including neighborhoods, attractions, hotels, tour operators, real estate agents, and restaurants who may also be competitors to each other. This usually requires an approach that is more conciliatory and inclusive than that found in the branding of most consumer products. For instance, being very specific with the positioning may unintentionally alienate many groups and cause controversy. The challenge is to not dilute the positioning to the point where the place loses its strongest competitive edge and ends up being seen as meaningless or irrelevant.

Before the planning of destination brand begins, it is imperative to encourage the endorsement and participation of the community's leading executives, opinion leaders, and public officials who are likely to be instrumental in the long-term health and delivery of the brand. Some of these people may not be directly involved in the ongoing brand management, but their decisions and support may have profound leverage and influence. They should be exposed to the basic concept of branding and its benefits, particularly that it is more than an advertising campaign, new logo, or slogan. Simply completing the brand strategy and then presenting it to the community leaders is likely to result in a very weak brand or, even worse, controversy. The objective of this chapter is to highlight the need to engage stakeholders in the brand planning for destinations from the earliest stages of the project. The chapter is based on excerpts from the book, *Destination Branding for Small Cities* (Baker 2007), which outlines consultative planning approaches to stimulate broad stakeholder engagement in the brand building process. Comments and quotations appearing in this chapter relating to specific cities are based on interviews conducted during the years 2006 to 2008. The chapter focuses mainly on the case of Durham (North Carolina, USA), amplified with examples of some other American cities.

STAKEHOLDER ENGAGEMENT FOR CITY BRANDING

Cities are dynamic with myriad agendas, visions, objectives, and egos—all in play at the same time. Most municipalities have multiple centers of influence, and while many individuals and organizations are very customer, business, and future-oriented, others may be firmly locked in the past or may not want to see any changes. Others are less concerned about economic benefits as they are about the social and environmental impacts that marketing the community may bring. Still others question why money is being spent on branding and marketing when there are pot holes in the streets.

Community-Based Branding

The marketing and branding of cities can be complex and controversial. To avoid or minimize controversy, political and opinion leaders should be encouraged to understand the branding assignment and embrace the many benefits that the strategy will bring. Communicating the benefits to local citizens and organizations will help in winning support and boosting community pride. When they fully grasp and support it, they are able to both deflect criticism and become influential champions, opening doors to signal that the project is important to constituents and the future of the city. At times, achieving the vision and delivering the city's brand promise requires a leader to break from the status quo and exert the influence of his or her office. The leader may need to support a call for new resources, new organizational structures, a review of relevant city ordinances, beautification programs, and performance reviews. In many respects, branding is also an exercise in change management and relies very much on healthy relationships, strong leadership, cooperation, and a genuine preparedness to adapt to new situations. A further challenge to the branding of destinations is satisfying the need for a long-term view. This can be particularly relevant to locations where political leaders are actively supportive of the brand development process, but their involvement is limited to a specific term. There needs to be sufficient awareness and conviction among both political and tourism leaders that the destination brand is able to withstand the periodic turnover in leadership and can sustain its momentum and relevance for both stakeholders and customers, including tourists.

Many places rush to define their new brand following one or two brainstorming sessions involving only their advertising agency and the DMO's staff. Equally as dangerous is when the agency presents a brand strategy comprising only a new logo and tagline to the DMO and stakeholders. Sometimes the approach is to first design the brand elements, then sell them to constituents. Efforts like these usually run out of steam very quickly or fail to ignite enthusiasm among stakeholders. When launched, more often than not, they do not have the support of key stakeholders because they were not treated as valued partners from the start. Sometimes it is not only a matter of what one does but the manner in which it is brought about. A collaborative and consultative approach is likely to lead to a much more accepted and sustainable brand. By adopting the principles of branding, cities are introducing a more strategically focused approach to their marketing. Branding should provide the organizing and decisionmaking framework to better orchestrate the messages and experiences emanating from the place. It should be strategic, not tactical, and approached with a long-term view. The overall process for formulating a brand strategy is much the same irrespective of the destination's size. However, individual elements and emphasis will vary according to the available budget, the size of the city, stage of development, market sophistication, complexity of its economic base, and the accuracy of its existing image in external markets. Each place brings its own relationships, politics, history, and attitudes.

The president or executive director of a DMO must be actively engaged in every aspect of the brand's development and breathe vitality into the assignment. The only way for the brand to take off is when the chief executive officer (CEO) and the board "get it" and have the passion, energy, skills, and vision to make it work. If he or she takes a passive role, the brand will almost certainly fail. This early buy-in will help to orchestrate a "soft landing" for the brand so that it will be well received, endorsed, and supported by key public, non-profit, and private sector organizations, stakeholders, and tourism industry partners. Understandably, there may be many legitimate distractions that consume the CEO's time. However, the brand is at the heart of what will influence every activity that the destination will be involved in for years to come and thus worth every minute that he or she can devote to it. Although the CEO may want to delegate aspects of the day-to-day management of the process to a marketing manager, the CEO must remain intimately involved in crafting the brand strategy.

Reyn Bowman, President of the Durham Convention & Visitors Bureau, encouraged broad community buy-in by facilitating Durham's brand planning using the *7A Destination Branding Process* created by Total Destination Management (Figure 1). According to him,

> Durham is an incredibly complex place. We initiated a process of one-on-one interviews, balanced focus group discussions, opinion research in key markets, a community survey and a representative Brand Advisory Board to ensure as much buy-in as possible. Additionally, once the brand was launched, we communicated periodic updates to hundreds of civic and business leaders and made presentations to local boards, civic clubs and organizations to help bring the brand to life and show people how to immediately incorporate it into their messages and operations. (Baker 2007:71)

Figure 1 The 7A Destination Branding Process.

The *7A Destination Branding Process* recognizes the special nature of community-based branding and the need for the ongoing engagement of constituents. This is essential to generate understanding and enthusiasm for the new brand. Importantly, it reinforces the need to build the brand from the inside out and ensures that planners are exposed to the heart and soul of the community. There are critical issues and questions that must be answered at each of the seven-stage process. The first stage is assessment and audit and aims to arrive at an understanding of what is the brand's place in the world. The second is analysis and advantage and examines what the city is to be known for. The third is alignment and focuses on establishing the brand's relationships. The fourth is articulation and planning and examines how the brand can be expressed visually and verbally. The fifth is activation and relates to the implementation of the brand strategy and answers the question of how the brand will come to life. The sixth is adoption and attitudes and aims to answer the question of how the stakeholders can support the brand. The seventh is action and afterward and relates to evaluation and focuses on how the brand will be kept fresh and relevant.

The rigor and speed with which a community is able to complete all stages is influenced by the community's size, its state of development, scope of the brand, politics, available budget, time, and the authority and autonomy with which the DMO has been empowered to make decisions. The challenge for the DMO is to orchestrate on-brand actions and messages that will ensure that the destination delivers the experiences that are inherent within their promise. Achieving this requires broad stakeholder support because partners and stakeholders throughout the destination must embrace the attitude that every time they are in touch with a customer is an opportunity to positively reinforce and build the brand through customer experiences. Despite their good faith and good intentions, communities can find this challenging because it takes passion, commitment, innovation and, most importantly a lot of collaborative behavior to sustain the required on-brand behavior.

Advisory Group and Stakeholders' Participation

A brand advisory group, representing a cross section of community and business organizations, should be assembled to oversee the brand planning process. Their main responsibility is to recommend approval and adoption of the brand strategy. Members should be carefully selected after a list of prospective candidates has been thoroughly evaluated. The group should ideally comprise 8–12 representatives, although there is no "correct" number. However, the more people in the group, the higher the risk that too many unrelated issues may start to play a role. This can slow the process down, impair the sense of cooperation and objectivity that is needed, and dilute the brand itself. The Pittsburgh Region Branding Initiative was the group responsible for overseeing the development of a brand strategy for Pittsburgh in 2002. It was surprising to see that it had 120 representatives on its Image Gap Committee. One wonders how each participant could make a truly meaningful contribution.

The advisory group's involvement should be woven throughout the brand planning process, especially at critical milestones. They may not necessarily be authorized to give approval or make major decisions, but they are an invaluable sounding board to provide guidance to the brand specialist and DMO executives. Members should be representative of the community and, as a group, recommend approval of the final brand strategy to the DMO. This will ensure that solutions do not lose touch with market situations, resources, implementation capabilities, politics, and the self-image and values of the city. The group's involvement should start with an intensive briefing and discussion on branding, the planning process that will be followed, its role, and a discussion of the members' aspirations for the project. Although some participants may be very experienced in marketing and branding, it is still advisable to provide this briefing. Starting with an informative presentation about branding cities ensures that everyone is on the same page. It is not unusual for advisory group members to develop a strong sense of ownership and pride in their contribution as the brand is defined. Their enthusiasm and commitment is priceless as the project moves forward. Many of them will eventually step forward to become active champions for the brand because they are so engaged and knowledgeable about all aspects of its creation. Hopefully, they will also come to see that the DMO cannot achieve its objectives alone and that all participants must work in an active partnership.

During the assessment stage of the planning process, canvassing the opinions of local constituents brings forward great ideas and perspectives and provides important clues as to where the "land mines" or likely trouble spots may be later in the process. Importantly, consultation is extremely valuable in clearing the way to reveal the brand. Within the community, there will be residents, business, and political and opinion leaders who will have comments, knowledge, and perspectives that should be considered. After they are identified, the level and nature of their involvement can be determined. Brad Dean, President and CEO of Myrtle Beach Area Chamber of Commerce (South Carolina, USA), has some excellent advice for those starting a brand planning process for their city:

> One nugget of advice that I wish someone had offered me is this: The brand effort does not belong behind closed doors, in an ivory tower or within the boardroom. Involve everyone— the stakeholders, the Web programmer, the mayor, the media—involve anyone and everyone who has a reason to care. Involve your mother-in-law if you have to. Just make certain that anyone who has a vested interest gets a chance to be involved.' We didn't do this and, lo and behold, we rolled out the new brand to a chorus of boos and jeers. A few of our county council immediately announced they hated the idea, and the media blasted us. All of this could have been avoided if we had involved some of the key people in advance. (Baker 2007:61)

The task of pulling participants together in a community with diverse political, cultural, and social interests as those found in Santa Monica (California, USA) would seem like an impossible task. But, according to Misti Kerns, President and CEO of the Santa Monica Convention & Visitors Bureau, "When you can bring together 11 different interest groups, from the right and the left, and have everyone agreeing on a single item, then I'd have to say that's success, and that's what our branding experience has done for our community" (Baker 2007:62). Creating opportunities to participate can range from membership in the brand advisory group, face-to-face interviews, attendance at a workshop, and an invitation to complete a survey or periodic briefings about the progress. Brand planners should not sidestep the opportunity to invite critics and even those who may be cynical about such projects. Engaging these constituents may provide an opportunity to change their opinions. Even if they choose not to participate, they may gain greater respect for one's efforts and provide support in other ways.

The brand planning process tends to gain credibility and support when the DMO reaches beyond "the usual suspects" to canvas the views of a wider range of constituents. The Greater Tacoma Convention & Visitors Bureau (Washington, USA) strongly supports the consultative route. According to the bureau's former Executive Director,

> The consultative planning process that we used generated incredible buy-in among our Board members, partners and stakeholders. It established the [the bureau] as a community leader and contributed directly toward a better understanding and working relationship. We were able to make changes that probably would not have been possible for years had we not used external assistance and developed a strategy that had been built on collaboration and engagement. (personal interview in 2003)

A destination brand is only as strong as its weakest advocate. The successful implementation of the brand strategy will require actions by more than just the chamber of commerce, city council, or convention and visitors bureau. It will require the long-term advocacy, passion, and support by dozens, and may be hundreds, of local individuals and organizations. Winning support for the adoption and use of a community's brand strategy can be very much about change and destinations may have to embrace many of those principles of change management. Brand leadership may call for changes in behavior and relationships for the DMO, its board, and partners. It may call for variations to structures, systems, recruitment, processes, attitudes, and management status quo. Preparing to deliver and manage a strong brand may directly impact on everything that the organization does.

There are possibly hundreds of prospective brand partners, stakeholders, and interested parties across the city—or at least parties who need to become interested. Consistent and repeated education and information is essential to maintain their focus, both as a refresher and due to frequent staff turnover in so many positions that affect the brand communications and delivery. Many agencies, organizations, individuals, and teams in the community are responsible for communicating the brand in one way or another in both official and unofficial capacities. For some, such as local government, DMO, chambers of commerce, and the tourism industry, it should be central to their destination or place marketing mission. There are others such as media, developers, real estate agents, and service staff who project a positive, and sometimes inadvertently a negative or dated, image of the city that need to understand the mission and realign their actions.

Most city governments do not think in terms of marketing, but they are often attuned to the related concept of enhancing and protecting the city's good name and encouraging business growth. Some individuals, such as politicians, sports stars, entertainers, business leaders, academics, and celebrities frequently find themselves in the role of official or unofficial ambassadors for a city, whether they set out to be or not. Then there are the hotels, attractions, tour operators, and others who are actively trying to entice tourists to the city; and so are the universities and colleges, retailers, developers, and employers. Each of them may be inducing outsiders to visit, invest, relocate, or study in the area. Every effort must be made to ensure that to the greatest extent possible, a common message or theme emanates from these stakeholders.

On the contrary, many communities make the mistake of not sufficiently informing and engaging external stakeholders and partners during the launch of the brand. This group, comprising meeting planners, relocation specialists, media, travel trade, and group travel operators, should be informed of the brand strategy and how they can support and use the brand as soon as possible. True success will only occur if key partners and stakeholders are motivated, totally understand the brand, know how to use it, and genuinely want to support it. A good example of using change management principles to successfully engage and harness the behavior of diverse local stakeholders to support the brand is in Durham where the convention and visitors bureau helped stakeholders see the need for the new approach. The bureau also recognized the need to educate all interested stakeholders in exactly what branding is, how it can relate to Durham, their organization, and what was needed to be done to achieve success. It was important for the bureau to build buy-in for the destination brand vision, ensuring that the stakeholders had a clear mission in mind and a unified approach. The formation of a brand advisory group comprised of influential and respected stakeholders including the mayor was created to oversee and guide the brand planning and adoption process. Important to their role was to communicate clearly and often to generate understanding and excitement and stimulate on-brand behavior among stakeholders. Importantly, each key stakeholder organization in the city conveyed its endorsement of the brand and also communicated this to its own constituents, informing them how they can play their part.

An important aspect of the approach adopted by Durham's convention and visitors bureaus was the way in which it approached organizations and individuals to gain their support to ensure that there were no barriers and hurdles that could interfere with the delivery of the city's desired brand experiences. A critical step was to firstly identify the most influential points in tourists' contact and experiences with the city to ensure that they were as satisfying as possible. Because of the random nature of the exchanges that tourists could have with a destination, this required engaging hundreds of organizations (such as local radio stations, service stations, and police) who may normally not see themselves as playing an important role in tourism or the image of the city. By being able to generate many short-term wins and broad community support, the bureau was able to create a positive atmosphere and further increase teamwork and collaboration. This ongoing engagement has stimulated stakeholders to stay aligned with the brand. In fact, they have a 30-member organization comprising volunteers called the Durham Image Watchers. This entity is constantly scanning the community and nationally to ensure that, wherever people are exposed to some aspect of Durham (whether it is in the media or everyday experiences in the city), they encounter an accurate and positive reflection of the brand. Many of the volunteers are retired and devote many hours a day to the task.

The Adoption Strategy

Successful brands are led from the top and owned at the grassroots and by customers including tourists. Communicating and delivering the community's brand promise cannot be the sole province of the DMO, city council, or chamber of commerce. It requires a shared responsibility. The branding objectives must engage leaders, organizations, and individuals who can orchestrate the on-brand behavior, regulations, policies, investments, and plans. Ideally, it should include city planners, architects, transport specialists, landlords, and developers, as well as elected, non-profits, government, and business leaders. A brand strategy frequently presents opportunities that require the DMO and its partners to adapt to new circumstances to attain their true potential. Effectively managing the new brand requires that there be no walls or "silos" in which people and organizations isolate their on-brand actions. Leaders should embrace changes, alleviate fear, and constantly evaluate how to create a better playing field for the brand to be a winner. Ultimately, success goes to those who pay attention to the politics, systems, processes, people, resources, and priorities that underpin their promises. It is not simply the hourly employees at the customer interface, or the executives and strategic priorities behind them, who are responsible for this. It is everyone.

The number one objective at this point is to encourage understanding, adoption, and correct use—one brand, many partners, and one voice. The adoption strategy should outline the goals, techniques, and messages that will boost support and use of the brand by stakeholders, residents, tourism partners, and other messengers. It calls for the need to identify the individuals and organizations most important to the brand's ongoing health and allow them to initiate the actions needed to fully adopt and support it. Their initial goals include the need to ensure that they understand the strategy including the Destination Promise™ and how to support the brand, including how to use its identity elements accurately and consistently. Many partner organizations will have to consider how they can best play their role in delivering outstanding brand experiences. After Durham's strategy was completed, President Reyn Bowman and Chief Operating Officer Shelly Green conducted 60 face-to-face meetings with government, community, business, and education leaders across the community. This enabled them to not only generate a clear understanding of the brand but also stimulate wide community acceptance and its use by groups as diverse as Duke University, the Research Triangle Park, the Durham Bulls baseball team, and neighborhood groups. The advice of John Cooper, President of Yakama Valley Visitors and Convention Bureau (Washington, USA), is:

> Plan to carefully orchestrate the launch with a detailed plan that includes media and community relations, the event launch format, and stakeholder briefings. You can't expect the brand to gain traction in the community without a concerted effort. Give consideration to who should speak at the launch and who are the best spokespersons to publicly lend their support to the effort. We found it very valuable to meet with the

editorial boards of newspapers and to treat all media equally in distributing information about the brand. No matter how much research, consultation and agreement there may have been in the creative process be prepared for the criticisms and possible misunderstandings. It pays to do your homework and prepare for the inevitable barbs with responses (which in some cases may be no response at all). Be sure that prime stakeholders are informed and are also ready to respond to possible criticisms with the suggested talking points. Encourage them to hold tight and ride out possible storms. (Baker 2007:166)

Although there are many tools in a destination marketer's arsenal, it is people who are ultimately the most influential and credible communicators of brand experiences. Behind the scenes, it takes people to drive the strategies, decisions, designs, creativity, management systems, and the policies that influence communications and the customer experiences. They may be marketers, urban planners, business and civic leaders, educators, and service professionals. In the case of a community it also involves political leaders, retailers, entrepreneurs, investors, and frontline staff to develop a compelling and sustainable brand. It is essential to make these stakeholders an integral part of the brand strategy to achieve the level of engagement to deliver the outstanding experiences promised by a brand.

CONCLUSION

The chapter illustrates a consultative model for destination brand planning. The model engages community stakeholders to generate their buy-in and support to build the brand from the inside out. Durham provides a fine case that has engaged the consultative approach to brand planning. Within the first year after implementing its new strategy, the city has registered many significant achievements in regard to brand adoption and use by community stakeholders. Community opinion surveys conducted by the Durham Convention & Visitors Bureau have revealed that 40% of its 250,000 residents are already familiar with the brand tagline, "Where great things happen™" and 97% of those believe that it makes them feel more positive about the city. Importantly, the brand has already been adopted and leveraged by more than 250 local organizations and companies. President of

Durham Convention and Visitors Bureau highlights the need for special care when focusing on the city's many customer groups:

> The overarching Durham brand has been embraced and activated by groups across the community as diverse as our tourism partners, universities, neighborhoods and dance companies because in the process of distilling it accurately, we identified elements which both external and internal stakeholders valued highly. We struck the right balance because it is now coming to life across the community and resonating positively with our key external audiences. (personal interview in 2007)

Through additional research, consultation, and creativity, Reyn Bowman and his team were able to encourage community support and enthusiasm for the brand. The primary tagline for Durham "Where great things happen™" was designed to encourage the whole community to adapt it to better connect with their particular audiences. For example, with prior approval partners can substitute other words for the word "things" in the tagline to reflect specific Durham strengths. Variations might include "Where great dance happens" or "Where great education happens" or "Where great discoveries happen." Durham-based Research Triangle Park dovetailed its new brand and tagline perfectly by adopting the line "The future of great ideas." Bowman indicates that:

> We have been able to generate such strong community support for the brand within the first year because we had adopted the philosophy that branding a community starts with broad based, balanced input from personal interviews, focus groups, surveys, briefings and educational communications. By their nature communities like Durham are fragmented, some more than others. When you've articulated a successful community brand for a place like this, it strikes people not like a lightning bolt, but rather like an Aha! —This really fits. That was our experience and it could not have been achieved without adopting a consultative and inclusive

approach from the start of our brand planning. (personal interview in 2007)

An essential yet frequently overlooked element of brand planning is broad community consultation and the adoption of change management principles to encourage the support and on-brand behavior that is needed for a successful city brand.

Chapter 15

DEVELOPING DISTINCTIVE CITY BRANDING
Cases of Anseong and Bucheon, South Korea

Jung-hoon Lee
Gyeonggi Research Institute, South Korea

Abridgement: There has been much research on city marketing, but some practical aspects remain unaddressed. One challenge is the development of a distinctive city identity. Traditional marketing tactics often ignore, deny, and marginalize the city identity. A more integrated and holistic approach is needed. As a complementary tool, city branding can overcome the shortcomings associated with traditional marketing. The purpose of this chapter is to show through case studies how two cities with different conditions went about developing their respective brand identities and illustrate how the identities were established through brand elements and promoted through coordinated marketing programs. Based on the two case studies, this chapter presents a process model for developing an identity in city branding. The model accommodates two different approaches to developing city identities. The first is applicable in the situation where a city is already strongly identified with its prominent existing heritage and cultural assets. The second is applicable in the situations where a city does not have prominent existing assets.
Keywords: city identity; city marketing and branding; cultural assets.

Tourism Branding: Communities in Action
Bridging Tourism Theory and Practice, Volume 1, 207–218
Copyright © 2009 by Emerald Group Publishing Limited
All rights of reproduction in any form reserved
ISSN: 2042-1443/doi:10.1108/S2042-1443(2009)0000001017

INTRODUCTION

Around the world, cities are increasingly relying on place branding to attract investment, industry, and tourism. The promotion of a city identity is regarded as a core strategy. The strategy emphasizes the peculiarity and uniqueness of a city and communicates a distinct city image that differs from others (Kampshulte 1999). There have been efforts to recreate places with preferred images (Holcomb 1993). Former industrial cities that have been restructured for the post-industrial service economy are in particular eager to develop a new identity to compete in the increasingly global marketplace.

City marketing is an established practice within urban management and has attracted the interest of many academic commentators from various disciplines. After decades of implementation, some aspects of it remain controversial and are subjected to criticism (Kavaratzis 2007). One criticism identifies an important phenomenon that the identity of a city often obscured in the process of re-imaging it through traditional tactics, resulting in the identity being ignored, denied, or marginalized (Griffiths 1998). Clearly, there is still a long way to go until a wider understanding of city marketing's potential is achieved, and a more integrated and holistic approach is adopted (Kavaratzis 2007). In this context, city branding has been proposed as a complementary tool (Kavaratzis and Ashworth 2005; Lee and Choi 2006) and can overcome the shortcomings associated with traditional city marketing. The purpose of this chapter is to show through case studies how two different cities went about developing their respective identities and illustrate how the identities were through brand elements and promoted through coordinated marketing programs, as opposed to ad hoc marketing tactics.

CITY BRANDING OF TWO CITIES

The cities examined in this chapter are Anseong and Bucheon, located near Seoul, South Korea (Figure 1). They have systematically developed respective identities (Lee 2004a; Park 2005) as part of their city branding efforts. Yet, the ways in which they have done so contrast with each other sharply and are thus useful for a comparative study of them as cases in city marketing and branding. The situations provide a practical model of developing city identity, which is a core strategy in branding cities. In Anseong, there already existed distinctive place assets, which have been

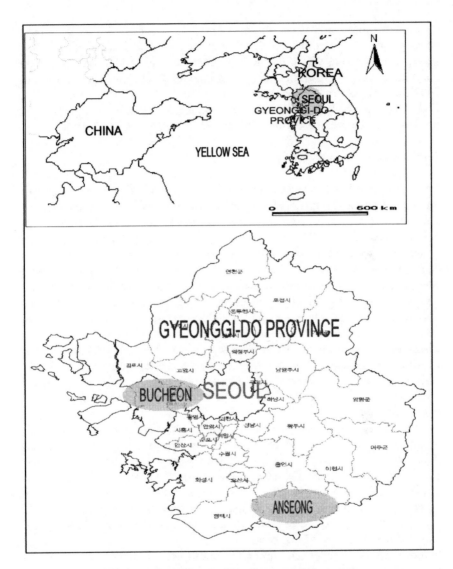

Figure 1 Locations of Bucheon and Anseong.

redefined and adapted by city marketers to develop an identity to promote the city. On the contrary, Bucheon had fewer place assets. An identity has been created through the development of new cultural assets. The case studies presented in the chapter are based on the review of administrative documents, interviews, and surveys. One was conducted for each city, investigating their distinctive characteristics and image associations. The survey for Anseong was done in 2006 on a sample of 900, including 300 inhabitants and 600 from outside. The survey for Bucheon was conducted in 2007 on a sample of 750, including 400 inhabitants and 350 from outside. The data was collected through face-to-face interviews by agents of a professional research company recruited by the city governments.

City Marketing and Branding

City marketing has evolved through several phases over time. These phases differ in the general approach toward marketing, as well as their level of refinement. Kavaratzis (2007) classifies city marketing practices as developing in three phases. The first phase is the fragmented place promotion undertaken by several independent actors with an interest in promoting a city. The next phase is the step toward the articulation of a marketing mix, which, apart from promotional measures, includes financial incentives and measures aimed at product development. Third, there is a realization of the significance of the image of the city together with recognition that an attempt to influence the image could become an effective way to coordinate marketing efforts. Therefore, it is observed that the desired image could provide the necessary target aimed at by marketing activities. It is this realization that has caused the recent popularity of city branding, which might well be the newest episode in the history of marketing applications (Kavaratzis 2007).

The goal of branding is to explore ways to add value to the basic product or service and thereby create brand preference and loyalty (Knox and Bickerton 2003). Currently, there is a general agreement in the literature that the brand is more than a name given to a product. It embodies a whole set of physical and sociopsychological attributes and beliefs (Kavaratzis 2004). Slogans and logos are useful practical instruments in a city branding strategy, although they do not constitute the entire strategy itself (Kavaratzis and Ashworth 2005). Many commentators have pointed out that a place brand represents corporate umbrella brand (Rainisto 2003). There are features that they have in common. Both have multidisciplinary roots, address multiple groups of stakeholders, have a high level of intangibility and complexity, need to take into account social responsibility, and deal with multiple identities (Kavaratzis and Ashworth 2005). A place or a city is typically more complicated and diverse than a corporate brand, and therefore, it is not easy to apply product branding theory to places or cities.

Nonetheless, corporate branding theory provides a useful reference to understand city branding strategies.

Balmer and Greyser (2002) suggest that the elements that constitute a corporate identity are strategy, structure, communication, and culture. They further suggest a test model for the relationship alignment of multiple identities. The multiple corporate identities in the model are composed of actual, conceived, communicated, ideal, and desired identities. He defines brand identity as covenanted. To promote a city as a brand, it is imperative to understand the role of brand identity, how to develop a distinctive one, and how to develop the equity of a city brand. Hankinson's (2004) place branding model provides an informative framework in this regard. His model focuses on brands as relationships for destination marketing. A place brand is represented by a core brand identity and four categories of relationships which extend its experience. The identity is the blueprint for developing and communicating the brand. In other words, the brand extends from the core to the periphery to include primary services, brand infrastructure, media, communications, and consumers. The extension is best described as a ripple effect where relationships gradually grow through a process of progressive interaction between the networks of stakeholders.

The Case of Anseong

Since ancient times, Anseong was a major transportation center and a node in the southern part of the Gyeeonggi region. The Anseong local market, traditionally called the "village market," was known to be one of the three biggest in South Korea where sellers of various specialties from all over Korea converged. This local market led to the development of a handicraft industry that included brassware. Its popularity was responsible for the creation of the famous term "Anseong machum," literally translated as "tailor-made in Anseong." The tide began to turn against the city in the late 1960s when the modernization and industrialization of South Korea started, which obscured Anseong's historical importance. When the developmental axis of industrialization failed to incorporate Anseong, the city was reduced to a backward agricultural area on the fringes of metropolitan regions. At the height of the country's industrialization, the people of this city maintained their conservative and clannish attitudes, raising another barrier to its inclusion in regional development (Anseong City 2007a).

Heritage Turned into Assets. South Korea adopted electoral local self-governance in the 1990s, which gave Anseong the impetus it needed to push itself out of comparative backwardness. It rediscovered its old traditions and cultural heritage as a valuable asset for regional development in the new era of local self-government. Its people began working on excavating and rediscovering antiques. The replicas of these antiques were also produced that contained some modern motifs. The first major city marketing momentum came in 1997 as designers revived the traditional image of "Anseong machum." This image developed into a brand name for its major agricultural and livestock farming products such as rice, pears, ginseng, beef, and other produces. The brand name led to remarkable results. Anseong's product sales jumped from 1.4 billion won (US$1 million) in 2002 to 47 billion won (US$47 million) in 2005 (Anseong City 2006b). Based on this phenomenal increase, a multi-partnered model venture became highly regarded as an exemplary success case for agricultural brands nationwide.

At the same time, Anseong started hosting the annual Namsadang Baudeoggi Festival (Figure 2) in an effort to promote itself. Based on a modern interpretation of an outstanding popular star Baudeoggi, the first and only female leader of a music and dancing troupe in South Korea, the festival is designed to immortalize Anseong in the minds of people and to attract tourists. The twin phenomena of agricultural brand development with the strong image of "Anseong machum" and the Namsadang Baudeoggi Festival became the corner stones for the city to develop a distinctive identity as part of its city branding.

Figure 2 Dancing at Baudeoggi Festival (left) with Anseong's New Logo.

From City Marketing to City Branding. To integrate the city's fragmented marketing activities, a branding strategy with a comprehensive marketing plan was started in 2005. It consisted of three steps, including the analysis of city potentials and distinctive identity, development of new slogan and logo, and formation of a task force to imbue the identity in city planning and practices. A variety of research activities revealed that Anseong machum, tailor-made brassware, grapes, and pears represent the city in the minds of both local people and those in neighboring regions. Its image as a producer of local agricultural specialties and as a garden city is found to be more distinctive among people in the neighboring regions than its own inhabitants. It was concluded that Anseong machum and local agricultural specialties are more representative of its identity. Together with its other cultural heritage, they are valuable assets for the city's future development (Anseong City and Metabranding 2006).

"Anseong, global city of arts, culture, and hometown to traditional craftsmanship," was chosen as the vision for the future Anseong. "City of Masters" became Anseong's brand slogan. This step was significant and differed from the city's previous marketing activities, which was not guided by a brand vision and stopped at developing a visual design and slogan. The new logo incorporating the slogan (Figure 2) is designed to present the distinctive identity of Anseong as its brand essence. It is used for all city marketing campaigns. The new logo is based on the motifs of brassware, the shape of the traditional main gate, curved lines of the *Taepyeongmu* (peace dance) and *Taeguk* (the ultimate limit of being), and a roundel of two interlocking commas suggesting the *yin* (shaded side) and the *yang* (brightly lit side). The logo design corresponds to the main motif of the national flag of South Korea—*Taeguk-gi*—which symbolizes harmony between the *yin* and the *yang*, the East and the West, past and future, and tradition and modernity.

Anseong organized a taskforce "Anseong Vision 2021" to promote brand leadership and symbolic government (Pedersen 2004). A specialist was invited to advise the taskforce. To encourage active participation, the city provided funding for overseas training and performance rating. Plans and ideas from the taskforce are considered as important guidelines and principles for the city's administration. The taskforce proposed 47 development projects in 7 sectors (Anseong City 2006a). It accomplished both individual and group objectives (Anseong City 2007b). The survey showed that 50% of the respondents said they were either "very satisfied" or "satisfied" with the taskforce's activities. Recently, residents are invited to the planning process as its members. Their participation in building the city's identity can strengthen their attachment to the brand. Pride and loyalty are the most important factors to increase brand equity.

The Case of Bucheon

During industrialization, de-industrialization, and urbanization, most countries experience identity change, although the speed of it may differ. The identity of a city is subject to change all the time as well (Pred 1984), accompanied by transformation in the city's social and economic characteristics, and in how people respond to changes in the world, the country, and the region (Lee 2004b). The formation of Bucheon city's identity was characterized by the structural processes of suburbanization and industrialization, which took place in many cities of Gyeonggi-do province near Seoul. While the development in the region varied from city to city and over time, Bucheon went through three stages: as pre-industrialization as agricultural suburbs of Seoul before the 1970s; industrialization as residential towns during the 1970s, the 1980s, and the early 1990s; and the post-1995 period. Its identity began to take shape in the late 1980s when it was transformed from a residential area to an industrial region comprising an important part of the Gyeongin Industrial Complex.

Developing Cultural Assets to Establish Identity.   Since 1985 and well before the inception of a local self-government system, Bucheon commenced with its "Cultural City Bucheon" policies. The city initiated three most important cultural programs: festivals, orchestras, and the launching of the city's logo featuring the peach flower. After 1995, the comics and animation industries were chosen to be the core cultural representation of Bucheon. Various marketing programs have since developed. First, the opening of the Bucheon Film and Cultural Complex became the base for the comics and animation industries. In 2003, an open-air set was built for a very popular TV series, "The Times of Heroes" (야인시대). The complex has become a famous attraction. Second, to promote Bucheon as a city of comics and animation, it has held a film festival with the theme of "Fantastic" (Figure 3) known as Pucheon Fantastic Festival or the Pifan. In its early days, many thrillers were shown at the festival. The current range of movies has broadened to include fantasies and comics. Third, to nurture the comics and animation industries, the city has invested in related infrastructure and human resources such as training programs. With these developments, Bucheon has emerged as a leader, only next to Seoul, in comics and animations, film industry–related institutions, festivals, and networks. Bucheon has actively

Figure 3 Bucheon Fantastic Film Festival (left) with Bucheon's New Logo (right).

carried out various projects needed to make it a cultural city including the construction of many museums.

Strengthening Identity through Branding Tools. Contemporary cultural assets are important characteristics of Bucheon today, bringing about significant strength to its new identity and image. If "A village of peach and a satellite city of Seoul" was the old identity of Bucheon, the new one claims to be something very different. Bucheon is now portrayed as a city of comics and animation industries equipped with advanced technologies and, perhaps more importantly, as a city of contemporary culture. The identity is represented by the Pifan, *Boksagol* (Peach Village), and the animation festival.

This multi-featured identity had its limitation, though, particularly when it is represented by the Peach Village. Bucheon addressed this limitation by developing a new city slogan through public submissions in May 2006. "Fantasia Bucheon" was chosen to present it as a city of culture, the comics, and animation industries, with robotic and molding industries. Respondents in the survey agreed that the slogan plays an important role in the popularity of its city identity and in the enhancement of its brand value. The slogan has been incorporated into the new brand logo (Figure 3). Public servants have favored modernistic color and shape of the logo and enjoyed using it in their documents and printed materials. Some local businesses and organizations have requested the city's permission to use its brand as a communal one of their products and activities.

A Process Model for Developing City Identity

The cases of Anseong and Bucheon provide important insights for city marketing and branding. The identities of the two cities have been developed under different conditions. In the case of Anseong, traditional cultural assets were redefined in the contemporary context and adapted to form its identity. This process is suited to cities that have an abundant traditional cultural heritage but are less developed economically than others in the region. The process also fits those wanting to promote culture and tourism industries in the competitive global economic environment. The key point of success in this case is an accurate evaluation of the city's external environment and internal strategic capability, within which the meanings of its traditional cultural heritage are interpreted and redefined. Anseong makes use of its unique heritage, Anseong machum, in the marketing of its agricultural products as the core of its brand identity. The creation of the slogan "City of Masters" populates the identity to all its marketing activities. Furthermore, Namsadang Baudeoggi Festival as a major marketing project adds equity to the identity based on Anseong machum and represented by the slogan of "City of Masters." A synergizing effect has been achieved.

The case of Bucheon shows that cities that do not have a distinctive heritage have to develop new cultural assets to amass a new identity and image. The cultural assets of Bucheon are classified into three types. The first is permanent and pure cultural and artistic establishments such as the birth of the Bucheon Philharmonic Orchestra and the construction of new museums. The second is the staging of seasonal cultural activities based on its existing cultural assets such as the Boksagol "Peach Village" Art Festival. The third relates to the creation of projects directly connected with contemporary cultural industries such as the Pifan, Pucheon International Student Animation Festival, Comics Information Center, Comics Museum, and Bucheon Film and Cultural Complex. Furthermore, the identity extends to and is extended by hi-tech and knowledge-based industries such as robotics and molding. Robotics is a core character of comics and animation.

In each of the two cases, innovative management tools and coordinated marketing activities are employed to support the city identity, such as the use of balanced score card system of Bucheon and the Anseong machum brand marketing campaign. The balanced score card is a strategic planning and management system that is used extensively in business and industry, government and nonprofit organizations worldwide to align business activities to the vision and strategy of the organization, improve internal and external communications, and monitor organization performance against strategic goals. Bucheon is the first local government that has successfully adapted it in South Korea. In so doing, the fragmented marketing practices of the past have been replaced by an intensive partnership system among many groups of stakeholders including local government, residents, businesses, not-for-profit organizations, and tourists. Active participation of community in identity building and communication process is considered to be a very important factor of successful branding.

The two case studies inform a process model for developing an identity in city branding (Figure 4). The model accommodates two approaches represented, respectively, by each of the cases. The first approach is applicable in the situation where a city is already strongly identified with its prominent existing heritage and cultural assets. The development of a new identity in branding, the city requires redefining the existing identity in the contemporary setting as in the case of Anseong. The second approach is applicable in the situations where a city does not have prominent existing assets. In branding, a new identity must be created by developing new cultural assets as in the case of Bucheon. Both approaches, however, call for engagement of different groups of stakeholders in the process and use of effective marketing programs to promote and strengthen the city identity.

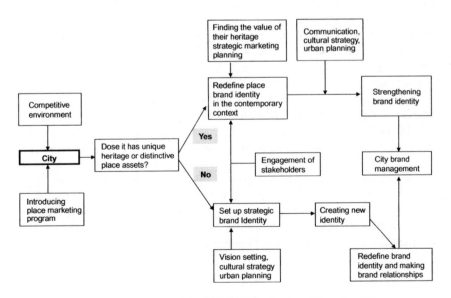

Figure 4 A Process Model for Developing City Identity.

The distinctive identity can serve as an umbrella brand under which related industries can prosper. Anseong's identity represented by the slogan of "City of Masters" is the value enhancer of its agricultural products and tourism industry. The Bucheon's identity represented by the slogan of "Fantasia Bucheon" directly benefits its comics and animation and robotics industries.

CONCLUSION

The cases of Anseong and Bucheon and resultant process model illustrate how a city identity can be developed using two different approaches. They only deal with the identity aspect, though, and are lacking in providing guidelines on how to develop a city brand. Dimensions and components of a full brand are missing. There remains a challenge to develop and implement other branding strategies to make the most out of the identity. As it is, brand leadership should be established to ensure that the identity be systematically reflected in the overall development plan of the city. It is critical that networking and communication are open among the diverse groups of stakeholders to maintain the consistency of the identity and its distinctiveness and to deliver an authentic experience. Branding strategies are needed to turn the established identity into a full city brand. City space and landscape should be rearranged so that people can experience the image. Current cultural projects and other programs need to be examined to see if they need tweaking for the future development goals of the city. The identity and image need to be used for the development of its culture and tourism industries.

The cases and the model neither contain any mechanism to assess if the identity can lead to measurable success of a city brand. An evaluation system for the process including implementation and feedback has to be established. The cases of Anseong and Bucheon represent two approaches to developing city identities. While the process model can be modified for use by other cities, other paths should be explored by taking into consideration each city's unique situations, both historical and contemporary. In spite of these limitations, the practices of Anseong and Bucheon as revealed in this chapter provide fine examples to develop identities for cities that bear the characteristics similar to either of the two cases.

Chapter 16

STRATEGIC BRANDING IN HOSPITALITY
The Case of Sol Meliá

Luís del Olmo
Sol Meliá, Spain

Ana María Munar
Copenhagen Business School, Denmark

Abridgement: This chapter analyzes the corporate branding of Sol Meliá, the 12th largest hotel chain in the world. It illustrates how branding has been moving upwards and becoming the core of the company's organizational structure and corporate strategy. The case shows that the company's branding process represents a high level of research and analysis, a strong relationship between brand strategy and financial management, and an increased involvement of customers and employees. The evaluation of the company's brand equity provides a new powerful tool to structure the company's long-term strategy and to strengthen its position in the marketplace. Furthermore, Sol Meliá's branding strategy illustrates a change toward an open-networking innovation culture. **Keywords:** corporate branding; hospitality; brand equity; innovation.

Tourism Branding: Communities in Action
Bridging Tourism Theory and Practice, Volume 1, 219–232
Copyright © 2009 by Emerald Group Publishing Limited
ISSN: 2042-1443/doi:10.1108/S2042-1443(2009)0000001018

INTRODUCTION

Brands are important to tourists. In the face of increased market expansion and diversification of products, brands save time, effort, and worry by facilitating tourists' decisionmaking. Brands also contain an emotional aspect as it may help tourists to project a desired social image and attitude (Anholt 2003). Brands can be found in almost all types of tourism goods (Cai 2002). However, this chapter focuses specifically on corporate branding in hospitality. The strategies of corporate branding have been changing over the past decades due to globalization processes. These main changes are a greater emphasis on corporate branding in order to strengthen corporate profiles, its prioritization versus product branding, and finally the raising of the responsibility of branding from middle to senior management (Hankinson 2007). These changes reflect an increased awareness of the relationship between innovative brand strategies and the improvement of competitive advantage.

Hotels sell a product that can only be enjoyed *in situ*. Unlike other products, tourists are not able to test the goods before purchase. They are also bound geographically to a place and to the culture and environment of the destination. Some similarities between a hotel product and that of a destination are the intangibility and perishability of tourists' experience. The hotel product of which consumption and production take place simultaneously includes a high risk, which is also a trait in the choice of a destination (Cai 2002). This feature demands of tourists a higher level of confidence and increases the relevance of their perception of the brand. However, there are many differences between destination branding and hotel branding. The hotel brand does not need to integrate the same level of diverse components necessary in the creation of an image of a destination, nor does it need as much to take into consideration the participation and cooperation of so many different stakeholders. Nevertheless, the making of a brand for a corporation faces other challenges.

In the case of corporate branding in hospitality, companies have to rise to the challenge of enhancing a coherent brand strategy for several product lines and must decide upon the degree of centralization and standardization. This can be exemplified through the difference that exists between creating a house of brands or a branded house. In the case of the branded house the corporate all-inclusive brand is the one that provides the strongest image and value. There is a strong centralization tendency and high standardization level throughout the company. In the case of the house of brands, the corporation pursues a more decentralized strategy: similar to an umbrella which covers multiple subbrands with its own strong image and attributes. The case of Sol Meliá which will be examined in this chapter is representative of a middle way between, on the one hand, a strong centralized house brand and, on the other hand, a group of independent subbrands.

Hotel corporations have also had to face many other challenges due to the evolution in information and telecommunications technologies, the expansion of e-commerce, and the decrease in importance of intermediaries. The possibility of addressing tourists directly has increased the relevance of brands to deliver consumer awareness and loyalty. Online presence is an important factor related to sales and communication strategy in hospitality businesses (Hashim and Murphy 2007). Hotels worldwide face the need to improve the image which tourists may have of their brands if they aspire to be competitive in the long term (Tepeci 1999). In addition, they must have an up-to-date e-business strategy that is coordinated with branding strategies.

As early as in the mid-1990s, hotel owners were advised to plan fully if their brand strategies were to deliver on the promise of customer access and loyalty (Cline 1996). However, transforming the internal and external perception of a brand is not an easy task. In most cases, it demands a new focus across the entire organization and the initiation of a challenging innovation process. The purpose of this chapter is to advance the study and practice of hospitality branding at a strategic level. To reach this aim, the chapter illustrates an innovative process of strategic branding through the case study of the global hotel chain Sol Meliá and examines the role of employees and customers in the branding process. Finally, the chapter presents a series of practical tools that can be used by practitioners and managers of the hotel sector.

INNOVATIVE PROCESS OF STRATEGIC BRANDING

Sol Meliá is a Spanish-based hospitality company whose history began in 1956 with the running of a single hotel in Majorca, Spain, by the founder Gabriel Escarrer Juliá. Today, thanks to a well-planned strategy of mergers and acquisitions, the company runs 406 hotels in 35 countries, with more than 80,000 rooms (Sol Meliá 2007a). This is the leading city and resort hotel chain in Spain and the leading hotel chain in Latin America and the Caribbean, the third largest hotel chain in Europe, and the 12th largest hotel chain in the world (Sol Meliá 2007b). With a clear growth and diversification strategy, Sol Meliá has expanded across the urban and resort tourist markets and entered new geographical destinations. Nowadays, the company manages a house brand *Sol Meliá*, which does not represent any hotel product but the corporation, and five different subbrands: *TRYP Hotels* with three and four star urban hotels, *Meliá Hotels and Resorts* with luxury hotels in urban and vacational areas, *Sol Hotels* with three and four star hotels in coastal destinations, *Paradisus Resorts* with luxury hotels in exotic destinations, and *Me by Meliá* which is the newest brand of the company with a few luxury experience-oriented hotels.

Being a company with more than 50 years of history and a multi-dimensional portfolio that included multiple brands, Sol Meliá was facing both increasing competition and the difficult task of managing the many uneven subbrands that the company had acquired during the expansion of the past decades. The organization's top management was aware of how important it was to handle a successful improvement and renovation of its brands to enhance its competitive advantage. An increase in the relevance of the house brand Sol Meliá began with the preparation of the company to be traded on the stock exchange in 1996. This task took form thanks to the recognition of the brand as a key strategic asset for the company. From then on and over the past few years, Sol Meliá has been innovating and developing its branding process, which has run parallel to the acquisitions strategy of the company and can be divided into two main periods.

The first period in the 1990s can be seen as that of brand portfolio's construction, while the second, beginning at the turn of the century, focused on brand image and value creation. All efforts during the first period aimed to build and give coherence to a highly diverse portfolio of hotels. The objective was to gain a stronger house brand identity while simultaneously coping with rapid expansion and the challenges and opportunities of e-commerce. Several strategies were tried during this period. In the first place, to deal with the high diversity of the hotels acquired by the company, Sol Meliá created several subbrands that represented different customer targets. The brand Meliá Hotels which had 79 hotels in April 1996 was divided into three groups: Gran Meliá, Meliá, and Meliá Confort, whereas the other brand of the company, Sol Hotels with 96 hotels, was divided into four minor types: Sol Elite, Sol Club, Sol, and Sol Inn. Furthermore, a new brand named Paradisus was created (Alvarez, Cardoza and Díaz Bernardo 2002). By the end of the 1990s, the corporation was managing up to seven different brands and subbrands, while it continued its international expansion in Latin America, the Caribbean, and Europe. In 1999, Sol Meliá had 262 hotels in 27 countries.

Although a lot of effort had been devoted to the establishment of the many subbrands, Sol Meliá planned to streamline its brand portfolio in the year 2000, following the Tryp Hotels acquisition. Tryp had added a total of 60 hotels, most of them urban properties in Spain, to the assets of the company. It was the opportunity to gain a stronger position in the urban market and to rethink its global brand strategy. At this point, the brand strategy of Sol Meliá moved into a second innovation process of optimization and identity creation. This chapter focuses mostly on this second period which began in the year 2000. The innovative process and its various phases were identified through the analysis of primary and secondary data gathered from inside and outside of the company, and through critical review of relevant literature. The structure of the chapter is divided into sections corresponding to different phases of the process. They are strategy, ideas and development, brand analysis, positioning, benchmark and standardization, implementation, and learning.

Strategic Phase

In the year 2000, Sol Meliá adopted a new strategic plan for the company centered on the needs and wishes of customers. Branding was seen by top management as a crucial tool to implement the new strategic vision. The research agency Infratest Burke was commissioned to carry out an in-depth study of its many brands and subbrands. The study showed that although the brands were recognized by customers, there was a lot of confusion regarding the different attributes of each of the brands and subbrands. On the basis of this analysis, the top management presented its new brand strategy in 2001, of which the main elements were a simplification and stronger differentiation of the brand portfolio. The relevance of the strategy to the top management of the company was not only stated in reports and press releases, but the company's marketing and sales department also expanded its analysis to identify external and internal forces affecting the corporate brand portfolio. Research on the customers, the competitors, and the tourism market in general was conducted and a process to reposition the multiple brands of the company was initiated.

The higher relevance that the brand had acquired for the general strategy of the corporation culminated in two main changes in its organizational structure. In the first place, brand management was separated from the sales function. Then in 2004, a new Brand Management Division with R + D activities and a strong strategic orientation was established. The main tasks of the new division were to review the situation and develop a rigorous strategy for this second period of brand positioning. The impact of the relevance of the brand on the organizational dimension of the corporation continued to grow as the process of repositioning and renewing the subbrands evolved. Finally, in 2007, the top management of Sol Meliá took the decision to change its departmental structure from one based on the geographical location of the hotels to that of an organizational configuration based on the different brands. The company is, in the year 2008, involved in the implementation of this complex task that aims to align the operational functions of the company to the branding strategy. From a strategic perspective, the case of Sol Meliá shows how the reforms conducted to date have brought a higher integration between brand and corporate strategy.

As mentioned previously, some companies that own multiple brands have attempted to market all of their types in an integrated message as a house brand whereas others have focused on each separately as a house of brands. Clearly, advantages can be seen in both strategies. There is a stronger supporting effect of one global brand on its weaker subbrands in the case of a house brand. The focused segmentation approach allows brands of differing quality and attributes to be positioned separately in the market in the case of a house of brands. Sol Meliá decided to go for a middle way approach in which the corporate brand acts as an umbrella and promotes standardization throughout the subbrands, while improving the identity and specific attributes of each brand to obtain a better positioning in its targeted market.

Ideas and Development

The organization's specific culture plays an important role in the phase of the idea development in an innovative process. In the 1990s, Sol Meliá had enhanced a corporate culture and a top management philosophy with a high level of creativity and strong entrepreneurial values. Internal and external resources were used to study the viability of the different strategic ideas regarding branding. Internally, the company's know-how covered the financial and economic analysis of the different proposals, whereas wider market and customer analysis was conducted by external consultants. In this phase, a systematic approach to the task of branding was put in place in the form of an action plan that included the following tools: brand analysis, positioning, benchmark and revenue, cost–benefit analysis, and profitability. Finally, a throughout evaluation of the results of this plan was to be attained by measuring customer satisfaction and benchmarking the evolution in relation to market competitors.

Brand Analysis

To examine the point of departure of the brand and aiming to get an accurate knowledge of customers' needs and wants, a rigorous analysis was conducted internally throughout the organization. First, a quantitative study of the evolution of the quality of the different departments of each hotel was made. The research methods included customer surveys, mystery shopping, and the examination of blogs and reviews on the Web. Second, for each one of the subbrands a qualitative study using focus groups of tourists was established, taking into consideration the different market segments with regard to nationality and the reason for traveling. Third, a study of the segmentation of the market targeted by each of the subbrands was compared to the evolution of the market demand over the previous years. Finally, the distribution channels and the pricing strategies of each brand were analyzed.

Externally the analysis included the following initiatives: an analysis of the economic situation of the countries where Sol Meliá's brands had an important presence, a study of the evolution of the destinations in which the brands had a high number of hotels and forecasts relating to the expansion strategy for the following years, and an examination of the competitive companies in relation to their differentiated attributes as well as to their financial performance. Furthermore, a report establishing the set of competitors in relation to each one of the brands was produced and the customer profile was analyzed using a psychographic and demographic classification.

All these different analyses and reports made it possible to establish a matrix of strengths, weaknesses, opportunities, and threats for each of the Sol Meliá subbrands. A series of weaknesses were identified and are summarized in Table 1. Some of the most important ones were the outdated style of the hotels, a lack of innovative products, and a low level of standardization. The extensive analysis laid the basis for the review process of the standards of the brand and for the positioning analysis. Furthermore, the customer research produced an unexpected outcome. It showed that there was a new customer segment of professionals who appreciated a high standard of living and luxury not targeted by the offers already in existence in the market. The management of Sol Meliá decided to target this specific market niche by building a new brand into its portfolio: Me by Meliá.

Positioning

The positioning initiatives that Sol Meliá took included, in the first place, a study of the segmentation of tourists as well as of the distribution policies

Table 1. Brand Analysis as Point of Departure

Tryp Hotels	Sol Hotels	Meliá Hotels and Resorts	Paradisus Resorts
Old-fashioned hotels	Products in decline phase	Old-fashioned hotels	Low brand identity
Low standardization	Low recognition of the brand by tourist and high by TTOO	A dominance of 50+ tourists	Low recognition of the brand by the market
High demand of IT by customers	Lack of activities and products suitable for families and 50+ tourists	Lack of IT offers for tourists	Good location but lack of guest experiences
Lack of innovative products in food and beverage	Lack of innovative products in food and beverage	Lack of innovative products in food and beverage	Good products and services but lack of differentiation
Lack of sport facilities	High competition by new vacational destinations with a lower price	Low quality of sport facilities and lack of wellness products	
Lack of offer of activities for city break tourists		High level of competition in the market	
		Lack of differentiation and diversification of products	

needed to reach each specific market segments. Moreover, it provided a price strategy for each brand aimed specifically at achieving a coherent and clearer image of the brand in the mind of targeted segments. Another important element at this stage was the enhancement of differentiation by defining new brand attributes. The aim in developing these attributes was to diminish the weaknesses detected in each of the brands. Its position would be strengthened to enhance customer satisfaction, improve sales, increase competitive advantage, create the potential to provide higher profit to the organization, and achieve greater awareness on the part of tourists.

In sum, the tendencies of the new attributes of the brands pointed toward a greater diversification of services, higher quality, cost control, and a more coherent modern image through standardization.

At this point, the company had established the brand analysis from a very broad perspective and had also decided on the positioning of each type. However, it was important to consolidate a system that allowed the benchmarking of them in relation to the revenues obtained and to the cost and expenditures of the company. To do this, the ratios taken into consideration were the average price, occupancy and revenue per available room (RevPAR), revenue for food and beverage, and other revenues for each brand and hotel, as well as their competitive benchmarks. This analysis not only allowed the company to define specific objectives for each brand to match the strategic positioning defined previously but also improved strategic decisionmaking regarding investments. Besides, the analysis helped to achieve a better control over the costs and expenditures by establishing a standard ratio per brand. The company could then analyze the performance of each hotel in relation to the standard and consequently achieve a high level of visibility of the hotel performance, allowing the establishment of specific actions addressed to reduce the difference between the actual performance and the standard. The standardization of prices and a strategic policy on costs helped to strive for efficiency without affecting the brand promise.

Implementation

The way in which the strategic innovation in each of the brands was implemented consisted of three stages. During the first stage, the new brand attributes and strategies were developed in a few pilot hotels. The second stage consisted of an evaluation and revision of the pilot projects and an improvement of the brand attributes and standards. In the third stage, the new brand attributes were to be implemented throughout the brand. The hotels to be included in the pilot projects were chosen among the ones that were performing well, had an innovative culture, and were of strategic value to the company. The idea was to establish these hotels as best practices to inspire the rest of the hotels of the brand and to secure several brand champions among the line managers and employees involved in the process. Although the customers were already incorporated into the process at the beginning of the idea creation through the focus groups and surveys mentioned previously, with the company top management had been very active in the development of the brand strategy from the very beginning, the middle management of the hotels was not actively participating in the branding innovation process until this point.

To enhance the commitment and active participation of the employees of the hotels in the pilot projects, a team of change management was set up in each hotel. These teams had to carry out the tasks of implementing the new brand image and its attributes, to help with the definition of the processes and standards that were needed for the implementation, as well as to evaluate the effects of these changes in relation to tourists. The work and evaluation of these teams were key elements to the successful implementation of the strategy in each of the brands. Once the pilot projects were finished, they were evaluated and the attributes and standards adjusted accordingly by the Brand Management Division and other departments when required.

A large number of innovative projects were carried out to develop the new attributes for each one of the brands. The most relevant ones are summarized in Table 2. Some of the most important innovations were the use of new logos and graphic identities, the creation of new types of rooms, new concepts for the food and beverage services, and the creation of an internal horizontal brand *Yhi Spa* representing the new spa and wellness offering. This diversification was encouraged, thanks to the forming of carefully selected cobranding partnerships with companies and well-reputed experts in the gastronomic world (such as Dani García), the fitness world (Lifefitness), as well as the entertainment sector (The Flintstones of Warner Bros). The final objective of this phase was to establish the appropriate standards to deliver the right experience and the right brand promise to tourists. The aim of the different attributes was to solve those problems identified during the phase of brand analysis as shown in Table 1.

All the four brands Sol, Tryp, Meliá, and Paradisus have initiated and implemented to a large extent their respective new brand strategies. In addition, Me by Meliá, a new brand with three hotels, has also been put into operation. In 2006, the new attributes were put into effect in 44 hotels, another 37 in 2007, and 55 more in 2008 and 2009. In the analysis of the attributes, a double tendency appears. First, there is an increase in the level of standardization within each brand and horizontally throughout the different ones. At the same time, there is an increase in the number of services and products offered, thus culminating in a greater diversification of products and services within the corporation and a clear boundary and positioning among the different brands of Sol Meliá.

Table 2. Innovations in Brand Attributes

Tryp Hotels	New image and logo	New rooms; premium, fitness and family	New services; fitness, IT, healthy breakfast	New programs of activities at the destination	New service of babysitting and activities for children
Sol Hotels	New image and logo	New family rooms; thematic rooms and large space rooms	New food and beverage concepts in restaurants and bars; *fun food*, theme areas for children	Co-branding partnership with The Flintstones, Warner Bros	New service programs: for families *Activity Fun*, sport activities *Sosport*, for 50+ *Seniors*
Meliá Hotels and Resorts	New image and logo	New high luxury services *The Level*; new spa and wellness brand *Yhi Spa*	New restaurants and bars with strategic partners	Program of leisure with specific activities related to the destination	
Paradisus Resorts	New image and logo	New modern and large rooms	New concept for couples *Romance* and new programs for families	New food and beverage concepts in restaurants and bars, new spa and wellness brand Yhi Spa	Co-branding partnership with The Flintstones, Warner Bros
Me by Meliá	Luxury class and exclusivity	Premium personalized service	Strategic partnerships for lounges and restaurants	Exclusive design and architecture, strategic partnerships	Exclusive music and IT services

Learning

The financial evaluation of the implementation so far shows a positive increase of the brands' RevPAR. The improvement of the gross operating profit in the year 2006 compared to that of 2004 is as follows: Tryp US$18.7 million with a brand equity of $362.6 million; Sol $9.3 million with a brand equity of $462.5 million; Meliá $121.1 million with a brand equity of $1238.3 million; Paradisus $53.6 million with a brand equity of $127.7 million. Sol did not increase its occupancy rate mostly due to the policy of higher prices applied as part of the new brand strategy.

Brand equity, which can be defined as the "differential effect that brand knowledge has on consumer response to the marketing of that brand" (Keller cited in Cai 2002:723), has been fully embraced in the general strategy by the company. Sol Meliá is a pioneer in the use of analytics to monitor brand equity in hospitality businesses. The company's measurement of this equity in 2007 was carried out externally by the firm American Appraisal. The study considered three main dimensions of brand equity creation: loyalty, awareness, and perceived quality. The valuation method used was the Royalty Relief Approach. The underlying premise of this method is that the brand value is based on the difference between owning the brand and licensing the brand (and therefore having to pay a royalty stream to use it). The evaluation concluded that Sol Meliá's brand portfolio had an equity of $2372.9 million. This valuation can be expected to improve the position of the company in the stock market by showing that its net asset value of a single share is over 30% higher than the average price per share.

It is too early to reach a conclusion on the final impact of the brand strategy launched by the company. In the coming years, the company will invest $460.2 million to continue with the implementation of the brand strategy, and its results will be better evaluated in several years time. Sol Meliá keeps on learning about brand strategy, primarily through the research and analyses that are carried out in the different departments, but most especially through the Brand Management Division which continues the examination of the external and internal factors that affect the corporation's brands. The process of innovating in branding will not finish just by implementing the new attributes in each of type. Strategic branding is understood by the management of the company to be an open-ended process that will help to enhance the company's brand equity and improve its competitive advantage. Changes in tourists' needs and wants and in the markets will constantly affect the performance of its brands. The company will have to react to those changes by learning more about its customers and its markets.

CONCLUSION

By the year 2000, Sol Meliá had a multiple portfolio of brands. Following the Tryp acquisition, Sol Meliá streamlined its portfolio and established four brands that were Tryp Hotels, Meliá Hotels and Resorts, Sol Hotels, and Paradisus Resorts. This was the start of a huge innovation process that is still being implemented. Over the years, the branding strategy of the company has become more closely linked to the main corporate decisions. Sol Meliá shows how branding has been moving upward from first being a niche of the marketing and sales department towards being a strategic asset and then becoming the core of the company's organizational structure and corporate strategy. The case illustrates an innovation process where branding affects all the departments from food and beverage to human resources. This type of branding strategy demands a high level of commitment by the higher echelon of the company as well as the enhancement of an innovative culture and business philosophy throughout the organization.

The purpose of this chapter has been to advance the study and practice of hospitality branding at a strategic level. The innovation process as practiced by the hotel chain Sol Meliá has included different phases. The analysis has provided insights on the way in which corporations in hospitality businesses develop and implement their branding strategies. The examination of the case has also presented a series of management tools that may be used by practitioners of the hotel sector. Furthermore, in the examination of this case, some specific features are worth mentioning. The full commitment of top management is required to put into place the adequate organizational structure to manage the innovation process. This leadership is vital in order to be able to carry on with the innovation. However, the involvement of top management alone is not enough. The active participation of both middle management and employees is a must in the development of standards and throughout the implementation phase. The establishment of a proper brand analysis and positioning demands a focus on tourists' needs and wishes obtained through the surveys, focus groups, and quality assessment.

Sol Meliá has emerged as a case in which the corporation strives to find a balance between being a brand house and a house of brands, with the difficulties and challenges that this decision entails. Looking at how the branding process was conducted, it is worth taking into consideration the high level of research and analysis that took place during the ideas and development phase prior to the decisionmaking and the strong relationship between brand strategy, and financial management. The use of analytics in the evaluation of the company's brand equity has provided top management with a powerful new tool to structure its long-term strategy and to strengthen its position in the marketplace.

Sol Meliá's branding strategy reflects a change toward an open networking innovation culture. This openness can be seen in the establishment of multiple and varied partnerships with other companies and experts and in the constant monitoring of the sociocultural changes of its customer base. The combination of brand attributes and a strategy of cobranding and partnerships at international level has generated both expansion opportunities and a strengthening and rejuvenation of its brands' images. It is too early to tell what will be the consequences in the long-term of this open brand strategy of Sol Meliá. However, it is important to stress that the branding process itself has been a valuable learning process for the company. It has gained tremendously in know-how and innovation capacity, and has managed to present a high degree of dynamism in an ever changing and demanding tourism market.

Acknowledgement

The authors wish to express their gratitude to Manuel Riego, Research and Development Manager at Sol Meliá Hotels & Resorts, for his help during the writing of this chapter.

References

Aaker, D.
  1991 Managing Brand Equity: Capitalizing on the Value of a Brand Name.
    New York: The Free Press.
  1996 Building Strong Brands. New York: Free Press.
  2004 Brand Portfolio Strategy: Creating Relevance, Differentiation, Energy,
    Leverage, and Clarity. New York: The Free Press.
Aaker, D., and E. Joachimsthaler
  2000 Brand Leadership. New York: The Free Press.
Aaker, J.
  1997 Dimensions of Brand Personality. Journal of Marketing Research 34(3):
    347–356.
Aas, C., A. Ladkin, and J. Fletcher
  2005 Stakeholder Collaboration and Heritage Management. Annals of Tourism
    Research 32(1):28–48.
Airfrance
  2007 Corporate Information <http://www.airfrance.com/corporate> (20 August).
Akis, S., N. Peristianis, and J. Warner
  1996 Residents' Attitudes to Tourism Development: The Case of Cyprus. Tourism
    Management 17(7):481–494.
Alexander, D.
  2000 The Geography of Italian Pasta. Professional Geographer 52(3):553–566.
Alvarez, J., G. Cardoza, and R. Díaz Bernardo
  2002 Estrategia de Marcas de Sol Meliá. Madrid: Instituto de Empresa.
Anderson, C.
  1970 The Political Economy of Modern Spain. Policy-Making in an Authoritarian
    System. Madison: The University of Wisconsin Press.
Anderson, J.
  1983 The Architecture of Cognition. Cambridge, MA: Harvard University Press.
Andreu, L., J. Bigne, and C. Cooper
  2000 Projected and Perceived Image of Spain as a Tourist Destination for British
    Travellers. Journal of Travel & Tourism Marketing 9(4):47–67.
Anholt, S.
  2002 Foreword. Journal of Brand Management 9(4/5):229–239.
  2003 Brand New Justice: The Upside of Global Branding. Oxford: Butterworth-
    Heinemann.
  2005 National Brand as Context and Reputation. Place Branding 1(3):224–228.
  2006 Why Brand? Some Practical Considerations for Nation Building. Place
    Branding 2(2):97–107.

Anseong City
  2006a Anseong Vision 2021 Development Plan (in Korean).
  2006b Report on 'Anseong Machum' Brand Marketing (in Korean).
  2007a 'Art-Culture City 2021' Plan for Future (T/F Team Report; in Korean).
  2007b 2007 Anseonng Vision 2021 T/F Team Operation Manual (in Korean).
Anseong City and Metabranding
  2006 Vision and Strategy for Anseong Place Marketing (in Korean).
Anthes, G.
  2006 IBM: Tapping Employee Brain Power. Computerworld, October 30.
    <http://www.computerworld.com/action/article.do?command = viewArticle
    Basic&articleId = 268098> (17 August 2007).
Ap, J.
  1990 Residents' Perceptions Research on the Social Impacts of Tourism. Annals
    of Tourism Research 17(4):610–616.
Ap, J., and J. Crompton
  1993 Residents' Strategies for Responding to Tourism Impacts. Journal of Travel
    Research 32(1):47–50.
  1998 Developing and Testing a Tourism Impact Scale. Journal of Travel Research
    37(2):120–130.
Araujo, L., and G. Easton
  1996 Networks in Socioeconomic Systems: A Critical Review. *In* Networks in
    Marketing, D. Iacobucci, ed., pp. 63–107. Thousand Oaks, CA: Sage
    Publications.
Azam, F.
  1999 NIKE: Nike Shoes and Child Labor in Pakistan <http://www.american.
    edu/TED/nike.htm> (20 August 2007).
Bagozzi, R.
  1975 Marketing as Exchange. Journal of Marketing 39(4):32–39.
Bagozzi, R.P.
  1982 A Field Investigation of Causal Relations among Cognitions, Affect,
    Intentions, and Behavior. Journal of Marketing Research 19(November):
    562–583.
Baker, B.
  2007 Destination Branding for Small Cities. Portland: Creative Leap Books.
Baker, D., and J. Crompton
  2000 Quality, Satisfaction and Behavioral Intentions. Annals of Tourism
    Research 27(3):785–804.
Balmer, J., and E. Gray
  2003 Corporate Brands: What are they? What of them? European Journal of
    Marketing 37(7/8):972–997.
Balmer, J., and S. Greyser
  2002 Managing the Multiple Identities of the Corporation. California Manage-
    ment Review 44(3):72–86.

Baloglu, S.
1997 The Relationship between Destination Images and Sociodemographic and Trip Characteristics of International Travelers. Journal of Vacation Marketing 3:221–233.
Baloglu, S., and D. Brinberg
1997 Affective Images of Tourism Destinations. Journal of Travel Research 35:11–15.
Baloglu, S., and M. Mangaloglu
2001 Tourism Destination Images of Turkey, Egypt, Greece, and Italy as Perceived by US-Based Tour Operators and Travel Agents. Tourism Management 22(1):1–9.
Baloglu, S., and K. McCleary
1999a A Model of Destination Image Formation. Annals of Tourism Research 26(4):868–897.
1999b U.S. International Pleasure Travelers' Images of Four Mediterranean Destinations: A Comparison of Visitors and Nonvisitors. Journal of Travel Research 38(2):144–152.
Barwise, P.
1993 Introduction to the Special Issue on Brand Equity. International Journal of Research in Marketing 10(1):3–8.
Bauman, Z.
1998 Globalization: The Human Consequences. Cambridge: Blackwell Publishers.
Baumol, W., R. Litan, and C. Schramm
2007 Good Capitalism, Bad Capitalism and the Economics of Growth and Prosperity. New Haven: Yale University Press.
Beck, U.
2000 What is Globalization? Cambridge: Polity Press.
Bedbury, S., and S. Fenichell
2003 A New Brand World: 8 Principles for Achieving Brand Leadership in the 21st Century. Viking: Penguin.
Beerli, A., and J. Martín
2004 Factors Influencing Destination Image. Annals of Tourism Research 31(3):657–681.
Bell, D.
2007 The Hospitable City: Social Relations in Commercial Spaces. Progress in Human Geography 31(1):7–22.
Bessière, J.
1998 Local Development and Heritage: Traditional Food and Cuisine as Tourist Attractions in Rural Areas. European Society for Rural Sociology 38(1):21–34.
Bhagwati, J.
2004 In Defense of Globalization. New York: University Press.

Bigné, J., M. Sánchez, and J. Sánchez
  2001 Tourism Image, Evaluation Variables and After Purchase Behaviour: Inter-
    Relationship. Tourism Management 22(6):607–616.
Biocca, F.
  1997 The Cyborg's Dilemma: Progressive Embodiment in Virtual Environments.
    Journal of Computer-Mediated Communication <http://jcmc.indiana.edu/
    vol3/issue2/biocca2.html> (28 October).
Blain, C., E. Levy, and B. Ritchie
  2005 Destination Branding: Insights and Practices from Destination Management
    Organizations. Journal of Travel Research 43(4):328–338.
Blichfeldt, B.
  2005 Unmanageable Place Brands? Place Branding 1(4):388–401.
  2007 Destination Branding: A Consumer Perspective. The 2nd International
    Conference on Destination Branding and Marketing, Macau, CD: 57–66,
    17–19 December.
Boulding, K.
  1956 The Image. Ann Arbour: University of Michigan Press.
Boyne, S., D. Hall, and F. Williams
  2003 Policy, Support and Promotion for Food-Related Tourism Initiatives:
    A Marketing Approach to Regional Development. Journal of Travel &
    Tourism Marketing 14(3/4):131–154.
Bramwell, B., and A. Sharman
  1999 Collaboration in Local Tourism Policymaking. Annals of Tourism Research
    26(2):392–415.
British Airways
  2007 "Dr Sleep Podcasts." <http://www.britishairways.com/travel/drsleeppodcasts/
    public/en_gb> (28 November 2009).
Brown, F.
  1998 Tourism Reassessed: Blight or Blessing? Oxford: Butterworth-Heinemann.
Brunt, P., and P. Courtney
  1999 Host Perceptions of Sociocultural Impacts. Annals of Tourism Research
    26(3):493–515.
Buhalis, D.
  2000 Marketing the Competitive Destination of the Future. Tourism Manage-
    ment 21(1):97–116.
  2003 eTourism: Information Technology for Strategic Tourism Management.
    London: Pearson.
Burns, P.
  2004 Tourism Planning: A Third Way? Annals of Tourism Research 31(1):24–43.
Burr, S. W.
  1991 Review and Evaluation of the Theoretical Approaches to Community as
    Employed in Travel and Tourism Impact Research on Rural Community
    Organization and Change. *In* Leisure and Tourism: Social and Environmental

Changes, A. Veal, P. Jonson, and G. Cushman, eds., pp. 540–553. Sydney, Australia: The World Leisure and Recreation Association Congress.

Butler, R.
1980 Tourism Area Life Cycle. Canadian Geographer 24(1):

Cai, L.
2002 Cooperative Branding for Rural Destinations. Annals of Tourism Research 29(3):720–742.
2007 A Tripod Model of Tourism Branding. Paper presented at the 10th Conference of the International Academy for the Study of Tourism: Then, Now and Future of Tourism Research, May 15–20, Mugla, Turkey.

Cai, L., R. Feng, and D. Breiter
2004 Tourist Purchase Decision Involvement and Information Preferences. Journal of Vacation Marketing 10(2):138–148.

Caldwell, N., and J. Freire
2004 The Differences between Branding a Country, a Region and a City: Applying the Brand Box Model. Journal of Brand Management 12(1):50–61.

Carman, J.
1973 On the Universality of Marketing. Journal of Contemporary Business 2:5.

Carter, S.
2007 The New Language of Business: SOA and Web 2.0. Upper Saddle River, NJ: IBM Press/Pearson.

Castells, M.
1996 The Information Age: Economy, Society and Culture. The Rise of the Network Society. Vol. 1, Oxford: Blackwell.
2001 La Galaxia de Internet. Barcelona: Plaza y Janés.

Castro, C., E. Armario, and D. Ruiz
2007 The Influence of Market Heterogeneity on the Relationship between a Destination's Image and Tourists' Future Behaviour. Tourism Management 28(1):175–187.

Čavlek, N.
2004 The Impact of Tour Operators in Tourism Development: A Sequence of Events. *In* Tourism Development: Issues for a Vulnerable Industry, J. Aramberri and R. Butler, eds. Clevedon: Channel View.

Chang, T., S. Milne, D. Fallon, and C. Pohlmann
1996 Urban Heritage Tourism: The Global-Local Nexus. Annals of Tourism Research 23(2):284–305.

Chen, P., and D. Kerstetter
1999 International Students' Image of Rural Pennsylvania as a Travel Destination. Journal of Travel Research 37(3):256–266.

Cho, Y.
2002 *Exploring web-based virtual tour experience: The effects of telepresence on destination image*. PhD thesis in Leisure Studies, University of Illinois at Urbana-Champaign, Illinois, USA.

Cho, Y., and D. Fesenmaier
   2001 A New Paradigm for Tourism and Electronic Commerce: Experience Marketing Using the Virtual Tour. *In* Tourism Distribution Channels: Practices, Issues and Transformation, E. Laws and D. Buhalis, eds., pp. 351–370. London: Continuum.
Cho, Y., Y. Wang, and D. Fesenmaier
   2002 Searching for Experiences: The Web-Based Virtual Tour in Tourism Marketing. Journal of Travel & Tourism Marketing 12(4):1–17.
Choi, H., and E. Sirakaya
   2006 Sustainability Indicators for Managing Community Tourism. Tourism Management 27(6):1274–1289.
Choi, Y., G. Miracle, and F. Biocca
   2001 The Effects of Anthropomorphic Agents on Advertising Effectiveness and the Mediating Role of Presence. Journal of Interactive Advertising 2(1):1–17.
Chon, K.
   1990 The Role of Destination Image in Tourism: A Review and Discussion. Tourism Review 45(2):2–9.
Cline, R.
   1996 Brand Marketing in the Hospitality Industry-Art or Science? <http://www.hotel-online.com/Trends/Andersen/Brand_Marketing.html>.
Coddington, A.
   1968 Theories of the Bargaining Process. Chicago: Aldine.
Cohen, E.
   1984 The Sociology of Tourism: Approaches, Issues, and Findings. Annual Review of Sociology 10:373–392.
Cohen, E., and N. Avieli
   2004 Food in Tourism: Attraction and Impediment. Annals of Tourism Research 31(4):755–778.
Coyle, J., and E. Thorson
   2001 The Effects of Progressive Levels of Interactivity and Vividness in Web Marketing Sites. Journal of Advertising 30(3):65–77.
Crockett, S., and L. Wood
   1999 Branding Western Australia: A Totally Intergrated Approach to Destination Branding. Journal of Vacation Marketing 5:276–289.
Crompton, J.
   1979 An Assessment of the Image of Mexico Vacation Destination and the Influence of Geographical Location upon the Image. Journal of Travel Research 17:18–23.
Danish Statistics
   2008a Population <http://www.statistikbanken.dk/statbank5a/default.asp?w = 1024> (1 October).
   2008b GDP <http://www.statistikbanken.dk/statbank5a/default.asp?w = 1024> (4 October).

Dann, G.
  1977 Anomie, Ego-Enhancement and Tourism. Annals of Tourism Research 4(4):184–194.
  1996 The People of Tourist Brochures. *In* The Tourist Image: Myth and Myth Making in Tourism, T. Selwyn, ed. Chichester: Wiley.
Dann, G., D. Nash, and P. Pearce
  1988 Methodology in Tourism Research. Annals of Tourism Research 15(1):1–28.
Davies, R.
  2003 Branding Asian Tourism Destinations-A Series < http://www.asiamarket research.com/columns/tourism-branding.htm > (20 August 2007).
Davis, D., J. Allen, and R. Cosenza
  1988 Segmenting Local Residents by their Attitudes, Interests, and Opinions Towards Tourism. Journal of Travel Research 27(2):2–8.
de Araujo, L., and B. Bramwell
  2002 Partnership and Regional Tourism in Brazil. Annals of Tourism Research 29(4):1138–1164.
de Chernatony, L.
  1999 Brand Management Through Narrowing the Gap between Brand Identity and Brand Reputation. Journal of Marketing Management 15: 157–179.
de Chernatony, L., and F. Riley
  1998 Modeling the Components of the Brand. European Journal of Marketing 32(11/12):1074–1090.
  1999 Experts' Views About Defining Services Brands and the Principles of Services Branding. Journal of Business Research 46(2):181–192.
de Chernatony, L., and M. McDonald
  2001 Creating Powerful Brands in Consumer, Service and Industrial Markets. Oxford: Butterworth-Heinemann.
De la Dehesa, G.
  2000 Comprender la globalización. Madrid: Alianza editorial.
D'Hauteserre, A.
  2001 Destination Branding in a Hostile Environment. Journal of Travel Research 39:300–307.
Dick, A., and K. Basu
  1994 Customer Loyalty: Toward an Integrated Conceptual Framework. Academy of Marketing Science 22(2):99–113.
Drucker, P.
  1992 The Age of Discontinuity: Guidelines to our Changing Society. London: Transaction Publishers.
du Rand, G., E. Heath, and N. Alberts
  2003 The Role of Local and Regional Food in Destination Marketing: A South African Situation Analysis. Journal of Travel & Tourism Marketing 14(3/4): 97–112.

Dwyer, L., and C. Kim
  2003 Destination Competitiveness: Determinants and Indicators. Current Issues
    in Tourism 6(5):369–414.
Eby, D., L. Molnar, and L. Cai
  1999 Content Preferences for In-Vehicle Tourist Information Systems: An
    Emerging Travel Information Source. Journal of Hospitality & Leisure
    Marketing 6(3):41–58.
Echtner, C., and B. Ritchie
  1991 The Meaning and Measurement of Destination Image. Journal of Tourism
    Studies 2(2):2–12.
  1993 The Measurement of Destination Image: An Empirical Assessment. Journal
    of Travel Research 31(4):3–13.
Ekinci, Y.
  2003 From Destination Image to destination Branding: An Emerging Area of
    Research. e-Review of Tourism Research 1(2):<http://ertr.tamu.edu/commen
    taries.cfm?articleid = 16>
Emerson, R.
  1976 Social Exchange Theory. Annual Review of Sociology 2:335–362.
Eroglu, S., K. Machleit, and L. Davis
  2001 Atmospheric Qualities of Online Retailing: A Conceptual Model and
    Implications. Journal of Business Research 54(2):177–184.
Estefanía, J.
  1998 La larga marcha. El País May 3.
Fakeye, P., and J. Crompton
  1991 Image Differences between Prospective, First-time, and Repeat Visitors
    to the Lower Rio Grande Valley. Journal of Travel Research 30(Fall):
    10–16.
Farquhar, P.
  1989 Managing Brand Equity. Marketing Research 1(3):24–33.
Farrell, B., and L. Twining-Ward
  2004 Reconceptualizing Tourism. Annals of Tourism Research 31(2):274–295.
Fasolo, B., R. Misuraca, G. McClelland, and M. Cardaci
  2006 Animation Attracts: The Attraction Effect in an On-line Shopping
    Environment. Psychology and Marketing 23(10):799–811.
Febas, J.
  1978 Semiología del lenguaje turístico (Investigación sobre los folletos españoles
    de turismo). Revista de Estudios Turísticos 57–58:17–203.
Ferguson, M.
  2008 Minister Welcomes New Tourism Australia Campaign. Ministry of Tourism,
    Australia <http://www.tourism.australia.com>
Fick, G., and B. Ritchie
  1991 Measuring Service Quality in the Travel and Tourism Industry. Journal of
    Travel Research 30(2):2–9.

Fiore, A., and H. Jin
2003 Influence of Image Interactivity on Approach Responses Towards an Online Retailer. Internet Research: Electronic Networking Applications and Policy 13(1):38–48.

Fiore, A., J. Kim, and H. Lee
2005 Effect of Image Interactivity Technology on Consumer Responses Toward the Online Retailer. Journal of Interactive Marketing 19(3):38–53.

Firth, R.
1967 Themes in Economic Anthropology. London: Tavistock Publications.

Fishbein, M., and I. Ajzen
1975 Belief, Attitude, Intention and Behavior: An Introduction to Theory and Research. Reading, MA: Addison-Wesley Publishing Company, Inc.

Flickr
2008a Photos of Amsterdam < http://www.flickr.com/photos/tags/Amsterdam > (4 September).
2008b Photos of Holland < http://www.flickr.com/photos/tags/Holland > (4 September).
2008c Photos of Paris < http://www.flickr.com/photos/tags/Paris > (4 September).
2008d Photos of France < http://www.flickr.com/photos/tags/France > (4 September).

Florida, R.
2002 The Rise of the Creative Class and How It's Transforming Work, Leisure, Community and Everyday Life. New York: Basic Books.

Florida, R., and Tinagli, I.
2004 Europe in the Creative Age < http://www.demos.co.uk/publications/creativeeurope >

Fodness, D.
1994 Measuring Tourist Motivation. Annals of Tourism Research 21(3):555–581.

Foley, A., and J. Fahy
2004 Incongruity between Expression and Experience: The Role of Imagery in Supporting the Positioning of a Tourism Destination Brand. Journal of Brand Management 11(3):209–217.

Fontana, J., and J. Nadal
1976 Spain: 1914–70. *In* The Fontana Economic History of Europe, C. Cipolla, ed. London: Fontana.

Fraga Iribarne, M.
1964 El turismo en España: Balance y Perspectives. Revista de Estudios Turísticos 1:5–50.

Framke, W.
2002 The Destination as a Concept: A Discussion of the Business-Related Perspective versus the Socio-Cultural Approach in Tourism Theory. Scandinavian Journal of Hospitality and Tourism 2(2):92–108.

Friedman, T.
2005 The World is Flat: A Brief History of the Globalized World of the 21st Century. New York: Penguin.

Frochot, I.
   2003 An Analysis of Regional Positioning and its Associated Food Images in French Tourism Regional Brochures. Journal of Travel & Tourism Marketing 14(3/4):77–96.
Galiana, M.L., and D.B. Timón
   2006 Los Centros de Interés Turístico Nacional y el despegue del turismo de masas en España. Investigaciones Geográficas (39):73–93.
Gallarza, M., I. Saura, and H. García
   2002 Destination Image: Towards a Conceptual Framework. Annals of Tourism Research 29(1):56–78.
Gartner, W.
   1989 Tourism Image: Attribute Measurement of State Tourism Product Using Multidimensional Scaling Techniques. Journal of Travel Research 28(Fall): 16–20.
   1993a Image Formation Process. *In* Communication and Channel Systems in Tourism Marketing, M. Uysal and D. Fesenmaier, eds., pp. 191–215. New York: The Haworth Press.
   1993b Image Formation Process. Journal of Travel & Tourism Marketing 2 (2/3):191–215.
Gaviria, M.
   1975 España a Go-Go. Turismo charter y neocolonialismo del espacio. Madrid: Turner.
   1996 La séptima potencia: España en el mundo. Barcelona: Ediciones B.
Gay, J.
   2004 Greece: Garden of the Gods. Athens, Greece: Athens News.
Gibson, C., and D. Davidson
   2004 Tamworth, Australia's 'Country Music Capital': Place Marketing, Rurality, and Resident Reactions. Journal of Rural Studies 20(4):387–404.
Gibson, J.
   1966 The Senses Considered as Perceptual Systems. Boston: Mifflin.
Giddens, A.
   1990 The Consequences of Modernity. Cambridge: Polity Press.
   2007 Europe in a Global Age. Cambridge: Polity Press.
Gitelson, R., and J. Crompton
   1984 Insights into the Repeat Vacation Phenomenon. Annals of Tourism Research 11(2):199–217.
Gnoth, J.
   1998 Conference Reports: Branding Tourism Destinations. Annals of Tourism Research 25(3):758–760.
   2002a Leveraging Export Brands Through a Tourism Destination Brand. Journal of Brand Management 9(4/5):262–280.
   2002b A Country-Can it be Repositioned? Spain-the Success Story of Country Branding. Journal of Brand Management 9(4/5):281–293.

Gnoth, J., S. Baloglu, Y. Ekinci, and E. Sirakaya-Turk
2007 Introduction: Building Destination Brands. Tourism Analysis 12(5/6): 339–343.
Goodall, B.
1993 How Tourists Choose their Holidays: An Analytical Framework. *In* Marketing in the Tourism Industry: The Promotion of Destination Regions, B. Goodal and G. Ashworth, eds., pp. 1–17. London: Routledge.
Goodrich, J.
1978 The Relationship between Preferences for and Perceptions of Vacation Destination. Journal of Travel Research 17(2):8–13.
Govers, R.
2003 Destination Image Evaluation: Part II. Eclipse: The Periodic Publication from Moonshine Travel Marketing for Destination Marketers 10:1–12.
Göymen, K.
2000 Tourism and Governance in Turkey. Annals of Tourism Research 27(4): 1025–1048.
Grace, D., and A. O'Cass
2002 Brand Associations: Looking Through the Eye of the Beholder. Qualitative Market Research 5(2):96–111.
Gray, B.
1985 Conditions Facilitating Interorganizational Collaboration. Human Relations 38(10):911–936.
Griffith, D., and Q. Chen
2004 The Influence of Virtual Direct Experience (VDE) on Online Ad Message Effectiveness. Journal of Advertising 33(1):55–68.
Griffiths, R.
1998 Making Sameness: Place Marketing and the New Urban Entrepreneurialism. *In* Cities Economic Competition and Urban Policy, N. Oatley, ed., pp. 41–57. London: Paul Chapman Publishing.
Gunn, C.
1972 Vacationscape: Designing Tourist Environments. Austin: Bureau of Business Research, University of Texas.
1988 Vacationscape: Designing Tourist Region (2nd ed). New York: Van Nostrand Reinhold.
Gursoy, D., and D. Rutherford
2004 Host Attitudes Toward Tourism: An Improved Structural Model. Annals of Tourism Research 31(3):495–516.
Gursoy, D., and K. Kendall
2006 Hosting Mega Events: Modeling Locals' Support. Annals of Tourism Research 33(3):603–623.
Hall, D.
1999 Destination Branding, Niche Marketing and National Image Projection in Central and Eastern Europe. Journal of Vacation Marketing 5(3):227–237.

2002 Brand Development, Tourism and National Identity: The Re-Imaging of Former Yugoslavia. Journal of Brand Management 9(4/5):323–334.
Hankinson, G.
    2004 Relational Network Brands: Towards a Conceptual Model of Place Brands. Journal of Vacation Marketing 10(2):109–121.
    2005 Destination Brand Images: A Business Tourism Perspective. Journal of Services Marketing 19(1):24–32.
    2007 The Management of Destination Brands: Five Guiding Principles Based on Recent Developments in Corporate Branding Theory. Journal of Brand Management 14(3):240–254.
Hanson, W.
    1999 Principles of Internet Marketing. Cincinnati: South-Western College Pub.
Harrison, J.
    1985 The Spanish Economy in the Twentieth Century. New York: St. Martin's Press.
Hashim, N., and J. Murphy
    2007 Branding on the Web: Evolving Domain Name Usage among Malaysian Hotels. Tourism Management 28(2):621–624.
Hashimoto, A., and D. Telfer
    2006 Selling Canadian Culinary Tourism: Branding the Global and the Regional Product. Tourism Geographies 8(1):31–55.
Hatch, M., and M. Schultz
    2003 Bringing the Corporation into Corporate Branding. European Journal of Marketing 37(7/8):1041–1064.
Held, D.
    1997 La democracia y el orden global. Barcelona: Paidós.
Held, D., A. McGrew, D. Goldblatt, and J. Perraton
    1999 Global Transformations: Politics, Economics and Culture. Cambridge: Polity Press.
Henderson, H.
    1999 Beyond Globalization: Shaping a Sustainable Global Economy. Bloomfield, CT: Kumarian Press.
Hills, K.
    2005 The Stakes of Doha, Foreign Affairs. New York: Council of Foreign Relations, December pp. 25–36
Hjalager, A.
    2007 Stages in the Economic Globalization of Tourism. Annals of Tourism Research 34(2):437–457.
Hjalager, A. and G. Richards, eds.
    2002 Tourism and Gastronomy. New York: Routledge.
Hoch, S., and J. Deighton
    1989 Managing what Consumers Learn from Experience. Journal of Marketing 53(2):1–20.

Holcomb, B.
1993 Revisioning Place: De- and Re-Constructing the Image of the Industrial City. *In* Selling Places-The City as Cultural Capital, Past and Present, G. Kearns and C. Philo, eds., pp. 133–143. Oxford: Pergamon Press.
Hopkins, C.D., M.A. Raymond, and A. Mitra
2002 Consumer Responses to Perceived Telepresence in the Online Advertising Environment: The Moderating Role of Involvement. Marketing Theory 4(1/2):137–162.
Howard, J., and J. Sheth
1969 The Theory of Buyer Behavior. New York: Wiley.
Howkins, J.
2001 The Creative Economy: How People Make Money from Ideas. London: Penguin.
Hu, Y., and B. Ritchie
1993 Measuring Destination Attractiveness: A Contextual Approach. Journal of Travel Research 32(2):25–34.
Huffington Post
2008 Starbucks Closing Stores Today. Huffington Post <http://www.huffington post.com/2008/02/25/starbucks-closing-stores-_n_88447.html> (25 February).
Hunt, J.
1975 Image as a Factor in Tourism Development. Journal of Travel Research 13(3):1–7.
Huxham, C., and S. Vangen
2000 Ambiguity, Complexity and Dynamics in the Membership of Collaboration. Human Relations 53(6):771–806.
Hyun, Y., and S. Han
2005 The Empirical Study of Eliciting Directly Influential Destination Images on Destination Choice: Simply Preferred Images and Leading Images. Korean Journal of Tourism & Leisure 17(3):23–42.
Hyun, Y., J. Wells, and H. Huh
2003 The Impact of the World Wide Web on the Future Marketing Roles of DMOs. International Journal of Tourism Sciences 3(2):17–39.
Hyun, Y., S. Han, and H. Huh
2005 The Empirical Study of the Structural Relationship between the Destination Image Formation and Tourist Behavior based on Familiarity Index: A Case Study of Ha Hoe in An-Dong. Journal of Tourism Sciences 29(1):147–167.
IgoUgo
2007a Homepage <http://www.igougo.com> (29 September).
2007b Les Galeries Lafayette <http://www.igougo.com/attractions-1595-f11-t20-things_to_do_in_Paris.html> (15 October).
Ind, N.
1997 The Corporate Brand. New York: New York University Press.

International Bank for Reconstruction and Development (IBRD)
  1963 The Economic Development of Spain. Baltimore: The Johns Hopkins Press.
Ioltravel
  2006 'Bloody Hell' Tourism ads Banned in the UK. Ioltravel. <http://www.
  ioltravel.co.za/article/view/3552402#> (09 March 2006).
Jafari, J.
  1987 Tourism Models: The Sociocultural Aspects. Tourism Management
  8(2):151–159.
  1990 Research and Scholarship: The Basis of Tourism Education. Journal of
  Tourism Studies 1(1):33–41.
Jamal, T., and D. Getz
  1995 Collaboration Theory and Community Tourism Planning. Annals of
  Tourism Research 22(1):186–204.
Jenkins, O.H.
  1999 Understanding and Measuring Tourist Destination Images. International
  Journal of Tourism Research 1:1–15.
Jensen, O., and T. Komeliussen
  2002 Discriminating Perceptions of a Peripheral 'Nordic Destination' among
  European Tourists. Tourism and Hospitality Research 3(4):319–330.
Jensen, R.
  2007 Amaprofferne Kommer! Dansk Oplevelsesøkonomi, 4 (1). Copenhagen:
  Dansk Oplevelse Okonomi.
Joppe, M., D.W. Martin, and J. Waalen
  2001 Toronto's Image as a Destination: A Comparative Importance-Satisfaction
  Analysis by Origin of Visitors. Journal of Travel Research 39(3):252–260.
Josiam, B., M. Mattson, and P. Sullivan
  2004 The Historaunt: Heritage Tourism at Mickey's Dining Car. Tourism
  Management 25(4):453–461.
Kahle, L., B. Poulos, and A. Sukhdial
  1988 Changes in Social Values in the United States during the Past Decade.
  Journal of Advertising Research 28(1):35–41.
Kampshulte, A.
  1999 Image as an Instrument of Urban Management. Geographica Helvetica
  54(4):229–241.
Kapferer, J.
  1994 Strategic Brand Management: New Approaches to Creating and Evaluating
  Brand Equity. New York: The Free Press.
  1997 Strategic Brand Management: Creating and Sustaining Brand Equity Long
  Term. London: Kogan Page.
Kavaratzis, M.
  2004 From City Marketing to City Branding: Towards a Theoretical Framework
  for Developing City Brands. Place Branding 1(1):58–73.
  2007 City Marketing: The Past, The Present and Some Unsolved Issues.
  Geography Compass 1:1–18.

Kavaratzis, M., and G. Ashworth
2005 City Branding: An Effective Assertion of Identity or a Transitory Marketing Trick? Tijdschrift voor Economische en Sociale Geografie 96(5): 506–514.

Keane, M.
1997 Quality and Pricing in Tourism Destinations. Annals of Tourism Research 24(1):117–130.

Keller, K.
1993 Conceptualizing, Measuring, and Managing Customer-Based Brand Equity. Journal of Marketing 57(1):1–22.
1998 Strategic Brand Management. Building, Measuring and Managing Brand Equity. Upper Saddle River, NJ: Prentice-Hall.
2003 Strategic Brand Management: Building, Measuring, and Managing Brand Equity (2nd ed). Upper Saddle River, NJ: Prentice-Hall.

Kiley, D., and Helm, B.
2007 The Short Life of the Chief Marketing Officer. Business Week, November 29.

Kim, H., and D. Fesenmaier
2008 Persuasive Design of Destination Web Sites: An Analysis of First Impression. Journal of Travel Research 47(1):3–13.

Kim, S., and J. Petrick
2005 Residents' Perceptions on Impacts of the FIFA 2002 World Cup: The Case of Seoul as a Host City. Tourism Management 26(1):25–38.

Kim, S., Y. Hyun, and J. Han
2006 The Structural Equation Modeling Approach to the Relationship between Tourism Destination Image Formation and Destination Loyalty Based on Tourist Information and Motivations: A Case Study of Beatles Theme City, UK. Journal of Tourism Sciences 30(2):299–319.

King, B., A. Pizam, and A. Milman
1993 Social Impacts of Tourism: Host Perceptions. Annals of Tourism Research 20(4):650–665.

Kivela, J., and J. Crotts
2006 Tourism and Gastronomy: Gastronomy's Influence on how Tourists Experience a Destination. Journal of Hospitality and Tourism Research 30(3):354–377.

Kivela, J., and N. Johns
2003 Restaurants, Gastronomy and Tourists: A Novel Method for Investigating Tourists' Dining out Experiences. Tourism 51(1):3–19.

Klein, L.R.
2003 Creating Virtual Product Experience: The Role of Telepresence. Journal of Interactive Marketing 17(1):41–55.

Knox, S., and D. Bickerton
2003 The Six Conventions of Corporate Branding. European Journal of Marketing 37(7/8):998–1016.

Koernig, S.
   2003 E-scapes: The Electronic Physical Environment and Service Tangibility. Psychology & Marketing 20(2):151–167.
Konecnik, M.
   2005 Customer-Based Brand Equity for a Tourism Destination: Conceptual Model and Its Empirical Verification. PhD dissertation in Business Administration, University of Ljubljana, Slovenia.
Konecnik, M., and F. Go
   2008 Tourism Destination Brand Identity: The Case of Slovenia. Journal of Brand Management 15(3):177–189.
Konecnik, M., and W. Gartner
   2007 Customer-Based Brand Equity for a Destination. Annals of Tourism Research 34(2):400–421.
Koonce, S., and J. Ferguson
   2007 New Longview Brand Not Exclusive to City-Officials Upset That 'Pure And Simple' Used for Other Towns. The Longview News-Journal, March 14.
Kotler, P.
   1972 A Generic Concept of Marketing. Journal of Marketing 36:46–54.
   1997 Marketing Management-Analysis, Planning, Implementation, and Control (9th ed). Upper Saddle River, NJ: Prentice-Hall.
Kotler, P., and D. Gertner
   2002 Country as Brand, Product, and Beyond: A Place Marketing and Brand Management Perspective. Journal of Brand Management 9(4/5):249–261.
Kotler, P., and G. Armstrong
   1996 Principles of Marketing (7th ed). Upper Saddle River, NJ: Prentice-Hall.
   2005 Principles of Marketing. Upper Saddle River, NJ: Prentice Hall.
Kotler, P., D. Jain, and S. Maesincee
   2002 El marketing se mueve. Una nueva aproximación a los beneficios, el crecimiento y la renovación. Barcelona: Paidos Ibérica.
Kotler, P., H. Haider, and I. Rein
   1993 Marketing Places, Attracting Investment, Industry and Tourism to Cities, States and Nations. New York: Free Press.
Kotler, P., J. Bowen, and J. Makens
   2003 Marketing for Hospitality and Tourism (3rd ed). Upper Saddle River, NJ: Pearson Education.
Kotler, P., S. Ang, D. Leong, and C. Tan
   1996 Marketing Management: An Asian Perspective. Singapore: Prentice Hall.
Kozak, M.
   2001 Repeaters' Behavior at Two Distinct Destinations. Annals of Tourism Research 28(3):784–807.
Krippendorf, J.
   1987 The Holiday Makers: Understanding the Impact of Leisure and Travel. Oxford: Butterworth Heinemann.

Lankford, S.
1994 Attitudes and Perceptions Towards Tourism in Rural Regional Development. Journal of Travel Research 32(2):35–43.

Larsen, D.
2007 Business Life has Not Discovered Podcasting, (in Danish in the original) Børsen, 4 September.

Lassar, W., B. Mittal, and A. Sharma
1995 Measuring Customer-Based Brand Equity. Journal of Consumer Marketing 12(4):11–19.

Laudon, K., and C. Traver
2001 E-Commerce: Business, Technology, Society. Boston: Addison-Wesley.

Lawrence, T., N. Phillips, and C. Hardy
1999 Watching Whale Watching: Exploring the Discursive Foundations of Collaborative Relationships. Journal of Applied Behavioral Science 35(4):479–502.

Lawson, R., J. Williams, T. Young, and J. Cossens
1998 A Comparison of Residents' Attitudes Towards Tourism in 10 New Zealand Destinations. Tourism Management 19(3):247–256.

Leadbeater, C., and Miller, P.
2004 The Pro-Am Revolution: How Enthusiasts are Changing Our Economy and Society <www.demos.co.uk> (15 October 2007).

Lee, C., Y. Lee, and B. Lee
2005 Korea's Destination Image Formed by the 2002 World Cup. Annals of Tourism Research 32(4):839–858.

Lee, G., J. O'Leary, and G. Hong
2002 Visiting Propensity Predicted by Destination Image: German Long-Haul Pleasure Travelers to the U.S. International Journal of Hospitality & Tourism Administration 3(2):63–92.

Lee, G., L.A. Cai, and J. O'Leary
2006 An Analysis of Brand-Building Elements in the US State Tourism Websites. Tourism Management 27(5):815–828. www.branding.states.US

Lee, J.
2004a The Third Way Strategy for Regional Development of Small and Medium Sized Cities-Merging Tourism and Cultural Industries Socio-Spatially into a Place. Tourism Management Research 8(3):257–297. (in Korean).
2004b Reconstructing the Methodology of Place Analysis for Positioning Unique Place Image in Regional Development. Geographical Journal of Korea 38(4): 479–495. (in Korean).

Lee, J.H., and S.H. Choi
2006 A study on Constructing Tourism Destination Brand Model. Gyeonggi Research Institute (in Korean).

Leonard, M.
1997 Britain: Renewing Our Identity. London, UK: Demos.

Lew, A.
   1987 A Framework of Tourist Attraction Research. Annals of Tourism Research 14(4):553–575.
Li, H., T. Daugherty, and F. Biocca
   2001 Characteristics of Virtual Experience in Electronic Commerce: A Protocol Analysis. Journal of Interactive Advertising 15(3):13–30.
   2002 Impact of 3-D Advertising on Product Knowledge, Brand Attitude and Purchase Intention: The Mediating Role of Presence. Journal of Advertising 31(3):43–57.
Lindberg, K., and R. Johnson
   1997 Modeling Resident Attitudes Toward Tourism. Annals of Tourism Research 24(2):402–424.
Litvin, S., and S. Ling
   2001 The Destination Attribute Management Model: An Empirical Application to Bintan, Indonesia. Tourism Management 22(5):481–492.
Lockie, S.
   2001 Food, Place and Identity: Consuming Australia's 'Beef Capital'. Journal of Sociology 37(3):239–255.
Lonely Planet
   2007 Homepage <www.lonelyplanet.com> (15 October).
Long, L.
   2004 Culinary Tourism. Lexington: University Press of Kentucky.
Luck, D.
   1969 Broadening the Concept of Marketing-Too Far. Journal of Marketing 33(3):53–55.
MacKay, K., and J. Campbell
   2004 An Examination of Residents' Support for Hunting as a Tourism Product. Tourism Management 25(4):443–452.
Martinovic, S.
   2002 Branding Hrvatska-a Mixed Blessing that Might Succeed: The Advantage of Being Unrecognizable. Journal of Brand Management 9(4/5):315–322.
Mathieson, A., and G. Wall
   1982 Tourism: Economic, Physical and Social Impacts. Harlow: Longman.
Mazanec, J.
   1994 Image Measurement with Self-Organizing Maps: A Tentative Application to Austrian Tour Operators. Tourism Review 49(3):9–18.
McCann, J., and C. Chiles
   1983 Design Guidelines for Social Problem-Solving Interventions/Comments/ Reply. Journal of Applied Behavioral Science 19(2):177–189.
McCool, S., and S. Martin
   1994 Community Attachment and Attitudes Towards Tourism Development. Journal of Travel Research 32(3):29–34.
McEwen, W.
   2001 The Power of the Fifth P. Gallup Management Journal 1(1):1–2.

McGehee, N., and K. Andereck
  2004 Factors Predicting Rural Residents' Support of Tourism. Journal of Travel
    Research 43(2):131–140.
McLellan, R., and K. Foushee
  1983 Negative Image of the United States as Expressed by Tour Operators Form
    Other Countries. Journal of Travel Research 22(1):2–5.
Merit, S., and T. Nielsen
  2006 Vinderkoncepter – Brugerdreven Innovation og Forretningsudvikling.
    Copenhagen: Børsen Forlag.
Middleton, V., and J. Clarke
  2001 Marketing in Travel and Tourism. Oxford: Butterworth-Heinemann.
Millar, M.G., and K.U. Millar
  1996 The Effects of Direct and Indirect Experience on Affective and Cognitive
    Responses and the Attitude-Behavior Relation. Journal of Experimental Social
    Psychology 32(6):561–579.
Miller, M., and T. Henthorne
  2006 In Search of Competitive Advantage in Caribbean Tourism Websites:
    Revisiting the Unique Selling Proposition. Journal of Travel & Tourism
    Marketing 21(2/3):49–62.
Milligan, J.W.
  1995 Are Banks Ready for Product Branding? United States Banker 105(April):
    39–41.
Milman, A., and A. Pizam
  1995 The Role of Awareness and Familiarity with a Destination: The Central
    Florida Case. Journal of Travel Research 33(3):21–27.
Milne, S., and I. Ateljevic
  2001 Tourism, Economic Development and the Global-Local Nexus: Theory
    Embracing Complexity. Tourism Geographies 3(4):367–388.
Mintz, S., and C. Du Bois
  2002 The Anthropology of Food and Eating. Annual Review of Anthropology
    31(1):99–119.
Mitchell, R., and M. Hall
  2003 Consumer Tourists: Food Tourism Consumer Behavior. *In* Food Tourism
    Around the World: Development, Management and Markets, M. Hall, L.
    Sharples, R. Mitchell, N. Macions, and B. Cambourne, eds., pp. 60–80. Boston:
    Butterworth-Heinemann.
Morgan, N.
  2003 Destination Branding and the Role of the Stakeholders: The Case of New
    Zealand. Journal of Vacation Marketing 9(3):285–299.
Morgan, N., and A. Pritchard
  2000 Advertising in Tourism and Leisure. Oxford: Butterworth Heinemann.
  2002 Contextualizing Destination Branding. *In* Destination Branding: Creating
    the Unique Destination Proposition, N. Morgan, A. Pritchard, and R. Pride,
    eds., pp. 10–41. Oxford: Butterworth-Heinemann.

2005 Promoting Niche Tourism Destination Brands: Case Studies of New Zealand and Wales. Journal of Promotion Managent 12(7): 17–33.

Morgan, N., A. Pritchard, and R. Piggott
2002 New Zealand, 100% Pure. The Creation of a Powerful Niche Destination Brand. Journal of Brand Management 9(4/5):335–354.

Morgan, N., A. Pritchard, and R. Pride, eds.
2002 Destination Branding: Creating the Unique Destination Position. Oxford: Butterworth-Heinemann.
2006a Destination Branding: Creating the Unique Destination Proposition. Boston: Elsevier Butterworth Heinemann.

Morgan, N., A. Pritchard, and R. Pride
2006b *In* Destination Branding, pp. 1–16. Boston: Elsevier Butterworth Heinemann.

Mulgan, G.
1998 Connexity: Responsibility, Freedom, Business and Power in the New Century. London: Vintage.

Munar, A.
2007 Rethinking Globalization Theory in Tourism. *In* Tourism Culture and Communication (Vol. 7, No. 2, pp. 99–115). New York: Cognizant Communication.

Munar, A.M.
2008 CAMPER: Walking into Tourism. *In* Cases from the Experience Economy, A. Sørensen and J. Sundbo, eds., pp. 44–55. Roskilde: CELF and Roskilde University <http://cof.ruc.dk/download/Casebook.pdf> (30 October 2009).

Murphy, L., G. Moscardo, and P. Benckendorff
2007 Using Brand Personality to Differentiate Regional Tourism Destinations. Journal of Travel Research 46:5–14.

Murphy, P.
1985 Tourism: A Community Approach. New York: Methuen.

Murphy, P., M. Pritchard, and B. Smith
2000 The Destination Product and Its Impact on Traveler Perceptions. Tourism Management 21(1):43–52.

Nickerson, N., and R. Moisey
1999 Branding a State From Features to Positioning: Making It Simple? Journal of Vacation Marketing 5:217–226.

Nield, K., M. Kozak, and G. LeGrys
2000 The Role of Food Service in Tourist Satisfaction. International Journal of Hospitality Management 19(4):375–384.

Official Online Tourism Office for Dublin
2007 Dublin Podcasts <http://www.visitdublin.com/multimedia/DublinPodcast. aspx?id = 275> (30 August).

Ohmae, K.
1990 The Borderless World: Power and Strategy in the Interlinked Economy. New York: Harper Business.

Ooi, C.
2004 Poetics and Politics of Destination Branding: Denmark. Scandinavian Journal of Hospitality and Tourism 4(2):107–128.
2006 Tales from Two Countries: The Place Branding of Denmark and Singapore. Copenhagen. Discussion Papers, 9. Asia Research Center, Copenhagen Business School: Frederiksberg (Denmark).

Oppermann, M.
2000 Tourism Destination Loyalty. Journal of Travel Research 39(1):78–84.

Ørestad
2008 Presentation <http://www.orestad.dk/index/uk_frontpage.htm> (1 October).

Pack, S.
2006 Tourism and Dictatorship: Europe's Peaceful Invasion of Franco's Spain. New York: Macmillan Palgrave.

Papadopoulos, N., and L. Heslop
2002 Country Equity and Country Branding: Problems and Prospects. Journal of Brand Management 9(4/5):294–314.

Park, N.
2005 Regional Development Make Use of Place Marketing: A Case of Bucheon City. Korean Society and Public Administration 16(2):341–362. (in Korean).

Park, O. J., X. Y. Lehto, and A. M. Morrison
2008 Collaboration between CVB and Local Community in Destination Marketing: CVB Executives' Perspective. Journal of Hospitality & Leisure Marketing 17(3–4):395–417.

Pearce, P.
1982 Perceived Changes in Holiday Destinations. Annals of Tourism Research 9(2):145–164.

Pearce, P., G. Moscardo, and G. Ross
1996 Tourism Community Relationships. Oxford, UK: Pergamon.

Pedersen, S.
2004 Place Branding: Giving the Region of Oresund a Competitive Edge. Journal of Urban Technology 11(1):77–95.

Perdue, R., P. Long, and Y. Kang
1999 Boomtown Tourism and Resident Quality of Life: The Marketing of Gaming to Host Community Residents. Journal of Business Research 44(3):165–177.

Pérez, E., and J. Nadal
2005 Host Community Perceptions a Cluster Analysis. Annals of Tourism Research 32(4):925–941.

Phelps, A.
1986 Holiday Destination Image: The Problem of Assessment: An Example Developed in Menorca. Tourism Management 7(3):168–180.

Pike, S.
2002 Destination Image Analysis: A Review of 142 Papers From 1973 to 2000. Tourism Management 23(5):541–549.
2007 Destination Image Literature 2001–2007. Acta Tourstica 19(2):107–125.

Pike, S., and C. Ryan
  2004 Destination Positioning Analysis Through a Comparison of Cognitive, Affective, and Conative Perceptions. Journal of Travel Research 42(4):333–342.
Pine, B., and J. Gilmore
  1999 The Experience Economy. Boston: Harvard Business School Press.
Poon, A.
  1996 Tourism, Technology and Competitive Strategies. Wallingford: CABI Publishing.
Porter, M.
  1990 The Competitive Advantage of Nations. Basingstoke: Macmillan.
Pred, A.
  1984 Place as Historically Contingent Process: Structuration and the Time-Geography of Becoming Places. Annals of the Association of American Geographers 74(2):279–297.
Prensky, M.
  2001 Digital Natives, Digital Immigrants < http://www.marcprensky.com/writing/ Prensky%20-%20Digital%20Natives,%20Digital%20Immigrants%20-%20Part 1.pdf> (12 May 2004).
Prentice, R.
  2004 Tourist Familiarity and Imagery. Annals of Tourism Research 31(4): 923–945.
Prentice, R., and J. Hudson
  1993 Assessing the Linguistic Dimension in the Perception of Tourism Impacts by Residents of a Tourist Destination: A Case Study of Porthmadog, Gwynedd. Tourism Management 14(4):298–306.
Pride, R.
  2002 Brand Wales: 'Natural revival'. *In* Destination Branding: Creating the Unique Destination Proposition, N. Morgan, A. Pritchard, and R. Pride, eds., pp. 109–123. Oxford: Butterworth-Heinemann.
  2007 A Challenger Approach to Destination Marketing. Keynote Presentation at the 2nd International Conference on Destination Branding and Marketing, Institute for Tourism Studies, Macau (SAR), China, December.
Prideaux, B., and C. Cooper
  2002 Marketing and Destination Growth: A Symbiotic Relationship or Simple Coincidence? Journal of Vacation Marketing 9(1):35–48.
Pritchard, A., and N. Morgan
  2001 Culture, Identity and Tourism Representation: Marketing Cymru or Wales? Tourism Management 22(2):167–179.
Rainisto, S.
  2003 Success Factors of Place Marketing: A Study of Place Marketing Practices in Northern Europe and the United States. PhD dissertation in Institute of Strategy and International Business, Helsinki University of Technology, Finland.

Ravinder, R.
  2003 Destination Image Evaluation: Part II. Eclipse: The Periodic Publication from Moonshine Travel Marketing for Destination Marketers 10:1–12.
Red Associates
  2006 Denmark: Analysis of Perceptions and Recommendations for a (Offensive) Global Marketing of Denmark (In Danish in the Original) <http://www.oem.dk/graphics/oem/Markedsf%F8ring%20af%20dk/Analyser/AnalyseDK.pdf> (17 August 2007).
Reed, M.
  1997 Power Relations and Community-Based Tourism Planning. Annals of Tourism Research 24(3):566–591.
Reid, D.
  2003 2003 Tourism, Globalization, and Development: Responsible Tourism Planning. London: Pluto Press.
Reiser, D.
  2001 Globalization: An Old Phenomenon that Needs to Be Rediscovered for Tourism? Tourism and Hospitality Research 4(4):306–320.
Ritchie, B., and M. Inkari
  2006 Host Community Attitudes Toward Tourism and Cultural Tourism Development: The Case of the Lewes District, Southern England. International Journal of Tourism Research 8(1):27–44.
Ritchie, B., and R. Ritchie
  1998 The Branding of Tourism Destination: Past Achievements and Future Trends. *In* Destination Marketing – Scope and Limitations, Reports of 48th Congress. pp. 89–116. St-Gall: AIEST.
Robertson, R.
  1995 Glocalization: Time-Space and Homogeneity-Heterogeneity. *In* Global Modernities, M. Featherstone, S. Lash and R. Robertson, eds. pp. 25–44. London: Sage.
Rodríguez, J.
  2007 El Plan de Estabilización de 1959. <http://www.juandemariana.org/comentario/1105/>.
Room, A.
  1992 History of Branding. *In* Branding: A Key Marketing Tool, J. Murphy, ed., pp. 13–21. Houndmills: Macmillan.
Ryan, C.
  1994 Leisure and Tourism: The Application of Leisure Concepts to Tourist Behavior—A Proposed Model. *In* Tourism: The State of the Art, A. Seaton, ed., pp. 294–307. Chichester, UK: Wiley.
Ryan, C., and D. Montgomery
  1994 The Attitudes of Bakewell Residents to Tourism and Issues in Community Responsive Tourism. Tourism Management 15(5):358–369.

Salazar, N.
  2005 Tourism and Globalization "Local" Tour Guiding. Annals of Tourism Research 32(3):628–646.
  2006 Touristifying Tanzania: Local Guides, Global Discourse. Annals of Tourism Research 33(3):833–852.
Salmon, K.
  1991 The Modern Spanish Economy: Transformation and Integration into Europe. London: Pinter Publishers.
Schlosser, A., D. Mick, and J. Deighton
  2003 Experiencing Products in the Virtual World: The Role of Goal and Imagery in Influencing Attitudes versus Purchase Intentions. Journal of Consumer Research 30(2):184–198.
Schmitt, B.
  1999 Experiential Marketing: How to Get Customers to Sense, Feel, Act and Relate to Your Company and Brands. New York: The Free Press.
Schroeder, T.
  1996 The Relationship of Residents' Image of their State as a Tourist Destination and Their Support for Tourism. Journal of Travel Research 34(4):71–73.
Seaton, A., and C. Palmer
  1997 Understanding VFR Tourism Behaviour: The First Five Years of the United Kingdom Tourism Survey. Tourism Management 18(6):345–355.
Selin, S., and D. Chavez
  1995 Developing an Evolutionary Tourism Partnership Model. Annals of Tourism Research 22(4):844–856.
Sheehan, L., and B. Ritchie
  2005 Destination Stakeholders Exploring Identity and Salience. Annals of Tourism Research 32(3):711–734.
Shih, C.
  1998 Conceptualizing Consumer Experiences in Cyberspace. European Journal of Marketing 32(7/8):655–663.
Simpson, K.
  2001 Strategic Planning and Community Involvement as Contributors to Sustainable Tourism Development. Current Issues in Tourism 4(1):3–41.
Sinclair, L.
  2008 New Tourism Australia Ad Campaign Launches Luhrmann Videos. The Australian <http://www.theaustralian.news.com.au/story/0,25197,24465048-7582,00.html> (8 October).
Skinner, H.
  2005 Wish You were Here? Some Problems Associated with Integrating Marketing Communications When Promoting Place Brands. Place Branding 1(3):299–315.
Smith, R., and W. Swinyard
  1982 Information Response Models: An Integrated Approach. Journal of Marketing 46(1):81–93.

1988 Cognitive Response to Advertising and Trial: Belief Strength, Belief Confidence and Product Curiosity. Journal of Advertising 17(3):3–14.

Snaith, T., and A. Haley
1999 Residents' Opinions of Tourism Development in the Historic City of York, England. Tourism Management 20(5):595–603.

SNTO (Spanish National Tourist Organization)
2000a Catálogo de Carteles Oficiales de Turismo del Centro de Documentación Turística de España. Madrid: Servicio de Publicaciones del Ministerio de Economía y Hacienda, Tomo I (1957 a 1979)
2000b Catálogo de Carteles Oficiales de Turismo del Centro de Documentación Turística de España. Madrid: Servicio de Publicaciones del Ministerio de Economía y Hacienda, Tomo II (1980 a 2000)
2005 Catálogo de Carteles Oficiales de Turismo (1929–1959). Madrid: Centro de Documentación Turística de España.
2007 Boletín Bibliográfico con Imagen de la Colección de Carteles de del Centro de Documentación Turística de España. Madrid: Instituto de Estudios Turísticos.

Sol Meliá
2007a History <http://prensa.solmelia.com/view_object.html?obj = 85,111,c,2615> (4 February 2008).
2007b About Sol Meliá <http://www.solmelia.com/solNew/groupinfo/jsp/ C_AcercaDe.jsp> (4 February 2008).

Sparks, B., K. Wildman, and J. Bowen
2001 Restaurants as a Contributor to Destination Attractiveness. Australian Journal of Hospitality Management 8(2):17–30.

Stanley, B.
2006 Australian Slogan Rankles Some. Wall Street Journal March 10:B1 and B6.

Stern, B., G. Zinkhan, and M. Holbrook
2002 The Netvertising Image: Netvertising Image Communication Model (NICM) and Construct Definition. Journal of Advertising 31(3):15–27.

Stern, E., and S. Krakover
1993 The Formation of a Composite Urban Image. Geographical Analysis 25(2): 130–146.

Sternthal, B., and A. Tybout
2001 Brand Positioning. In Kellogg on Marketing, D. Iacobucci, ed. Chichester: Wiley.

Steuer, J.
1992 Defining Virtual Reality: Dimensions Determining Telepresence. Journal of Communication 42(4):73–93.

Stiglitz, J.
2003 Globalization and Its Discontents. New York: W. W. Norton.

Suh, K., and S. Chang
2006 User Interfaces and Consumer Perceptions of Online Stores: The Role of Telepresence. Behaviour & Information Technology 25(2):99–113.

Sutton, W.
   1967 Travel and Understanding: Notes on the Social Structure of Touring. International Journal of Comparative Sociology 8:218–223.
Taiwan Tourism Bureau
   2007 2006 Annual Survey Report on Visitors Expenditure and Trends in Taiwan. Taiwan: Ministry of Transportation and Communication.
Tamames, R.
   1968 Introducción a la Economía Española (2nd ed). Madrid: Alianza Editorial.
Tasci, A., W. Gartner, and S. Cavusgil
   2007a Measurement of Destination Brand Bias Using a Quasi-Experimental Design. Tourism Management 28(6):1529–1540.
Tasci, A., W. Gartner, and A. So
   2007b Branding Macao: An Application of Strategic Branding for Destinations. Paper Presented at the 2nd International Conference on Destination Branding and Marketing, Institute for Tourism Studies, Macau (SAR), China, December.
Tellström, R., I. Gustafsson, and L. Mossberg
   2006 Consuming Heritage: The Use of Local Food Culture in Branding. Place Branding 2(2):130–143.
Temprano, A.
   1981 Cambios Demográficos y Crecimiento Económico en la España Desarrollista. *In* Crecimiento económico y crisis estructural en España (1959–1980), R. Carballo, A. Temprano, and M. Santín, eds. Madrid: Akal.
Teo, P., and B. Yeoh
   1997 Remaking Local Heritage for Tourism. Annals of Tourism Research 24(1):192–213.
Teo, P., and L. Li
   2003 Global and Local Interactions in Tourism. Annals of Tourism Research 30(2):287–306.
Tepeci, M.
   1999 Increasing Brand Loyalty in the Hospitality Industry. International Journal of Contemporary Hospitality Management 11(5):223.
Teye, V., E. Sirakaya, and S. Sönmez
   2002 Residents' Attitudes Toward Tourism Development. Annals of Tourism Research 29(3):668–688.
Timothy, D., and G. Wall
   1997 Selling to Tourists: Indonesian Street Vendors. Annals of Tourism Research 24(2):322–340.
Tosun, C.
   2002 Host Perceptions of Impacts: A Comparative Tourism Study. Annals of Tourism Research 29(1):231–253.
Travel Industry Association of America
   2005 Traveler's Use of the Internet. Washington, DC: Travel Industry Associate of America.

TravelBlog
   2007 Homepage <http://www.travelblog.org/> (15 October).
Travis, D.
   2000 Emotional Branding: How Successful Brands Gain the Irrational Edge.
   Roseville: Crown Business.
Trip Advisor
   2007a Ozi Traveller31, Good Location But Nothing Else ...! <http://www.
   tripadvisor.com/AllReviews-g186338-London_England.html> (10 September).
   2007b Homepage <www.tripadvisor.com> (10 August).
   2007c A Trip Advisor Member, Worst Motel in s. Taloe (pics) <http://
   www.tripadvisor.com/ShowUserReviews-g155987-d281277-r4455866-Roadside_
   Inn-Lake_Tahoe_California.html> (16 October).
Um, S., and J. Crompton
   1990 Attitude Determinants in Tourism Destination Choice. Annals of Tourism
   Research 17(3):432–448.
United Nations
   2008 World Population Prospects, Urban <http://data.un.org/Data.aspx?d =
   PopDiv&f = variableID%3a17> (1 October).
United Nations Conference on Trade and Development
   2008 Creative Economy. United Nations 2008 <http://www.unctad.org/
   Templates/Webflyer.asp?intItemID = 4494> (2 June).
Urde, M.
   1999 Brand Orientation: A Mindset for Building Brands into Strategic Resources.
   Journal of Marketing Management 15(1–3):117–133.
Urry, J.
   2001 Globalising the Tourist Gaze. Department of Sociology, Lancaster
   University, Lancaster LA1 4YN, UK <http://www.comp.lancs.ac.uk/sociol-
   ogy/papers/Urry-Globalising-the-Tourist-Gaze.pdf> (28 October 2009).
   1990 The Tourist Gaze. London: Sage.
   2003 Global Complexity. Cambridge: Polity.
Van der Berg, L., J. Van der Meer, A. Otgaar, and C. Speller
   2008 Empowering Metropolitan Regions Through New Forms of Cooperation.
   European Institute for Comparative Urban Research. Euricur/Ashgate:
   Rotterdam.
Vazquez, R., A. Del Rio, and V. Iglesias
   2002 Consumer-Based Brand Equity: Development and Validation of a
   Measurement Instrument. Journal of Marketing Management 18(1/2):
   27–48.
Velarde F.J.
   2001 Informes y Perspectivas: la Economia Española en el siglo XX. Estudios
   Economicos de Desarrollo Internacional. Euro-American Association of
   Economic Development <http://www.usc.es/~economet/reviews/eedi115.pdf>
   (28 October).

Vernon, J., S. Essex, D. Pinder, and K. Curry
  2005 Collaborative Policymaking: Local Sustainable Projects. Annals of Tourism
    Research 32(2):325–345.
Vidal Villa, J.M.
  1981 España y el imperialismo. *In* Crecimiento económico y crisis estructural en
    España (1959–1980), R. Carballo, A. Temprano, and M. Santín, eds. Madrid:
    Akal.
Virtual Tourist
  2007 Homepage <http://www.virtualtourist.com> (30 August).
Visit Denmark
  2008 Danmark på Bloggen <http://www.visitdenmark.com/NR/rdonlyres/
    811A0400-98D0-4A92-9610-34EC5C249814/0/Danmarkpåbloggen.pdf>   (5
    October).
Vriens, M., and F. Hofstede
  2000 Linking Attributes, Benefits and Consumer Values. Marketing Research
    12(3):4–10.
Wahab, S., and C. Cooper
  2001 Tourism in the Age of Globalization. Oxford: Routledge.
Walsh, J., U. Jamrozy, and S. Burr
  2001 Sense of Place as a Component of Sustainable Tourism Marketing.
    In Tourism, Recreation and Sustainability: Linking Culture and the Environ-
    ment, S. McCool and R. Moisey, eds., pp. 195–216. Oxon, UK: CABI
    Publishing.
Wang, N.
  2000 Tourism and Modernity: A Sociological Analysis. Oxford: Elsevier.
Wang, Y., and D. Fesenmaier
  2007 Collaborative Destination Marketing: A Case Study of Elkhart County,
    Indiana. Tourism Management 28(3):863–875.
Wansink, B.
  2003a Response to Measuring Consumer Response to Food Products. Sensory
    Tests that Predict Consumer Acceptance. Food Quality and Preference
    14(1):23–26.
  2003b Using Laddering to Understand and Leverage a Brand's Equity.
    Qualitative Market Research: An International Journal 6(2):111–118.
Ward, L., and J. Russell
  1981 The Psychological Representation of Molar Physical Environments. Journal
    of Experimental Psychology 110:121–152.
Weiermair, K., and M. Fuchs
  1999 Measuring Tourist Judgment on Service Quality. Annals of Tourism
    Research 26(4):1004–1021.
Weisman, R.
  2008 Under Expedia, Trip Advisor Flourishes as Travel Sites Boom. International
    Herald Tribune, September 5.

Westwood, S., N. Morgan, A. Pritchard, and E. Ineson
1999 Branding the Package Holiday: The Role and Significance of Brands for UK Air Tour Operators. Journal of Vacation Marketing 5(3): 238–252.
Wikitravel
2007a Homepage <http://wikitravel.org/en/Main_Page> (15 October).
2007b Project Page <http://wikitravel.org/en/Wikitravel:The_traveller_comes_ first> (16 October).
Williams, A., and A. Palmer
1999 Tourism Destination Brands and Electronic Commerce: Towards Synergy? Journal of Vacation Marketing 5(3):263–275.
Williams, J., and R. Lawson
2001 Community Issues and Resident Opinions of Tourism. Annals of Tourism Research 28(2):269–290.
Williams, P., A. Gill, and N. Chura
2004 Branding Mountain Destinations: The Battle for 'Placefulness'. Tourism Review 59(1):6–15.
Williams, P., R. Penrose, and S. Hawkes
1998 Shared Decision-Making in Tourism Land Use Planning. Annals of Tourism Research 25(4):860–889.
Wolf, M.
2004 Why Globalization Works. New Haven: Yale University Press.
Wonderful Copenhagen
2008a Corporate Information <http://www.wonderfulcopenhagen.dk/content/ dk/hvem_er_vi/mission_vision_og_strategi> (4 October).
2008b Monocle's Ranking of Life Quality of Cities <http://www.visitcopenhagen. com/content/tourist/news/news_and_events/copenhagen_rated_worlds_best_ life_quality> (4 October).
2008c DitKøbenhavn <http://www.visitcopenhagen.dk/content/turist/hvad_ sker_der_i_byen/ditkobenhavn> (4 October).
Wood, R.
2000 Caribbean Cruise Tourism: Globalization at Sea. Annals of Tourism Research 27(2):345–370.
Woodside, A., and S. Lysonski
1989 A General Model of Travel Destination Choice. Journal of Travel Research 27(4):8–14.
World Bank
2006 World Development Report. <http://www.siteresources.worldbank. org/INTWDR2006/Resources/477383-1127230817535/082136412X.pdf> (16 November 2008).
2007 Global Monitoring Report 2007. <http://web.worldbank.org/external/ default/main?contentMDK = 21256862&menuPK = 3413296&theSitePK = 3413261&piPK = 64218883&pagePK = 64218950> (28 November 2009).

World Tourism Organization (UNWTO)
  2007a UNWTO World Tourism Barometer. 5(2).
  2007b Tourism Highlights <http://www.world-tourism.org/facts/menu.html>
    (23 October).
  2008 World Tourism Barometer <http://www.unwto.org/facts/eng/pdf/
    barometer/UNWTO_Barom08_2_en_Excerpt.pdf> (21 September).
World Trade Organization (WTO)
  2007 Tonga Becomes the 151st Member of WTO, Press/488, 27 July <http://
    www.wto.org/english/news_e/pres07_e/pr488_e.htm> (4 September).
Worldwatch Institute
  2004 The State of the World (in Catalan in the Original). Barcelona: Centre
    Unesco de Catalunya.
Wright, A., and J. Lynch, Jr.
  1995 Communication Effects of Advertising versus Direct Experience when Both
    Search and Experience Attributes are Present. Journal of Consumer Research
    21(4):708–718.
Wright, S.
  2007 What's the Deal with Americans Ripping off Our Tourism Slogans? <http://
    cblog.brandcanadablog.com/2007/11/30/whats-the-deal-with-americans-ripping-
    off-our-tourism-slogans.aspx>.
Yoo, B., and N. Donthu
  2001 Developing and Validating a Multidimensional Consumer-Based Brand
    Equity Scale. Journal of Business Research 52(1):1–14.
Young, C., D. Corsun, and S. Baloglu
  2007 A Taxonomy of Hosts Visiting Friends and Relatives. Annals of Tourism
    Research 34(2):497–516.
YouTube
  2007 Catmairo, Bora Bora Ibiza Junio 2007. <http://www.youtube.com/watch?
    v = tnkvhs_mMEQ> (16 August).
Zhang, J., R. Inbakaran, and M. Jackson
  2006 Understanding Community Attitudes Towards Tourism and Host-Guest
    Interaction in the Urban-Rural Border Region. Tourism Geographies 8(2):
    182–204.

About the Authors

Julio Aramberri, Ph.D., is Professor of Tourism at Drexel University (Philadelphia, Pennsylvania, USA. Email: ja43@drexel.edu). Previously, he worked for the Spanish Tourist Office in different capacities including the CEO position (1987–1990). He has recently been appointed to be the dean of the School of Cultural Studies at Hoa Sen University, Ho Chi Minh City, Vietnam. His areas of research are marketing, consumer behavior, and the sociology of travel and tourism. He has also published in other areas such as political sociology, US life and culture, and global challenges.

Bill Baker is President of Total Destination Management (Portland, Oregon, USA. Email: billb@destinationbranding.com). The company specializes in the branding and tourism marketing of cities. In the past 30 years, he and his team have developed hundreds of successful destination marketing strategies for countries, states, cities, and regions of all sizes. Previously, he held executive positions with the Australian Tourist Commission for more than a decade shaping Australia's brand identity in North America and Europe. His research interests include destination marketing and branding. Bill Baker is the author of Destination Branding for Small Cities, published in 2007.

Miguel Angel Bañuelos is Chairman at BBDO Spain (Madrid, Spain. Email: miguelangel.banuelos@bbdo.es). He began his professional career 40 years ago and has been working at BBDO for more than 30 years. He has served as a full member of the main advertising festivals around the world including Cannes Lions International Advertising Festival (Cannes), Festival Iberoamericano de la Publicidad (FIAP), and Latin American Advertising Festival (El Sol). Miguel Angel Bañuelos was president of the Asociación Española de Agencias de Publicidad (AEAP) in 2008 and a conference maker in several Spanish and Latin-American universities.

Liping A. Cai, Ph.D., is Professor and Director of Purdue Tourism and Hospitality Research Center, Purdue University (West Lafayette, Indiana, USA. Email: liping@purdue.edu). He specializes in branding and conducts applied research in consumer behavior and experience, rural tourism, and emerging markets. He is a governor-appointee to the Indiana Tourism Council, and the senior academic advisor to the Sloan Foundation Travel & Tourism Industry Center for the study of China market. He serves as a regional editor and on editorial boards of seven international journals and has authored or coauthored of over 200 scientific papers for journals, books, and international conferences.

Luís del Olmo is Chief Global Marketing Officer and Member of Executive Committee of Sol Meliá (Palma de Mallorca, Spain. Email: luis.del.olmo@ solmelia.com). Sol Meliá is Spain's leading hotel company and the 12th largest hotel company in the world with 350 hotels and 85,000 rooms in 30 countries in 4 continents. Luís joined Disneyland Paris in 1989 as a key member of the pre-opening executive team. He led multidisciplinary groups to develop and implement successful marketing and sales initiative and distribution strategies that resulted in achieving the first year's objectives of 12 million visitors to Euro Disney, Paris.

William C. Gartner, Ph.D., is Professor in the Applied Economics Department at the University of Minnesota (Minneapolis, St. Paul, Minnesota, USA. Email: wcg@umn.edu). His research interests are branding, image, economic impact, and tourism development. Bill has worked extensively in Asia, Europe, Latin America, and West Africa. He is a fellow of the International Academy for the Study of Tourism and is currently a visiting professor at the University of Ljubljana (Slovenia), Munich University of Applied Sciences (Germany), and University of Zagreb (Croatia) and has served as honorary dean for the Faculty of International Tourism, Macau University of Science and Technology.

Martin Yongho Hyun, Ph.D., is Assistant Professor in the School of Hospitality and Tourism Management at Catholic University of Daegu (Gyeongbuk, South Korea. Email: martinhyun@cu.ac.kr). He has expanded his marketing communication background to web and mobile destination marketing. He has currently conceptualized the mobile-mediated virtual experience (VE) in tourism. In addition, he is interested in developing the VE-based tourism communication model through the application of Elaboration Likelihood Model and the optimistic package of mobile service for tourists. His research interests also include IT-based tourism development, virtual destination branding, and online and mobile destination marketing.

Lars Bernhard Jørgensen is Managing Director for Wonderful Copenhagen (Copenhagen, Denmark. Email: lbj@woco.dk). After earning his M.Sc. in public administration and before taking the current position in 1994, Lars Bernhard Jørgensen worked for several public offices including the Danish Embassy in Paris, Ministry of Energy, Ministry of Economic and Business Affairs, and Ministry of Foreign Affairs and as Secretary to the Prime Minister. He has also served on the board of numerous companies and has been the driving force in the development of the capital's tourism and a diligent participant in the debate on Copenhagen's international profiling.

Alexandros Kouris is CEO of November Holdings (Athens, Attika, Greece. Email: alexandros@altervision.gr). The company is the shareholding entity of Altervision and Edg Designlab and Critical Publics London. In 2007, he co-directed a team of consultants to produce Greece's new 5-year destination marketing strategy and branding system. He is the author of the book titled "Destination Brand Equity – A Toolkit for Marketing to Visitors." He has over 16 years of experience in senior positions in international networks of TBWA, BBDO, and JWT. He holds a degree in business from the American College of Greece and professional qualifications from CIM and INSEAD.

Jung-hoon Lee, Ph.D., is Research Fellow of Gyeonggi Research Institute (Suwon City, South Korea. Email: jhoon@gri.re.kr). Currently, Dr. Lee is working for the Presidential Office of South Korea in the area regional development affairs. His area is in charge of government agenda for regional and municipal competitiveness. He received his doctoral education in the Department of Geography at Seoul National University with an emphasis on socio-cultural geography and regional development. He has written extensively on regional tourism and cultural development and marketing and branding cities and regions. He specializes in developing brand assets and identities.

Xinran Y. Lehto, Ph.D., is Associate Professor in the Department of Hospitality and Tourism Management at Purdue University (West Lafayette, Indiana, USA. Email: xinran@purdue.edu). Dr. Lehto's research centers on cross-cultural and cross-cohort consumer behavior, decision making, and marketing communication strategies. She is actively engaged in interdisciplinary research and is a research faculty fellow and partner with Purdue Center on Aging and the Life Course and the Purdue Center for Families. Dr. Lehto had 7 years of professional experience as a marketing executive with the China National Tourism Administration and as a senior planning executive with Chan Brother Travel Inc. in Singapore.

Yi-Chin Lin, Ph.D., is Assistant Professor in the Graduate School of Hospitality Management at National Kaohsiung Hospitality College (Kaohsiung City, Taiwan. Email: yclin@mail.nkhc.edu.tw). She received her doctoral education in hospitality and tourism management at Purdue University, USA. Her research interests center on destination marketing and branding, tourism and hospitality marketing, and consumer behavior. Much of her work focuses on the relationship between food and tourism. She teaches undergraduate and graduate courses in the areas of travel and tourism management, hospitality marketing management, restaurant operations management, consumer behavior, and qualitative research.

Ana María Munar is Associate Professor at the Center for Tourism and Culture Management, Copenhagen Business School (Frederiksberg, Denmark. Email: amm.tcm@cbs.dk). She holds a Ph.D. in Business and Economics from the University of the Balearic Islands (Spain). Her research interests are in tourism and information and communication technologies (ICT), globalization processes, destination branding, and policy and trends in tourism education. Her latest work focuses on the use of ICT and destination branding. She was the director of the European Convergence Office of the University of the Balearic Islands and has extensive experience on the development of educational programs.

Ignacio Ochoa is CEO at BBDO Spain and General Manager at BBDO Consulting and Tiempo BBDO Madrid (Madrid, Spain. Email: ignacio. ochoa@bbdo.es). He was account director in JWT Madrid and joined Tiempo BBDO Madrid in 1987. Following a successful experience in Tiempo BBDO Madrid, he founded his own company, De Federico Valmorisco y Ochoa (DFVO), which he later sold after it became the second largest local advertising agency in Spain. He has helped Miguel Angel Bañuelos launch and consolidate BBDO Consulting in Spain. Ignacio is author of advertising dictionaries, photography, and sociology books and also co-author of humor books.

OunJoung Park is Ph.D. Candidate in the Department of Hospitality and Tourism Management at Purdue University (West Lafayette, Indiana, USA. Email: opark@purdue.edu). Her research interests are collaborative destination marketing and consumer behaviors in the fields of online tourism information searching, family travel, and hotel and restaurant markets. She has taught hospitality marketing course as a graduate instructor. She also has been conducting consulting projects and provided marketing advice for university dining services, lodging, student leisure, and catering and events. She worked in Westin Hotel in Seoul, South Korea, in the areas of hotel revenue management and event planning.

Maja Konecnik Ruzzier, Ph.D., is Assistant Professor in the Marketing Department of the Faculty of Economics at Ljubljana University (Ljubljana, Slovenia. Email: maja.konecnik@ef.uni-lj.si). She teaches courses related to general marketing principles and tourism marketing and branding. Her special research interest is in the area of destination branding. She is an external expert to the "I feel Slovenia" brand development team that undertook Slovenia's first systematic branding program in 2007. Dr. Maja Konecnik Ruzzier presently works on transferring her teaching and research expertise and experience into Slovenian business practices.

Mitja Ruzzier, Ph.D., is Assistant Professor of entrepreneurship and Vice Dean for research and scientific work of the Faculty of Management Koper at the University of Primorska (Koper, Slovenia. Email: mitja.ruzzier@ fm-kp.si). His research interest lies in the area of internationalization, international marketing, innovation, patenting, small- and medium-sized enterprises, and entrepreneurship. His articles were published in scientific publications such as Entrepreneurship and Regional Development, Transformations in Business and Economics, and Canadian Journal of Administrative Sciences. He teaches courses related to entrepreneurship and international business. He also works part-time as consultant for many companies.

Vicenta Sierra, Ph.D., is Associate Professor in the Department of Quantitative Methods at ESADE, Ramon Llull University (Barcelona, Spain. Email: vicenta.sierra@esade.edu). She is an expert of statistical methods in both teaching and research aspects. She began her research work with the specialization in statistical techniques for single-case designs. Her scope of expertise has been expanded to various applied fields. Most recently, she has directed her research toward the mathematical and statistical analyses of social systems, human resource management, group dynamics, and interpersonal perception.

Asli D. A. Tasci, Ph.D., is Assistant Professor of Hospitality and Tourism Marketing in the School of Tourism and Hospitality Management at Mugla University (Mugla, Turkey. Email: adatasci@yahoo.com). Her B.A. is from the Middle East Technical University in Turkey and her MS and Ph.D. are from the Department of Parks Recreation and Tourism Resources at Michigan State University. She was visiting assistant professor in the School of Hotel and Tourism Management at Hong Kong Polytechnic University during the academic year 2007–2008. Her primary area of research interest is in image and branding as they relate to hospitality and tourism.

Josep-Francesc Valls, Ph.D., is Professor in the Department of Marketing Management at ESADE (Madrid, Spain. Email: josepf.valls@esade.edu). He founded the ESADE Tourism Management Centre in 1990 and was the center's director until 2004. He is a visiting professor at Luigi Bocconi, Milan; Antonio de Nebrija, Madrid; UNIA, Andalusia; Altos Estudios Turísticos, Havana; and UCA, Managua. Professor Valls is author of seven books and many research articles. He is also chapter contributor to other tourism and leisure books. He is currently working on the research topics of European leisure style, destination branding, pricing, and responsible growth and planning of cities and destinations.

AUTHOR INDEX

SUBJECT INDEX